UNHOLY UNION

UNHOLY UNION

When Rugby Collided with the Modern World

Michael Aylwin
with Mark Evans

CONSTABLE

CONSTABLE

First published in Great Britain in 2019 by Constable

1 3 5 7 9 10 8 6 4 2

A CIP catalogue record for this book
is available from the British Library.

ISBN: 978-1-47213-069-3 (hardback)
ISBN: 978-1-47213-068-6 (trade paperback)

Typeset in Electra Lt Std by SX Composing DTP, Rayleigh, Essex
Printed and bound in Great Britain by Clays Ltd, Elcograf S.p.A.

Papers used by Constable are from well-managed forests
and other responsible sources.

Constable
An imprint of
Little, Brown Book Group
Carmelite House
50 Victoria Embankment
London EC4Y 0DZ

An Hachette UK Company
www.hachette.co.uk

www.littlebrown.co.uk

For Vanessa

Contents

Part 1

Out of Chaos

I

The Diamond at the Heart of It All

There are those who will tell you rugby is a simple game, but that is just because they are desperate to believe it. Rugby is not simple. Rugby is the most complicated sport in existence, whose mysteries not even the most immersed can fathom, still less agree upon. This should come as no surprise. Just look at all those players on the pitch. Just look at those weird configurations: the twisting, seething scrum; the flailing lineout. See how the players smash into each other. Just look at that ball.

All sports need their philosophers. Usually, they're French. In rugby, the French have cornered the philosophy market. In France, they call rugby *L'Ovalie*, but *L'Ovalie* refers not just to rugby but to everything that is not quite right, everything awkward, ugly. Beautiful. *L'Ovalie* is life. *L'Ovalie* is you and me. We love it, even as it drives us mad.

By the mid-19th century, various types of football had emerged. One day, they came together with the perfectly reasonable aim of becoming an association, united by what the rest of the sporting universe had long ago recognised to be the optimum shape of ball – simple, round and sure of bounce, whose very purity was an escape from the messy truth of life. If a family tree of footballs could be plotted, the branch of that sweet, round ball would begin and end there, as if no more need be said.

But there remained within that gathering a wilful, belligerent lot who would not accept the integrity of the round ball. For reasons no other sport has quite discerned, rugby insisted upon a ball that was angular and impossible to second guess, which meant nothing could be taken for granted, nothing could run in a straight line. Nothing could be simple.

Rugby's branch of the tree did not end with rugby. It gave rise to sport after sport, as if trying to escape its own madness, as if it knew there was something wrong with itself, the game with the only ball in the cosmos not to be round. New versions were born in far-off lands – America, Canada, Australia – until the most traumatic split of all.

When rugby league smashed itself free to join the others, it left behind a sport that would not come out of the 19th century. For a hundred years, rugby union dug in its heels, crushing rebellions, squaring off against progress. The other sports galloped away into the 20th century. They experimented with professionalism. They restructured themselves, found out who they were.

But rugby held out and held out, until suddenly, on the very edge of the 21st century, it let go . . .

Our subject is what happened next. What does it do to a sport to be catapulted across an entire century in one shot? And not just any sport. This, the game that values brutality as highly as skill, that divides opinion as surely as it unites, whose ball does not even know its own bounce. If any sport should try to skip a hundred years, rugby was never it. And yet it was, because which other sport harbours a soul so contradictory as to need to make such a leap in the first place?

Rugby is deep into the fallout. Sports enter clutch periods that make or break them. This book is nothing if not a proposition that rugby is in one now, as it tries to rationalise the warping pressures of its journey into the 21st century. The repercussions continue to sweep throughout the structures, up and down, from elite to community, far and wide, from Gloucester to Suva. Players are stressed physically, institutions financially. Stereotypes are challenged and overturned, just as much as they are reinforced.

The world still does not know what to make of rugby. Rugby does not know what to make of itself.

It might help to draw out two separate strands. So tangled up with each other have they become that an indifferent world all too easily sees them as one. First, there is rugby as happens on the pitch. Then there is rugby as embodied by the blazer.

We can be too dismissive of the former. Rugby beats itself up over the success its sibling has gone on to enjoy, that round ball having taken over the world. 'Rugby will never be as popular as football' is a familiar refrain. It is true that certain fundamental qualities mitigate against rugby's mass appeal, but its primordial accent on confrontation renders it very attractive too. If we could aggregate all the sports that constitute rugby's branch of the family, the oval ball gains the continents of North America and Australasia among its territories.

If only a missive could be sent back to the blazers of the 19th century. 'Look what you could have become,' it might read, 'if you'd only let go.' But that would be to misunderstand the mindset of rugby's Victorian administrators and those who followed. The twenty-first-century notions of consumerism and popularity did not feature in their universe. Theirs was the contrary attitude, doubling down on their control of a pastime, where others let theirs fly. And so evolved a phenomenon as convoluted as it is divisive.

A hundred years of insularity will do that to a sport. For almost all of the 20th century, rugby focused in on itself, cultivating weird customs and policies that took little account of the outside world, which all too many of its governors considered an inconvenience from which to turn away. By the time the call came to open up at last to the dynamics of the high 20th century, rugby's solipsism had long ago polarised opinion beyond it. Suddenly, the sport found itself with an audience to win over and an esoteric ritual with which to do it.

Some love rugby precisely because it is so complicated; some love it for far simpler qualities, the elemental crunch of collision, the ballet of speed and skill.

Some loathe it.

Rugby, the simple word, let alone the game and the cult that surrounds it, is charged with such conflicting energies and preconceptions, here adored, there despised, often within the same town, the same street, the same house. In some parts of the world dismissed as a toff's sport, in others revered by the working class, in others again played by barefoot devotees under swaying palms. A sport crystallised from out of that argument over a football in the 19th century and within a few decades torn apart by another, whence emerged a third sport, persisting with the same name, now distinguished by an alternative suffix and a very new dynamic.

Rarely in the history of sport, or even thought, can a movement have broken away from the dictatorship it objected to with such animosity as rugby league did from rugby union – and yet insisted on retaining the same name. It is the name of the public school on whose field a game evolved some two centuries ago, a detail, along with the associated stereotype, that many cannot or will not see past. And yet in so many locations around the world, as far removed from an English public school as can be conceived, from the south of France to the south of Africa to the remotest islands of the South Pacific, rugby is a ritual something close to religion.

The subject of this book is the union code, which will be referred to throughout as rugby. There are no apologies for this. It seems absurd that rugby league would want to retain that link with the twisted mess it left behind, let alone with the public school that created it. In the same way rugby football left the name football to the association code when it broke away, why would rugby league not leave the name rugby to the union. Indeed, in Australia, where rugby league is king and the politics less complicated, the two sports are known as league and rugby respectively.

If only such simplicity could pertain to rugby in general, but our subject has been pulled in many directions over the years, bulging and creaking under the stresses and, when they have become too great, scarred by the subsequent upheavals, few as momentous as that wrought by the decision, at the tail end of the 20th century, to open the sport to professionalism after more than a hundred years of brutish intransigence on the subject. Today we find rugby between eras, unable to shake off that elitist stereotype, even as the new imperative to find affinity with the people takes hold.

And yet the game, the specific activity on the field, when lifted clear and cleaned of the soil of politics and prejudice, deserves so much better. How galling that rugby, the game, should be seen as an elitist pursuit, when really it brings together so many different types – of body and of class – and coaxes harmony from them. The wonder is it has not taken the world by storm over the past century and a half.

To cast rugby as elitist is a travesty. That false impression is no more than the legacy of the goons who used to run rugby's affairs. If ever there were a Victorian killjoy to ruin a sport's life, the historical Rugby Football Union (RFU) and its various offshoots have been it. Of all the world's major sports, rugby was the last to be allowed out like a grown-up – in 1995 to be precise, decades, even centuries, after the rest of them had turned professional. Its administrators not only held out for more than a hundred years but suppressed all attempts to institute a culture of remuneration with such inflexibility that any image of arrogance and bigotry became inevitable – and some might say well earned.

There were further repercussions to the rigid stance of the 'gentlemen amateurs'. Once they had cast a cloak of purity around rugby – or at least the perception of one – their precious sport started to attract the approval of some distinctly unsavoury types. Vichy France, Nazi Germany (Albert Speer was a notable proponent) and Fascist Italy (Mussolini likewise) nurtured continental Europe's major rugby powers in the 1930s. In the 1980s, Argentina and Romania became forces to reckon with, as tools of, respectively, the junta and Nicolae Ceauşescu's communist regime.

And then, of course, there was apartheid South Africa.

Rugby has a long and troubling history with the wrong sort, successive totalitarian regimes finding much to approve of in the sport's manly virtues and the amateur ideal.

But this is a troublesome conundrum. However backward, however elitist a defence of the amateur way might appear, it is not without merit. Most of the problems rugby wrestles with today can be traced back to the plunge into professionalism. Many were uneasy about that, even as it was about to happen. They had good reason. A plunge is a plunge and cannot be taken by degrees at the best of times, but by holding off until basically the 21st century, by which time the information age had properly taken hold, professional rugby was forced to establish itself in a more demanding, consumer-led culture than other sports had contended with during their conversions. Once taken, all defining vectors at once became quantitative, all notions of the qualitative lost in the headlong rush.

The result has been as ugly as it has, at times, been impressive, but the attempt to transform a sport from a concern not unfamiliar to the 19th century into one fit for the 21st has rendered rugby a special case. And after these whirlwind first decades, developments are set to unfold with even greater speed in who knows what direction, whisking rugby further and further away from that rough and ready diversion of which a certain class of Victorian was so protective.

So they should have been. If it is possible to strip away the preconceptions of class and culture that have dogged rugby for its first 130 years or so, we will see that, behind it all, there is – there has always been – a jewel of which those chauvinistic Victorians were rightly proud. The very fact that swathes of working-class men in the north of England were prepared to walk out and incubate a rival, just so they could carry on playing without the interference of those guardians, is its own kind of back-handed compliment.

But there's no doubt, either, that rugby is not quite as light-footed as the world's favourite sport, the beautiful game – association football. The Sibling.

Beauty may be in the eye of the beholder, but one element distinguishes football from more or less any other team sport under the sun and is surely the source of its attractiveness – and that is simplicity. That round ball, a patch of grass, two goals. Pass the ball to anyone you like anywhere on the field. Stick it in the other team's goal and it is worth a point. Most points wins. If you're really pushed, you don't even need the grass or the goals. Jumpers for goalposts will do, or rocks, or bollards, and a street has proved the breeding ground for many an international player. The offside law is the only convoluted aspect, about which many jokes have been cracked, but really, as offside laws go, it is as simple as they come. No one cracks jokes about rugby's offside law – or laws, since there are so many different ways to be caught – because it is just not funny.

Here rugby has undoubtedly been at a disadvantage. It is far harder to strike up an impromptu game, impossible if it is to be the full-fat 15-a-side version. There are too many specialist positions with too many physical and technical requirements. And with all those offside laws, not to mention the encyclopaedia of others, you need a referee. Even if you were to forgo the full-fat version, with its set pieces and penalties, there would still be discomfort in the idea of hurling yourselves at each other, often at high speed, without the endorsement and support of some sort of institution, be it medical or just official. And you wouldn't want to try it at all in the street or on asphalt.

These days the rise of touch rugby is addressing this aspect, as is sevens the specialist restriction. In 2019, a five-a-side version, Rugby X, was introduced into the mix. It is no coincidence, either, that these forms of the game have proliferated since 1995, thrust forward on a campaign diametrically opposed in attitude to that of the blazers, sent out into the world like sweetly packaged samples to lure in the uninitiated – and, in the case of sevens, who knows, one day to become yet another rival for the public's attention. But these bite-sized versions of rugby are much further removed from the 15-a-side version than a kick-around in the park is from 11-a-side football.

In short, rugby is too dangerous and too complicated to have had a chance of competing against football when the battle for hearts and minds was being waged at the turn of the last century. The elitist Victorians, not to mention the fascists of the 20th century, would be nodding vigorously. Rugby is dangerous, or at the very least it hurts. And if you hope to gain mastery of the laws (not that anything like a majority of players, then or now, would claim to have acquired that), you need a certain level of intelligence. That, you suspect, is precisely what the blazers and dictators valued so much about it. The imperative to make the sport popular did not exist back then. Indeed, rugby's very exclusivity was both inevitable and desirable – a kind of filter, sifting those who had fibre and education from those who did not. How rugby's new missionaries would have despaired, had they been around then, at so small-minded an attitude.

The truth is that pain is an integral part of the rugby experience, but, far from acting as a tool for elitism, it should – and does – serve as just the opposite, a great leveller universalising an experience throughout a body of players more various in shape, aptitude and role than can be found in any other team sport. The gathering of a team in the changing room before a rugby match is an experience intensified by the expectation of pain, or at least of the ferocity of the struggle to come, which all will feel, whatever their class, whatever their role in the team. It is the gladiatorial frisson, which unites all those who play confrontational sports.

What unites rugby players further is the variety of those roles. Is there a sport that so eloquently calls on as various a collection of contributors? League shares the gladiatorial nature but lacks the diversity of player type; American football has the diversity, but each player is so blinkeredly specialised, the game regularly stopped to bring certain of them on or off, that many have neither hope nor ambition so much as to touch the ball.

Rugby, in contrast, is a symphony of moving parts, spread across the spectrum of body types, each fulfilled, each reliant on the others and their very different aptitudes, from the battered yeomen of the front row who graft in unseen, ungodly places, through those who leap high, who grapple low, who smash, who shape and manipulate, to the rock stars who bask in glory on the wide outside. All human life is in a rugby team, and all as important as each other. The changing room after a game is a beautifully equal place, where prop can look across at wing and wing across at prop in gratitude and admiration for qualities completely alien to each other but equally valuable.

When players retire from rugby this redemptive communion in the changing room is often cited as the aspect they miss most. Likewise, the delicate trudge from changing room to bar, limbs battered, face bloody and raw, each elementary movement a contortion of pain avoidance, there to immerse oneself deeper into the communion with the first drink of the day.

Sometimes the antics thereafter have made rugby still more repellent to right-thinking humans. Post-match raucousness has damaged its reputation almost as much as association with the public school and created as many barriers, but this is hardly a stain unique to rugby. The phenomenon of the anti-social clique is universal. When a sizeable collection of people, particularly of the same sex, convenes under a single, obvious banner such as that of a rugby club, the impression of a division between them and the outside world is natural and inescapable. The results are far from endearing, whether the offending collectives are rugby teams, stag or hen parties, students, work colleagues or simply other sports teams. Perhaps it's a size thing. Rugby players may come in many different shapes, but some are very big, and there are generally at least 15 partaking in any one session. Such groups will tend to make an impression, even before they have started drinking, and it may not always be favourable. Indeed, the effect can be quite unnerving.

It is not surprising, then, that rugby has suffered from an image problem. Chuck in a few accents accounted 'posh', and the charge of a sport for Hooray Henrys follows inevitably. Rugby is indeed played by a disproportionate number of posh people, and not just in England. That is a function of the number of private schools that have made it their chosen sport, which is itself a legacy of those protective Victorians and the practical considerations that can sometimes make organising a match seem more trouble than it is worth. But the number of posh people in rugby remains a minority, just not as much of one as in the wider world.

In the areas where the game has been allowed to breathe – New Zealand, France, the South Pacific, to name just a few – it has seeped into the local culture and drawn in a cast of characters from across the spectrum not just of body types but of personality and class. Even in England, your typical town club rings out to the strains of hod-carrier, sparky, policeman, lawyer, teacher, tree surgeon, each with no care for who the other is or where they come from. Many don't even know. They come together to be in each other's company and play the sport they love, with no tomorrow or yesterday – and no judgement, bar (in less charitable cases) of the ability to throw a pass, make a tackle or hold up a scrum.

No, rugby is not for the elitist or insular. And if it has ever seemed to the uninitiated to be closed off in such a way, that is a harrowing failure on the part of those responsible, be they blazered administrator or beered-up goon. For the rugby team is nothing less than a utopian model of diversity and cohesion, which no walk of life should look on without envy or admiration. And that is down to rugby itself, its very nature, for so long obfuscated by the schemes and priorities of those whose chauvinism was a betrayal of that.

Which, in theory, should render it primed for uptake by the people, now the screen has been dismantled. Great strides have indeed been made in that direction, but rugby has stepped out to find a whole new set of problems, exacerbated by that century missed. The peculiar furnace of prejudice and politicking from which it emerged the century before cannot be passed over lightly. In any attempt to investigate the state of the modern game, it pays to pause for a while to consider its twisted origins.

One legacy of that treacherous time still burns brightly, a legend so pristine and evocative as to be etched in gold. No other sport bears a blazon like it. No other sport has felt the need.

II

The Hero Who Ran into Thin Air

The 2015 World Cup opened to a breathtaking ceremony at Twickenham Stadium, the centrepiece of which was a film depicting the birth of rugby. To the strains of 'I Vow to Thee, My Country', a bird's-eye view of the fields of Rugby School forms the backdrop to the words, 'One boy breaks a rule, creates a game, becomes a legend.' The film builds to the moment said boy catches a ball, which comes at him from out of a clear sky. Amid the exhortations of team-mates, opponents and spectators, his expression changes from uncertainty, through resolution to self-discovery. In defiance of established practice, he bounds off from the field, through the school gates to freedom, where his image in the film segues into sepia-tinged sequences of the legends to come, Gareth Edwards, Serge Blanco, David Campese et al, running with the freedom of expression pioneered by that bold lad those many decades earlier. The footage was beautiful and affecting and made one feel emotional just to be associated with the sport of rugby.

Symbolically, William Webb Ellis has more than served his purpose. But to hope to know where rugby has come from, it helps to know how his name came to adorn the World Cup. A collection of alumni from Rugby School responded to the break-up of their game in 1895 with the creation of the most brilliant foundation myth in all of sport, which has since worked on so many levels that corporations today would pay millions for PR as effective.

We all know the story: in 1823, William Webb Ellis was playing in a game of football at Rugby School when he took the ball in his hands and ran with it, thus creating a new sport. The boy has become a hero to certain types of rugby fan, his intervention symbolic of the sport's no-nonsense manliness, doing away with the delicate posturing of football, cutting to the chase. So much so that someone somewhere decided to name the sport's highest prize after him. Every four years the best teams in the world gather to contest for the Webb Ellis Cup. As the profile of the World Cup grows with each instalment, so the boy in that field all those years ago bestrides the rugby world ever more surely as the hero who created it.

The only trouble is, he didn't.

For those pig-headed about their romance, the best we can say is that William Webb Ellis went to Rugby School and was there in 1823 as a 16-year-old, but it's more than possible the 1823 date was chosen retrospectively as consistent with his time at the school. Also in his favour is the testimony of one Reverend Thomas Harris, who remembered him 'perfectly' as an 'admirable cricketer' who was 'generally regarded as inclined to take unfair advantages at Football'. But Harris's testimony goes on to deal a fatal blow to the Ellis myth, which the history creators have ignored, purposely or not.

Harris's observation that he took 'unfair advantages at Football', one of only two first-hand references to Ellis we know of, was offered in May 1895, some 72 years after the alleged incident. The other first-hand evidence of Ellis's character is a mildly derogatory reference in a contemporary letter, which seems to imply he received help from his mother with his entry for a Latin prize. In other words, he wasn't much liked and was, indeed, considered a bit of a cheat.

The foundation of the birth-of-rugby myth comes in the form of two letters and an article, written between 1876 and 1880, by Matthew Bloxam, a solicitor and antiquarian of Rugby, who went to the school from 1813 to 1820. The first letter was written in 1876 to the *Standard*, in response to correspondence speculating over the origins of rugby football. In that first letter, Bloxam wrote of his belief that the practice of 'running in', i.e. running with the ball in an attempt to cross the opposition line, developed during the headmastership of Thomas Arnold, which means some time between 1828 and 1842. But in a letter to the *Meteor*, Rugby School's magazine, in October 1876, he announced that he had made further enquiries, which yielded the identification of Ellis as the first boy to run with the ball. In this letter, he dated the incident to the second half of 1824. Four years later, in an article for the *Meteor*, he had changed that to the second half of 1823. Four years later again, in a talk he delivered to the school, he gave the date as 1825, which was actually after Ellis had left. In the end, posterity adopted the 1823 date, but no one really knows when it happened – least of all, it seems, the man who supplied us with the story in the first place.

Ellis's crime was not the violation it would be today. The football the boys were playing at Rugby School bore little resemblance to the game we now recognise (i.e. soccer). Ellis did not, for example, pick up the ball in the penalty area and leg it while the ref peeped furiously on his whistle. For a start, there were no refs, or even teachers. Football was a controversial pastime that the masters of Rugby School, like other public schools of the time, allowed the boys to play to let off steam. The masters themselves would steer well clear. Public schools in those days were a wild west of arrogant, hormonal teenagers, many of aristocratic stock, who resented being told what to do by teachers of invariably lower social standing. So, the football the boys were playing was presided over by themselves and almost certainly anarchic in nature.

Indeed, to the modern eye, it might already have looked more like what we know as rugby, an indeterminate number of players on each side basically fighting each other, kicking indiscriminately at each other's shins, over the rights to a ball that might not be anywhere near them. Occasionally someone would actually kick the ball, and if you caught it on the full you were allowed to call a temporary halt to the madness by shouting, 'mark', much as you can today under the right circumstances. The opposition would then advance to a point level with your mark, while you retreated a few yards further and decided what to do with the hot potato, which was a pig's bladder. This is the rule Ellis is said to have broken.

'On catching the ball,' wrote Bloxham in his 1880 article, 'instead of retiring backwards, [Ellis] rushed forwards with the ball in his hands towards the opposite goal, with what result as to the game I know not, neither do I know how this infringement of a well-known rule was followed up, or when it became, as it is now, a standing rule.'

It is all a bit vague, as you might expect. Bloxam's second-hand (or possibly even more tenuous than that) testimony, delivered nearly 60 years after the event, would be thrown out of any self-respecting court in the land, now or then. Which is not to say Ellis never ran with the ball. On the no-smoke-without-fire principle alone, it is perfectly possible that he did. But to suggest he was the only boy to do so, or even just the first, is much more of a stretch, while the notion that a new sport was created by his single, transformative act is next to inconceivable and not borne out by what we know.

The boring truth is that football, whatever the code, evolved gradually. If anything, it was association football that required most of the 'inventing'. The sketchy details of historic, pre-19th-century football to which we have access suggest a variety of interpretations of what might happen between human foot and ball, almost all of them sounding like closer approximations to modern rugby than soccer. In other words, high on violence and low on finesse.

Harpastum, as played in the Roman Empire, is usually cited as one ancestor of football – and that sounds very much more like rugby. But in Britain, where codified football would emerge, there seem to have been as many versions of the game in the Middle Ages as there were pairs of villages who fancied a bit of argy-bargy. This tradition has become known as 'folk football'. The rules were lax and the object rudimentary, with the local terrain exercising a loose influence on both. A typical summary might be that, on Shrove Tuesday, Village A and Village B fought, often in their thousands, over a ball, with each endeavouring to carry it to the other's green. These games, as well as the more impromptu, smaller-scale versions that sprang up in between the major festivals, were violent and dangerous and considered a menace, not to mention a distraction from more militarily useful pastimes, such as archery and swordsmanship. Edicts banning football were frequently passed by the kings of the Middle Ages.

By the time the public schools sank their teeth into their various interpretations, the sport had not progressed much further towards the modern versions. Only fleeting impressions are available of each school's code in the early decades, but by the middle of the 19th century they were starting to set the rules down. What is noticeable is how much each game seems to differ from soccer today. All of them involved some form of handling, a legacy that remains in soccer in the form of the goalkeeper, but an option for every player in the mid-nineteenth century.

In later constructing the Ellis legend, Rugby School claimed for its code the defining characteristic of running with the ball, but they might just as easily have claimed the H-shaped goals. No one knows when they were invented – first mention is made in *Tom Brown's School Days*, based on the experiences of its author, Thomas Hughes, at Rugby in the 1830s. Modern observers might point to the scrum as rugby's signature, but loose interpretations of that practice have been a feature of various types of football for centuries, including the Eton field game, which contains within it some of the features we could recognise as part of soccer. Another salient characteristic of rugby is the strict offside law, from which developed the famous requirement to pass backwards, but most of the public schools in the 19th century required everyone on a team to be behind the player with the ball or consider himself out of the game. In the Football Association's first set of rules, drawn up in 1863, this strict interpretation of the offside law was enshrined as Rule No. 6.

Many of the distinctive features of rugby were the norm in football, rather than the exception. A more apposite question is, 'Who invented soccer?', since it seems to stand more distinct from all the haphazard, brutal expositions of football in history.

One might even say that, come the great split of 1863, the game played at Rugby could have more easily unified the schools as association football (from the first part of which name is derived the term 'soccer'), while what we know now as soccer evolved from the breakaway sport of Eton football. 'You watching the eton tonight?' the refrain might have gone.

For the Eton field game required the ball to be shot into a goal under a certain height. It also featured dribbling and allowed for the pass to a player in front, or 'passing on'. In 1867, association football's offside law was amended to allow the latter practice, transforming the nature of soccer. Yet even the Eton field game had (still has, for it continues to be played at the school) among its methods of scoring points the 'rouge', which is when the ball is touched down over the opposition's goal-line – in effect, a try.

To attempt to untangle rugby from all the competing versions of football in the mid-19th century is an enterprise doomed, and to reduce the source of its idiosyncrasies to the single act of a boy in a field in 1823 no more plausible than a fantasy. What we can say is that modern rugby developed directly from that version of football played at Rugby School, where the laws were set down for the first time in 1845. By then, Rugby's was just one of several interpretations of football spreading across the country, transmitted by the development of railways and the proselytising of various devotees.

In 1863, at a pub in Holborn, a meeting was convened of what would become the Football Association. The aim was to establish some sort of order to the playing of football. Over the course of the next few weeks, the fledgling FA canvassed views from clubs and public schools alike, as they attempted to synthesise the rules.

The suggestion that it is Rugby's version that could have emerged as the FA's official code is not so fanciful. At one point, in the saga of meeting and counter-meeting, running with the ball and the controversial practice of hacking – essentially, kicking an opponent's shins – were in, by a vote of 10 to nine at the fourth meeting. What appears to have been sharp practice by Ebenezer Cobb Morley, secretary of the FA, whose idea the whole enterprise was, prevented those two rules being accepted, thus leading to the split. At the fifth meeting, Morley's minutes from the fourth conveniently left out the fact that running with the ball and hacking had been passed, prompting F. W. Campbell of the Blackheath Football Club to move to have the minutes rejected. Alas, the personnel at the fifth meeting was different from that at the fourth, and his motion was denied. Campbell insisted that the loss of hacking would 'do away with all the courage and pluck from the game, and I will be bound over to bring over a lot of Frenchmen, who would beat you with a week's practice'. But his was a losing cause. Running with the ball and hacking were dropped when the trial rules were drawn up at the sixth and final meeting (although it is worth noting that fair catches, touching the ball down over the goal-line for a free kick at goal and the strict offside law were included). Campbell withdrew Blackheath from the FA at that sixth meeting. Other clubs favouring the Rugby rules joined the breakaway, and soccer was free to develop into the dribbling, non-handling game we know today.

By 1871, hacking had been dropped by those playing the breakaway sport, too. The potential for injury, while all very well for schoolboys, made it an unreasonable risk for working men to endure. Still, there remained variations in the rules played even by the breakaway clubs, so 21 of them met on 26 January of that year, in much the same manner and under the same pretences as those forming the FA had done, this time in a hostelry off Pall Mall, to form the Rugby Football Union.* In June of the same year, three lawyers, all old boys from Rugby School, drew up the first official set of laws (because they were lawyers, they decreed rugby be played by laws not rules) of rugby football.

At this point, nobody had heard of, or mentioned, William Webb Ellis.

Momentum gathered over the following decades, and rugby as we know it began to emerge. The first 15-a-side game was played in the Varsity Match of 1875; by the early 1880s, players were passing the ball to each other; by the 1890s, sides were settling on the practice of fielding four three-quarters and only eight forwards.

Old Rugbeians were everywhere – in the England team, on the RFU committees, in charge of clubs the country over. But, alas, others were becoming better at the sport – and they weren't even public schoolboys. The working-class men of the north, their bodies and attitudes hardened by life in pit or factory, turned out to have more than a natural aptitude for rugby. The popularity of the sport in the north escalated, pulling in sizeable crowds and money for the legion clubs that had established themselves. The best players were under pressure to take time off work. They wanted to be paid for it, but this did not sit well with the gentlemen of the RFU.

The Reverend Frank Marshall was president of the Yorkshire Rugby Union and a maniacal scourge of what became known as broken-time

---

* Most of the clubs present no longer exist, but among the surviving founders, all necessarily from in or around London, are Blackheath, Harlequins and Richmond. Legend has it that the Wasps guy went to the wrong pub and got too drunk to find his way to the correct one. Without a mobile he was stuck, so Wasps forfeited their right to be a founding club.

payments in the north. He even suspended his own club, Huddersfield, on suspicion of payments to players. He, incidentally, had put together a formidable tome in 1892 entitled *Football: the Rugby Union Game*, which documented all aspects imaginable of the sport at that early stage of its life. William Webb Ellis, whose name was technically in the public domain by then, was not mentioned once.

Reverend Marshall had bigger fish to fry, as the RFU's avenging angel of the north. The mutual resentment between the northern clubs and the RFU was palpable, the latter holding their meetings in London and dictating to the former, despite there being more players among the former. In 1893, two trains' worth of northern representatives descended for one such meeting to propose the motion that broken-time payments be made lawful. It was in vain. The RFU had gathered proxy votes from more than a hundred clubs against, and the motion was defeated. The idea of absent committeemen overruling those who had travelled miles to be there was more than a little symbolic.

And so the way was paved for the next split in codes. In 1895, 22 clubs from Yorkshire and Lancashire seceded from the RFU to form the Northern Rugby Football Union (which would in time become the Rugby League), a new body that allowed payments for broken time. Rugby football in England was in chaos. The national team's form collapsed there and then (they would not win the Home Nations Championship again until France joined in 1910), but the amateur ideal of the gentleman-player had been under threat for some time and was now officially breached. The much-loved pastime of an ancient school was running out of control, further and further away from its spiritual guardians.

It was against this backdrop that a sub-committee of Old Rugbeians was formed to investigate the origins of their sport in July 1895, a month before the great schism in the north was finally consummated. Nominally, the sub-committee was responding to the findings of a book published eight years earlier that held forth, erroneously they felt, on the history of the game played at Rugby. Again, the book made no mention of Ellis, but our latest committee did recall the pair of mentions the boy had received in the school magazine from Bloxam, the second of which had been aired some 15 years earlier. Could it be their game had been born suddenly from such a simple, romantic gesture as a boy running with the ball one day – and on the very field they had graced themselves in their youth?

If only they had thought to investigate earlier. Ellis was 23 years dead by then – and, worse, Bloxam seven. Bloxam had spent nearly all his life in Rugby, living for much of it literally across the road from the school. His brother ran one of the boarding houses next door. He lived for eight years after the publication of his second mention of Ellis in the *Meteor*, and twelve after the first, ample time for Old Rugbeians to make enquiries if they had been genuinely interested. As it is, they left it until that calamitous year for rugby, 1895, before mobilising. Too late.

Still, they knew a good thing when they heard vague rumours about it, so they set about contacting as many living old boys as possible who had played football at Rugby School in the first half of the century. This was far from an exhaustive sample. All but one had played after Ellis left, and there was agreement among them on one point – they had never heard of him.

The most damning testimony came from Thomas Hughes himself, the author of *Tom Brown's School Days*. Hughes was a keen and influential player at a time when the game was beginning to find itself. His famous novel included a detailed description of a football match set in the 1830s, a numerically unequal contest between scores of boys in a big field, 17-year-olds colliding with 12-year-olds, and much pain and violence besides, and so on for two hours. At one point there's a goal. It is possible to infer from the colourful account that running with the ball is allowed, even perhaps practised at one point, but the details are vague, and most of the interludes between mauling and hacking seem to involve kick-chasing and/or dribbling.

Hughes was rather more explicit on the matter of running with the ball in the letter he sent in reply to the sub-committee's enquiries in 1895. 'In my first year, 1834,' he wrote, 'running with the ball to get a try . . . was not absolutely forbidden, but a jury of Rugby boys of that day would almost certainly have found a verdict of "justifiable homicide" if a boy had been killed running in. The practice grew, and was tolerated more and more, and indeed became rather popular in 1838–39 from the prowess of Jem Mackie, the great "runner-in".'

Hughes went on to describe Mackie as 'fleet of foot as well as brawny of shoulder' and very difficult to stop. His success that season was instrumental in legitimising the troublesome tactic of running with the ball. Three seasons later, when Hughes was captain, they 'settled it (as we believed) for all time' by decreeing the practice lawful. Hughes could not remember signing anything to make it official, but when the rules were first written down in 1845 running in was included, some 22 years after Ellis had supposedly invented it.

Mackie is an interesting character, and it would surely be more appropriate, if we had to indulge in this exercise, to attribute to him the birth of rugby. At least we have here first-hand evidence, corroborated elsewhere, that his contribution was key to the development of the sport.

Alas, he was expelled from Rugby at the end of 1839, after some of the younger boys had let off fireworks and smashed up the wares of a travelling merchant who made the mistake of venturing into the school grounds. Mackie was guilty of nothing more than failing to stop them, but an expulsion is an expulsion and a stain against one's name when sub-committees draw up their conclusions. Worse than that, he was Scottish. And a politician. The legend of William Webb Ellis, the English boy who became a priest, would have seemed far more appealing.

If only it were as well supported by the testimony of first-hand witnesses – which is to say, at all. Hughes, in his letter to the sub-committee, flatly replied to their enquiry about the Ellis tradition that it 'had not survived to my day'. He and the 13 other witnesses from the 1830s did agree, though, that running with the ball was a feature of football at Rugby, albeit rarely practised, until Mackie mastered it, for fear of the reprisals meted out to one's shins.

And so to the one man the sub-committee tracked down who had been a contemporary of Ellis's, if five years younger. The Reverend Thomas Harris began by stating that in his time at Rugby, from 1819 to 1828, 'picking up and running with the ball in hand was distinctly forbidden'. So, even if Ellis had been the first to run with the ball, his single act did not create a new sport.

Harris then went on to deal with Ellis himself. And he wasn't particularly kind, fellow man of the cloth or not. 'He was an admirable cricketer, but was generally regarded as inclined to take unfair advantages at Football. I should not quote him in any way as an authority.'

It is rather dismissive of a supposed hero. There is no doubt, though, the slight that he took 'unfair advantage' might be consistent with this idea that he ran with the ball. The sub-committee pressed Harris further on the point but, in a second letter, he could add no further details on Ellis himself. 'You must observe that I was several years his junior, and had not either reasons or opportunities for closely observing his manner of play.'

His next paragraph is instructive. 'I may add that in the matches played by boys in the lower part of the School, while I was myself a junior, the cry of "Hack him over" was always raised against any player who was seen to be running with the ball in his hands.'

It is worth dwelling on this observation. Harris now seems to be suggesting that boys *did* run with the ball in the 1820s, even if it was not allowed. He is not specific on dates, other than to say that boys were known to indulge while he was in the 'lower part of the School'.

Suddenly, we have visions to rival that of Ellis with the ball tucked under his arms, and they must be roughly contemporaneous.

We know Harris entered the school in 1819. More important to our enquiries, though, is when he left the Lower School. In other words, what is the timeframe for his memories of boys running with the ball at Rugby School?

In those days, the Upper School began in the Lower Fourth Form. It appears Harris was a particularly precocious pupil. According to the archives at Rugby School, he entered the Sixth Form in 1825 at the tender age of 13 – and he entered the Lower Fourth, i.e. left 'the lower part of the School', in 1822, aged 10. Which means that, if we are to take his words at face value, there were boys running with the ball at Rugby School *more than a year before* William Webb Ellis was supposed to have invented the practice, and possibly as many as four. The only testimony we have from a first-hand witness, therefore, undermines the very legend it played such a crucial role in building up.

The very best we can say of the contention that Ellis was the first to run with the ball is that it is conjecture seized upon by those anxious to develop a founding myth. That he didn't invent a new sport, however, is incontrovertible. What became rugby evolved over the ensuing decades, when a number of distinctive features crystallised, of which running with the ball was but one.

William Webb Ellis left the school in 1825 and, as far as we know, never touched a football again in his life. He was a scholar, however, albeit described by Bloxam as 'of fair average abilities'. With or without the help of his mum he won an exhibition to Brasenose College, Oxford, where, consistent with the recollection of him as an 'admirable cricketer', he batted at number three in the first Varsity cricket match, in 1827. After leaving Oxford, he went into the church and was the rector of parishes in London and Essex. When he contracted tuberculosis in 1871, he moved to the south of France for the winter and died there in January 1872, aged 65, a year after the Rugby Football Union was formed. He almost certainly knew nothing about it. The RFU certainly knew nothing about him. His grave was discovered in 1957, and its new and improved headstone is now a French-maintained shrine for rugby fans the world over, while he spins in his box six feet beneath it.

His legend was clinched, though, not by the speculations of Bloxam, or even those of the sub-committee of Old Rugbeians, who published their findings in 1897 under the title *The Origin of Rugby Football*. In February 1900, a plaque was erected on the Doctor's Wall at Rugby School, overlooking the famous field where it all evolved, which describes how a boy many years earlier with 'a fine disregard for the rules' had first taken the ball in his arms and run. It was a genius stroke of PR, uniting in one concrete memorial the school's ownership of the sport and the romantic ideal of a young lad expressing himself with an audacity considered integral to rugby's character.

Rugby School was losing control of its beloved game in the 1890s. Whether the sub-committee of Old Rugbeians investigated the William Webb Ellis tale as a direct response to this will remain open to debate, but the erection of the plaque telling of his deed was a plain attempt to remind the world where it all started. To take ownership of the sport in such a way is Rugby School's prerogative, since the game undoubtedly developed there. They were wise enough, though, to know that the story of a field is nowhere near as compelling as the story of a boy. They needed a personality to pin it on – didn't really matter who it was – and the passing reference to a rumour voiced nearly 20 years earlier about an act another 60 or so before that sounded perfect. The plaque went up and the legend was born. As with the most poignant legends, it has grown and grown, until it became currency so universally recognised that the boy's name now adorns the sport's highest prize.

It is a travesty that the World Cup is named after such a flimsy legend. Like so many of the other travesties in rugby we shall go on to consider, it owes its roots to the determination of a ruling class to retain control of their sport. Rugby could and should have been embraced without qualification by millions around the world, whoever they are, wherever from, but the chauvinism, often brutal at times, with which rugby's international administrators protected their interests has left a poisonous legacy. Naming the World Cup after Ellis was a final, curious nod by rugby to those elements of its past best left behind, just as the future presented itself so suddenly.*

When the football equivalent was initiated, they renamed its trophy a few years later after Jules Rimet, a man who had worked tirelessly to make the event happen. There are countless people in rugby's history more deserving of such an honour. In 2015, New Zealand won the Webb Ellis Cup for the third time. Surely they have earned the right to keep it, as Brazil did the Jules Rimet Trophy in 1970. Now that rugby has shaken off the blazers of Empire, well might we retire William Webb Ellis to the mists of myth and legend and come up with a new standard for the global game, which bears the name of someone more appropriate.

The Jonah Lomu Cup, for example. Now, there is someone who very definitely ran with the ball. There is someone who changed the sport for ever.

---

* And why is it called the Webb Ellis Cup anyway? His surname was Ellis; Webb was just his middle name. It would be like naming a trophy after Ma'a Nonu and calling it the Allan Nonu Cup – yes, Allan really is Ma'a Nonu's middle name.

Part 2

A Formation of Bodies

III

None Shall Pass:
Annexation by an Empire

This notion of taking up the ball and running is powerful. Hence William Webb Ellis. Hence Jonah Lomu. The Ellis legend may be of such stuff as dreams are made on, but there is no arguing with the substance of the legend that rocked the rugby world in 1995, exactly 100 years after the only other transformation of the sport to compare. Indeed, it is tempting to posit Lomu as the force that unleashed the professional era on a sport that had so stubbornly denied it. The shadowy negotiations of men in suits might have paved the way, but Lomu captured the imagination and allowed rugby to throw itself open with a certain confidence, even a flourish, 10 weeks later.

There is a poetry as poignant as it was devastating in that tumultuous day in Cape Town, 18 June 1995, when Lomu clinched his place in the pantheon and rugby's, finally, in the consciousness of the wider world. The International Rugby Board made its announcement on 26 August that year that rugby would become an open game, but by then it was little more than confirmation the sport was ready to take advantage of the new dynamic. The day Lomu tore through an England team as startled as anyone by the dimensions he seemed to be opening up was the one that changed everything, at least from a sporting perspective, more so even than the politically marvellous events of the following weekend in Johannesburg.

So many of the energies that had both riven rugby and fuelled it came together on that field on the edge of the world. That it should be a boy (for Lomu had just turned 20) not only from New Zealand, the tiny, distant nation who had run away with the sport, but descended from the islands even tinier and further away in the wide Pacific who have come to supply the world with its most outrageous talent; that the day should fall a hundred years after those other disadvantaged folk, rich of talent if not circumstance, had taken up their ball and run off to form a new sport altogether; that the chastened, the devastated, opposition should be none other than England, the imperial power who had given the world the sport then tried so adamantly to keep its energies in check – the symbolism was profound from whichever angle viewed.

In the 170 years between the two legends, many more have arisen along rugby's tempestuous journey towards the 21st century. The peculiar antagonism of matters on the field seems to have yielded similarly fractious attitudes off it. Taken together, the sport has proved a fertile arena for the production of heroes.

The first were those who took rugby out into the world. The football codes were quick to spread their respective gospels beyond Britain. Rugby was at the forefront, reaching many nations before The Sibling did, even those, such as the Netherlands and Brazil, whose culture would become so bound up with soccer. It spawned whole new sports in others too. Had anyone been in position to make such a judgement in the third quarter of the 19th century, there would be little reason not to think that rugby would be the sport, if any, to acquire world domination within a hundred years. Chest-beating was very much the modus communicandi of the football codes, and the rhythm pounded out by rugby was the louder across the world after the two went their separate ways. One might even argue that very machismo proved the sport's undoing, had either any conscious designs at that stage on taking the world.

The reasons for soccer's eventual pre-eminence will remain a matter of debate. The sheer simplicity of the sport that would emerge – and its versatility – must have played some part, but rugby was further stymied by the very intransigence of its own administrators, which they no doubt imagined at the time proved them superior in the muscular ways of the public school. The attitudes of the FA and the RFU towards professionalism were not dissimilar. The FA instituted a maximum wage for its players, which lasted until 1961, so was never comfortable with the idea of the remuneration of the players, but it, crucially, relented on the question 10 years before the RFU did not.

The parallels were uncanny. By 1884, 30 northern football clubs were threatening to form a breakaway league so that their working-class players might be paid. In 1885, after much agonising, the FA agreed. In so doing, it loosened its grip ever so slightly, and in time its bird flew.

The RFU was not so lenient. Indeed, it saw what had happened to football and vowed all the more determinedly that the same would not happen to rugby. And so the mood was set for a story of fury, repression and defiance. Wherever we follow the various trails rugby beat into the world the same sort of dynamic recurs, best described as conflict, the classic tension between authority and the rebel. Public schoolboy introduces rugby into new land; natives start to wake up to it; classes unite; arguments and/or rebellions ensue.

If it were possible to be more Victorian than the RFU, the Scottish Rugby Union did its best, until the working men in the Borders expressed their grievances by inventing another concept, seven-a-side rugby, which may yet prove as much of a nemesis to the original as any of the other codes that have broken away in impatience. And the Borders clubs invented rugby's first league, which was another development that displeased the authorities, who considered competitions to be almost as much a contravention of the amateur ideal as payment. It was another stubborn point of resistance that, for all the rebel competitions that broke out around the world, would hold back rugby in the mother country. The FA Cup (est. 1871), the Football League (1888) and the lack of equivalents in rugby's founding nation furthered football's advantage as much as professionalism, if not more.

The dynamic was repeated time and again – in Ireland, where Dublin played the role of overlords, Ulster defied them and Munster simply threw open the doors to everyone; in Wales, where rugby rose from the soil like the coal and the RFU came as close as it ever did to countenancing, or at least conveniently overlooking, payments to players; in France, where Paris and the cities and communes of the south-west clashed furiously with each other, transmitting their centuries-old animosity through the explosive combination of rugby and the railways that proliferated, uniting them as surely as the increased contact provoked.

In farther-flung lands, with greater or lesser regard for the sensibilities of the English, the same antagonism developed between tradition and the disregard of it. In Australia, rugby's first landing precipitated the sport that would become Australian rules. Its instigator, Tom Willis, an Old Rugbeian, reckoned improvements could be made to rugby and thought nothing of making them. Having headed south to Melbourne with the rest of the gold rush, his code took hold unanswerably in the southern states of Australia, leaving a familiar struggle to unfold in New South Wales and Queensland between the 19th century and the fast-approaching 20th, which in rugby's universe meant between union and league. The struggle was decisively won by the latter, the pioneering Australians caring not for anything so intangible as the amateur ideal and rather taking to the accent integral to league on running rather than set piece. Why wouldn't they accept payment to play it? And so the world's dominant league nation was born.

The sporting pre-eminence of the Australians in general seems stymied largely by their own prowess. Aussie rules never spread much beyond those southern states in the 20th century, an era critical for the expansion of any sport, because the locals perfected it to such a degree there was no point in playing anyone else – and certainly for anyone else in playing them. That confined a healthy contingent of Australia's finest sportsmen to a sport only they played. The same was true, to a lesser extent, with league.

A similar story unfolded in North America. The USA had even less concern for the British and their traditions than the Australians. And they had even less regard for the scrum, doing away with it, like the Canadians, in favour of the two straight lines of the scrimmage and poignantly bypassing all the aggro in and around by simply flinging the ball over the top to players so far upfield as to cause a union man to splutter in his claret. And so was born what would become the world's most lucrative competition, the National Football League, albeit in a sport confined, again, more or less exclusively to itself.

Actually, rugby did have its chance to take the American stage – and who knows what that might have meant for the condition of the sport today. A recurring theme for the codes of football derived from Rugby School's version in the early stages, which has never been shaken off (and may bring them down yet), was the concern and dissent over the violence inherent. As in the Middle Ages, when folk football was considered a public menace, so certain codes in the 19th century and early 20th evoked criticism for the danger to those playing, never more so than American football in 1905, when a season of deaths on the field precipitated a crisis in the sport. One of the responses was to introduce that signature forward pass to circumvent the brutality of the defences, but another saw rugby, which had never quite caught on in the 19th century, start to regather, finding traction in California particularly.

In the years that followed, American rugby teams performed admirably at home and away against the Australians, who were rocked at around the same time by their own split into league and union.

As ever, though, it was rugby's special breed of direful angels, the nemesis of so many aspiring nations since, who killed off any hopeful buds the sport may have been nurturing in the world's largest market. Rugby in America was summarily crushed by the All Blacks.

They had toured in 1906, playing two exhibition matches in California against British Columbia, just as America was digesting the 18 deaths and 150 serious injuries of the season before. Both matches were routs, but there was much admiration then for the All Blacks and, by extension, rugby. When they returned, however, in 1913, American rugby was starting to dream. This time, the inevitable routs were not so well received, as the black crusaders swept all before them, simultaneously brandishing their expertise and the beauty of rugby when perfected, while killing off what little chance the sport might have had of gaining traction more widely at that precarious juncture in its development. Humiliation at anything does not sit well with Americans. Their rugby was not as far advanced as they had hoped. By the end of the decade, any institutions that had adopted the game, most of them in California, had reverted to American football.

Had a nation as vast and commercial as America embraced rugby early on, the dynamics driving the sport would surely have created yet more tensions between the new world and the old, the professional and the amateur. As it is, by the time rugby's tale had unwound into the 20th century, the sport had taken firmly in just the home nations, France, and the outer reaches of what had been the British Empire: New Zealand, South Africa and Australia. For most of the 20th century, rugby was quite happy with its modest reach, or at least the dominant voices at administrative level were, the old world vying on the field with the new, who, while always demonstrably better at the game, remained manageable from an ideological and economic point of view. But by the 1980s the radicals on the fringes of the old Empire were agitating for a World Cup. Professionalism was by then an open secret in certain parts of the world, not least South Africa, where political isolation allowed the culture of remuneration that had been developing anyway to mature still further. Nearly a hundred years after the great split, confronted by an increasingly aggressive global sports marketplace, not to mention the machinations of member unions, the members of the International Rugby Board (IRB) were constantly having to remind themselves why amateurism was so important. Increasingly, they could not remember.

In 1985, they voted in favour of a World Cup (well, France, New Zealand, Australia and South Africa did; Ireland and Scotland voted against, while England and Wales could not decide). Now rugby had its showpiece international event. Professionalism was sure to follow. The first Rugby World Cup was won by New Zealand on home soil in 1987, in a popular but gentle warm-up, and the second by Australia in England in 1991, when the commercial possibilities started to become apparent. Both were without South Africa.

Which set the scene for the convergence of all the energies in 1995, when the third edition not only welcomed South Africa back into the fold after the fall of apartheid but actually took place there. Professionalism in rugby was a done deal by now, the only question remaining whether it be rebel or authorised, the same tension as ever. Backstage, the negotiations raged, but even onstage the feeling pervaded that everything was changing. Never was that impression more boldly realised than in the shape of Lomu, the boy from the mean streets of Auckland, born of a Tongan line.

The image of his trampling over England's Mike Catt in the semi-final is one of the most famous action shots in rugby. Indeed, the unfortunate Catt's travails are captured from such a variety of angles and moments in time by the developing technology that we can chart his indignity minutely; so too the magnificence of his nemesis, exotic, ferocious, from another time and place, while the crumpled Catt, whose bowed head never raises above Lomu's waist, flings his hands upwards and forwards throughout, part in self-defence, part, it is tempting to infer, in worship. Catt – or you and I, as an astonished world came to view him when the vignette swept across the globe – looked what he was, a regular-sized human blown away by the new reality.

Another hero representative of the times was his captain, Will Carling. England actually played quite well that day, scoring more points than they ever had against the All Blacks in their 45–29 defeat, but playing quite well was no longer going to cut it. New physical powers had here been unleashed. Carling perfectly encapsulated the transition between the two eras, a dashing public schoolboy of army stock who walked in palaces but retained a twinkle in the eye and the lightness of mind to see where things were going. He had found himself at the centre of a storm himself a few weeks before the tournament, when he had questioned in an interview the efficacy of a system by which '57 old farts' (viz the RFU) continued to administer a sport on the brink of the 21st century. The RFU stripped him of the captaincy for the jibe, then reinstated him, but it knew the old ways were at an end. Carling was himself towards the end of a career that had ushered in the televisual possibilities for rugby, if not quite yet the financial, but when he came face to face with that new century he was as shell-shocked by Lomu as anybody. 'He's a freak,' he famously quipped after the match, 'and the sooner he goes away the better!'

Carling's latter remark amounted to a come-and-get-him plea to league on behalf of international union players everywhere. Lomu, he reckoned, would be right up league's street – and had a 19-stone behemoth who could run a sub-11-second 100 metres burst on to the stage 10 to 15 years earlier, he almost certainly would have ended up in league, as had Va'aiga Tuigamala only two years earlier, at 17 stone, the man to pave the way. But now rugby was armed with a mandate to make money out of such assets – and of course to pay them. Lomu was going nowhere.

His trail of destruction in the semi-final was astonishing, but so too was the fact it did not continue into the final. The brave new era reached yet another height the following weekend, when rugby transcended the sporting universe to touch the historical. If the image of Lomu laying waste to the English is as famous as any in rugby, that of Nelson Mandela presenting the World Cup to Francois Pienaar, South Africa's captain, sits comfortably alongside any in history. Pienaar was another hero to bestride the eras, a square-jawed, steel-eyed Afrikaner whose belief in an enlightened future for the Rainbow Nation was as ardent as his resolve to throw himself in the way of the new breed of rugby player. He wasn't the only one with such resolve in the South Africa team that took on the All Blacks in the final in Johannesburg. If England had been taken unawares by quite how destructive Lomu could be, even to a team good enough to dispatch champions Australia the previous round, South Africa were as well versed in his powers as everybody else had become in the intervening week. When Mandela and Pienaar reached across the dais and the years to shake hands after a suffocating final in the thin air that was more of a throwback to rugby's past – and no less compelling for that – it was hard to discern which of the two was the more natural statesman, Pienaar effortlessly drawing in the 43 million people of South Africa, whatever their colour, just as tribute was paid to the 15 he had led on the pitch. The moment felt historic – and if you had any acquaintance with rugby it was a surreal experience to witness the sport's association with it.

It marks an appropriate point to take stock. South Africa might have been surprise winners, but the finalists that year were the two teams who had dominated rugby's first hundred years since the split with league, which might be considered an unlikely dominance if the wider world is anything to go by. The success of New Zealand

and South Africa would have been facilitated by rugby's limited reach across the globe, but by this stage the world according to team sport boiled down to football and the rest. Of the rest, rugby's establishment in those eight nations represented actually quite a respectable reach. The link was the Commonwealth and the English language, *Tom Brown's Schooldays* inspiring enthusiasm for rugby wherever it was read. And in the very obvious exception, France, rugby owed much to the enthusiasm of Baron de Coubertin, more famous as the founder of the modern Olympics, whose love for the book and the British seems to have bordered on idolatry.

When the IRB (as it was then; World Rugby as now) voted on the idea of the World Cup in 1985, the result was 10–6 in favour, 16 votes shared equally between those eight nations, who alone constituted the body governing the sport around the world. It is not as if rugby was played exclusively in those countries – when that first World Cup was held, nine other nations were invited (to make up 16, with South Africa in isolation) – but they were, literally and metaphorically, the only ones who counted, a set-up consistent with that tension between exclusivity and democratisation that has fuelled and distorted rugby throughout. The tale of the IRB is as illustrative of this as any face-off between aristocrat and worker – and the influence of the public school is felt keenly at every turn.

The IRB began life, inevitably, because of an argument. And, inevitably, it was an argument about the labyrinthine laws. The 1884 Calcutta Cup match on a freezing day in Blackheath had been won by an England goal, but the preceding try was bitterly contested. One of the Scotland players passionately owned up to having knocked the ball backwards with his hands in the build-up to the try. In those days, the Scottish were adamant that knock-ons of any kind were illegal, whether forward or backward, and much of the argument centred on the fact the English were not so sure about the backward bit, a typical point of ambiguity from which, one senses, the simpler code of football did not suffer. There was no advantage in those days, so by the letter of the law play should have stopped, but the English argued that to have done so would mean Scotland benefiting from their own infringement.

The argument raged – on the pitch for nearly half an hour (play eventually resuming with no decision reached, although the kick at goal was allowed to proceed) and then in letters and correspondence to newspapers for more than a year. The Irish referee is said to have left it until that evening to decide one way or the other. In the end, he sided with the English interpretation.

Scotland were having none of it. They refused to play the following year's fixture and in 1886 effectively buddied up with their fellow Celts, who sympathised with any attempt to defy the English overlords (even if, on this occasion, the English surely had a point), to form the International Rugby Football Board. Scotland, Ireland and Wales appointed themselves the guardians of the laws of the game and invited – practically defied – the English to join. Needless to say, they refused. No one played England for a couple of years.

It all feels rather familiar. Even the IRB, though, knew that a championship without England, who had more than three times as many clubs as the others combined, lacked a certain credibility. In 1890, an independent arbitrator decreed that the English should join the IRB and abide by its laws – but with the fairly significant proviso that their numerical superiority be recognised by the incorporation of six English members and two from each of the other three unions.

And so was born an institution, led as it was by the RFU, as brutal and chauvinistic as any in rugby's brutal, chauvinistic history. The IRB pre-dated its football equivalent, FIFA, by 14 years and, attitudinally, by about 1,400. The French, naturally, wanted to join in the early 20th century but were not allowed because it occurred to the IRB when the matter was raised that only English-speaking nations were. New Zealand, Australia and South Africa wanted to join, but they couldn't because, well, they were mere colonials and needed to know their place, particularly as they did not seem to know it on the pitch. At one point, British Columbia applied to join, but it didn't stand a chance because it wasn't even a country. It was not until 1948 that the three from the south were admitted to the IRB and not until, incredibly, 1978 that the French were. Meanwhile, FIFA (Fédération Internationale de Football Association), whose very name is French (although the home nations remained aloof there, too, if only for a year before joining), counted among its multilingual membership nearly 150 nations. By 1978 it was already on its 11th World Cup.

At least by the time the French had brought the IRB's membership up to eight, a more equitable distribution of power had been instituted, so that those 16 votes were shared equally, but rugby remained a sport, even in 1995, administered by a small clique of unions who knew what was in their interests and, just as importantly, what was not. It is a moot point whether they wanted their sport to expand. Certainly, it is possible to imagine the uneasiness of any number of committee men as the realities of the 20th century began to overtake them, let alone those of the 21st already appearing on the horizon.

The question is, how much has changed? When a status quo has been allowed to develop that institutes the interests of a minority so deeply into a system of governance, expansion beyond that minority – genuine, transformative expansion – faces so many obstacles as to become inherently compromised, even preventively so. The constitution of the IRB has evolved since then, but gradually, and never once in such a way as to threaten the mandate of what rugby has unashamedly come to refer to as the Tier 1 nations.

No other sport – and surely not many institutions – has considered it normal, healthy or even anything other than offensive to its membership to formalise any stratification in such terms. There are now 10 Tier 1 nations, which is progress of sorts from the original eight, Italy and Argentina having joined rugby's two major annual international tournaments (the Six Nations and the Rugby Championship) in the 21st century. But if you are of a World Cup standard and not in that club you are in Tier 2, should there be any doubt about your right to self-respect. There then follows the swathe of Tier 3 nations, analogous to cricket's non-Test nations, who are, in rugby terms, works in progress.

It is a profoundly discouraging arrangement, which does nothing to dispel the impression that rugby's administration remains as much of a clique as it has always been. Likewise, one might add, the name of the governing body that oversees rugby in the country with the biggest image problem of all, England. Everyone understands and (to a greater or lesser extent) respects the fact that the English were the first to play the game and establish a union, but to continue to go by the title of the Rugby Football Union lays the game's most powerful organisation open to all the accusations of arrogance it spends so much of its time elsewhere trying to undo. As a microcosm of rugby's wider struggle in the 21st century, it is apt. Admirable intentions abound, as do policies, but the old instincts remain deep-rooted and give themselves away time and again, sometimes with details like nomenclature, sometimes with insidious attitudes that belong indeed in another century. With a title like that, the RFU might as well rebrand itself as THE Rugby Football Union, but how easy it would be to change instead to the English Rugby Union. The message that would send out is generous and egalitarian. The same might be said of the Football Association.

Football, though, has democratised far more effectively, so that the balance of power is spread more or less evenly across the globe – at international level, anyway – and any airs and graces of an individual member obliviously swept away. The constitution of FIFA is simple: 211 members; 211 votes. This set-up undoubtedly has its drawbacks – if airs and graces can be easily missed in so unwieldy an organisation, so too, it seems, can corruption – but the speed with which football has developed in Africa, Asia and North America cannot be wholly put down to the simplicity of the sport itself. World Rugby's constitution is just not set up for such growth.

By the 2003 World Cup, that constitution had evolved – a bit. With membership of the IRB having exploded to 95, the 16 votes had expanded to 21. The original eight, known as the foundation unions, still had their two, but now five others had been invited to the table – Italy, Argentina, Japan, Canada and FIRA (Fédération Internationale de Rugby Amateur, now Rugby Europe), an alliance of European nations formed in 1934. Just the one vote each, mind. Then three others had been invited, if not quite to the table, to the edges of the room at least. Representatives from the regional associations of Africa, Asia and Oceania were granted 'observer' rights at council meetings. 'I will have no talking rights at the meetings,' Philip Muller of Samoa, the Oceania representative, explained to, of all newspapers, the *Observer* during the 2003 World Cup. 'I have to be asked before I can contribute.'

Fifteen years later, World Rugby had become more enlightened. In 2017, with a membership of 123 the total vote had expanded to 48. The Tier 1 nations had loosened their grip a little, but not much. They had three votes each, so a majority of 62.5 per cent. Japan, now a bona fide World Cup host, had two, while Canada, Georgia, Romania and the USA had one, with two each for six regional associations, the two continents of America having joined FIRA, Africa, Asia and Oceania, now all happily ushered in from the walls. A year later, to much rejoicing, Fiji and Samoa were finally given places at the table in their own right, to bring the total vote up to 50.

As one might expect, World Rugby is becoming more sophisticated as it settles into the crazy journey it has been launched upon by the slingshot from 19th century to the 21st. The arrogance of the set-up, predicated as it was almost exclusively upon the foundation unions, remained insufferable for several years into the professional era. That 2003 World Cup in Australia was a case in point. The fixture list was a scandal, with the foundation unions enjoying for the most part a schedule of matches regularly spaced out, their multimillion-dollar operations transitioning smoothly from weekend to weekend, while the Tier 2 mob, underfunded and understaffed, deprived in many cases of even the basic right to pick their best players, had to fit in and around them, sometimes playing four matches in 15 days, sometimes two. Things have improved on that front, although the impression is difficult to shake that lobbying from media and, well, those Tier 2 folk sitting not so quietly around the edges of the room was at least as responsible as any desire to do the right thing.

World Rugby is doing its best to emerge into the light. There has been, and continues to be, more than the odd goonish slip along the way, but those in government, whether of sport, business or state, are constantly being pulled up and ridiculed for such. Maybe governance is harder than it looks. Rugby, through the missionary work of its governing body, is striving more frenetically than ever to expand. Yet World Rugby, with all its enthusiastic, hopeful, almost childlike proclamations of progress – millions invested, millions participating in the unlikeliest parts of the world – now comes across as the camera-conscious, spin-doctored politician who wishes (which of us doesn't) they were more powerful than they are, a kind of Tony Blair darting enthusiastically around the feet of George Bush.

Because, governing body of the global sport though it may be, World Rugby is not the biggest beast in the pen. Sprawled across the same patch of turf it has occupied for decade after decade, there lies a monster that predates everything and answers to no one.

The Six Nations does what it wants. And the Six Nations is a mean mother-fucker.

Every now and then the mask slips. Like any other arena in the twenty-first century, rugby has become monopolised by the anodyne and inoffensive, the politically correct and the perfectly reasonable, from the dutiful utterances of players coached not to say a word out of place through the polished press releases, all the way up to the magnanimous administrators who speak such sense so calmly, not a hair out of place, each opinion carefully put together and road-tested before delivery. There are exceptions, but you know who they are at any given moment because they are in the news. No wonder the majority are so careful.

The former chief executive of the Six Nations, John Feehan, was one who was unafraid to speak his mind, particularly in the cracks between press conferences during the annual extravaganza, when no publicity is bad publicity. He attracted considerable criticism during the 2017 championship on the perennial issue of Six Nations expansion, when he admitted the championship was a closed shop with no responsibility towards the development of the sport beyond its frontiers. He said much the same thing at the launch the year before, when he proclaimed to, of all papers, the *Independent*: 'It is not [our] job to provide solutions for Georgia, Romania or anyone else.'

The temptation is to rail against the arrogance of such a position, the complacency and exclusivity – and, God knows, many have done just that, the airwaves abuzz at the time with condemnation for the ancient institution. Take a step back, though, to see past the end result of so unattractive an attitude, and the inevitability of the Six Nations' position cannot be denied. The Six Nations is a closed shop; it is the biggest, baddest tournament out there, generating sums the others, the World Cup included, can only dream of; and it is all these things, not only because it is played in rugby's most populous region, but because it is suffused with history and soul and many other intangibles that may not sit squarely with the shiny, populist 21st century but lend an institution gravitas and confidence – and make deeper the dent it hollows out in its patch of turf.

The Six Nations, in its various guises, has always been there. What creates the tension is the rise of so many competing interests as rugby continues the surge into its new era. The old ways are entrenched, the formulae set, but the clamour of the new is loud, and the incompatibilities ugly to behold. John Feehan is right. The Six Nations is run by itself, for itself. The interests of 'the game' do not feature in its remit beyond the extent to which its prosperity is threatened by neglecting those interests.

The Six Nations is by far the biggest institution in rugby. The revenues of its participants dwarf those of even the World Cup – and therefore World Rugby, which surrenders 52 per cent of its profits anyway to, well, the Tier 1 unions. World Cup years are the only years World Rugby makes any profit. Its revenue from the four-year cycle 2012–16 was £389 million, £345 million of it in 2015. Its net revenue from that year's World Cup, the highest-earning yet, was £190 million, the best part of £100 million of which went back to those Tier 1 unions. The revenue of the Six Nations unions, meanwhile, across the same period (excluding the £280 million the RFU brought in from hosting the World Cup) was more than £1.8 billion. It is impossible to discern how much of that was generated by the championship itself. Only Italy specify their receipts from the Six Nations (€72.4 million out of €180.5 million, or 40 per cent), but that excludes their sponsorship deals, to which their participation in the Six Nations would be integral. Wales used to list the proportion of their match income (tickets and broadcast revenue) that came from the Six Nations – and it amounted, depending on the year, to between 55 and 65 per cent – but that also excluded commercial revenue, catering and hospitality. Six Nations Limited distributes £100 million a year to its participants from central funds (broadcast deals and sponsorship), and it would not be unreasonable to guess that the unions collectively make at least the same again from their involvement.

All of which places in perspective World Rugby's heft. The revenue of the RFU alone over that four-year period was nearly £700 million, a billion if you include its receipts from the World Cup. If World Rugby in its current guise represents rugby's attempt to grow itself and undo the decades of insularity, the Six Nations is the immovable object it will continually butt up against. The Six Nations represents the past.

No one has consciously contrived such a situation, but the situation is no less impossible to undo for that. Another ancient institution locked into the calendar are the Lions, whose 12-yearly cycle of tours to Australia, New Zealand and South Africa has become fundamental to the ongoing viability of those three nations. But, why, the cry will continue to build over the next few decades, should they be the only ones who benefit? If rugby continues to grow in Argentina, Japan and America, for example, they will soon demand inclusion in the roster – and not just as an amusing diversion on the way to the main event. It is very difficult to see how such movements with the times could be effected without damaging, possibly ruinously, those very foundation unions whose control of the sport is so entrenched, even as they try to grow it. And so one would have to conclude they never will be effected – at least not until those new players become powerful enough to overthrow the traditions, which is not looking likely any time soon. This is the legacy of that century of chauvinism – a sport that means well but doesn't really know how or even whether to expand.

Does rugby really want to grow? It seems a ridiculous question to ask in an era when the land grab for resources and attention is more ferocious and ubiquitous even than it was in the age of Empire in which the sport was formed. But ask any of the foundation unions, in a quiet moment over brandy or schooner, what they really, really want from the near future, and it is likely they will each have their own concern, none of which will feature the promotion of rugby in, say, China. Most of them will cite the economic dominance of England and France as their most immediate preoccupation, while England and France will cite the maddening, eternal quest to beat the All Blacks as theirs. The theory is perfectly plausible that no one with any genuine power in rugby – in other words, no one in the foundation unions, who still hold the reins – actually wants rugby to expand beyond its traditional heartlands, because they *are* its traditional heartlands.

Another moment when the mask slipped was when the then chief executive of the RFU, Ian Ritchie, was asked in 2016 about the idea of Twickenham sharing its gate revenue for a home match, not this time with a tiny nation such as Samoa or Tonga, desperate for extra funds, but with mighty – in playing terms at least – New Zealand. His reply was that New Zealand should 'go and build a bigger stadium', a statement so toe-curlingly arrogant and out of touch it might become rugby's answer to 'let them eat cake'. Who knows, perhaps Ritchie's comment, controversial though it might have been, was born of just the sort of strategic spin-doctoring mentioned earlier, for it was based on some indisputable realities, as Ritchie spelt out at the time. No team in rugby's current set-up is due a share of the host's revenues. England would not receive any from their tour of Australia that summer; the Lions would not from theirs of New Zealand the following year. Tellingly, he also referred to England's problems beating southern-hemisphere teams as further reason not to surrender extra funds to make them, theoretically, harder to beat yet. The most powerful union in world rugby had no interest in helping others keep their operations sustainable, even their oldest friends. And why should they, it might reasonably be argued, certainly in any paradigm where dogs are at liberty to eat dogs?

As an intelligent man, though, Ritchie would have known how disingenuous his recommendation was, as if anyone could build themselves an 82,000-seater stadium and fill it. He may have nominally urged New Zealand to do so, but he was speaking just as defiantly to the rest of the rugby world. If the Six Nations is the game's most powerful institution, the RFU is its most powerful player, now consistently generating close to £200 million in revenue a year. The French union tends to net about £100 million, and the next biggest do well to break £80 million in a non-exceptional year (New Zealand generated £133 million when they hosted the Lions in 2017 – then again, the RFU generated £407 million when it hosted the World Cup two years before that). Ritchie proclaimed his union's ability to sell out its 82,000-seat stadium as the result of its own hard work and investment, rather than a function of England's population of 56 million, or of Twickenham's situation in a city twice as populous as the whole of New Zealand.

This is why New Zealand, let alone any of rugby's lesser lights, are so concerned about the future. For it is not only governance that continues to shape the rugby world, but increasingly, now the professional dynamic has been unleashed, demography. Professionalism turns a sport ever more starkly into a numbers game, and rugby's numbers are overwhelmingly in Europe, more specifically in England and France.

New Zealand, no matter the miracles they consistently produce on the field, know that only too well.

IV

The Naturals:
Souths Pacific and Africa

The All Blacks don't believe in dickheads. It's the secret to their success, apparently. They've written books about it. Take a half-decent rugby player and give him a broom to sweep out the sheds. That's all there is to it.

Others, perhaps dissatisfied with this explanation for one of sport's, let alone rugby's, most extraordinary phenomena have delved a little deeper. Every time the All Blacks are in town, the cry goes up to weary writers from sports editors half interested in rugby, who think no one has ever considered it before, and television producers much the same, to go out in search once more of what it is, what it really is, that makes them so good, what it means to be an All Black, blah, blah, blah. Cue the latest in the archives of beautifully written long reads, each more poetic than the last, and stunningly shot films of misty mountains with the spirit of forefathers oozing down their slopes. And here's the crumbly changing room Richie has always been the last to emerge from, and still is, broom in hand, to sweep away the dickheads.

It's all bollocks, of course. There isn't a rugby team on earth that welcomes dickheads. No country without mountains or forefathers or pride in the jersey. Rugby's a religion there – as it is in Wales, or white South Africa, or southern France, or, at a push, the west of England.

The fact is they are just better than everyone at rugby, and they almost always have been. When the All Blacks were in London in 2013, one intrepid reporter, searching their hotel for the press conference, stumbled upon the room where the All Blacks had just held a team meeting. On the whiteboard, which no one had thought to wipe down, was written in a bold hand: 'We are the most dominant team in the history of the world.'

The revelation caused a stir at the time, revealing a certain bravado in a camp supposedly defined by the virtues of humility. Tempting though it is to cite this as a loosening of the no-dickhead policy, the infuriating truth for everyone else is that, whichever way we measure it, whoever wrote that message was basically right. This tiny little land on the fringes of the known world has produced a team, a phenomenon, that has dominated their sport like no other. When the claim was scribbled on that whiteboard they were about to complete an unbeaten calendar year, the first Test team to do so in the professional era. Over the 510 matches of their history to that point, New Zealand boasted a 78 per cent win record. But that was nothing. Over the following years, which would take in their third World Cup triumph – at Twickenham in 2015 – their win record would hold steady at around 90 per cent.

The population of New Zealand is – count them – 4.8 million. At the turn of this century it was 3.8 million; at the turn of the last, when rugby's journey was only just unfolding, it was 0.8 million. To have dominated a code of football like that for so long, with so little behind them, defies analysis. Hence all those long reads and documentaries.

Usually, they end up talking about culture. Schools rugby, certainly, is big in New Zealand, unofficial academies long before the notion occurred in Europe, not dissimilar to college football in America. The same is true in South Africa, who are New Zealand's nearest challengers as rugby's dominant nation, albeit some way adrift (historical win record of 65 per cent to New Zealand's 79 per cent). New Zealand also go in for weight-graded rugby, as opposed to age-graded, so that, as far as possible (which isn't always very far in the sparser rural communities), children play against children roughly the same size, allowing them to focus on skill rather than physical domination. All of these are plausible contributing factors, but do not feel quite sufficient to explain the disparity.

The synthesis in their culture of Maori and Anglo-Saxon starts to feel a bit more like it, certainly in the professional era, when all the misty bollocks tends to get squeezed out in the end. The Polynesians are God's gift to rugby, genetically disposed to collision sports like no other people. They have been enhancing New Zealand teams for almost as long as rugby has been played there, even if they were a little slow to embrace the sport, its introduction coming so soon after the wars between the Maori and the colonists. That said, the Originals, the first New Zealand team to blaze a trail across the UK, in 1905, whose success cemented rugby in the consciousness of a young, proud nation, contained only two players of Maori descent, Billy Stead and Billy Cunningham, who were an eighth and a quarter Maori respectively. New Zealand today would be half the team they are without the influence of their Polynesians, but if the All Blacks' pre-eminence was secured in the early 20th century they were a predominantly Anglo-Saxon concern then. The Maori gave the All Blacks the haka and their first superstar in George Nepia, but it wasn't until the mid-1980s that Wayne Shelford taught the shuffling Anglo-Saxons how to do justice to the pre-match ritual for which the All Blacks are now almost as famous as for the rugby. Suddenly the All Blacks seemed suffused with Maori spirit. Their rugby soared still higher on the back of it.

That is now. The phenomenon of the All Blacks, though, was built largely by the white man, as were the Springboks of South Africa and the Wallabies of Australia. Built, in other words, by people just like those back in the motherland who, throughout almost the entirety of rugby's history, have not been able for the life of them to understand how it is those colonial upstarts keep winning. But maybe that is the very reason. Those in the motherland stayed at home. Anyone with any get-up-and-go got up and went, ending up in places like New Zealand, South Africa and Australia.

There are two ways for a nation to become good at sport, one through a natural disposition, the other through the throwing of resources at the problem. In the late 20th century, Team GB, before they were called that, were virtually an embarrassment. They secured one gold out of 15 medals at the Atlanta Olympics in 1996, which was a nadir but not unrepresentative of their middling performances during most of the 20th century. Sixteen years later, they secured 29 golds out of 65 at their own Olympics, then 27 golds out of 67 in Rio de Janeiro four years later, second only to the USA. This transformation was not achieved by a sudden eruption of sporting talent, nor even by the renaming to Team GB. It was the result of hundreds of millions of pounds of lottery funding and a millennial epiphany regarding the virtues of the sporting life.

If there were a way, though, of whittling out the enhancements of the resource vector, which is generally a function of policy and economic clout, to get at the underlying 'talent' per capita of a nation for sport, we would surely see the colonial nations represented well among the best. In 1962, Sports Illustrated made a hopelessly unscientific, if entertaining, attempt to answer the question, ranking the nations of the world, quite arbitrarily some might argue, across an equally arbitrary choice of 40 sports, picking a top three for each. Unsurprisingly, the American magazine's study found the USA to be top scorers in absolute terms, a nose ahead of the Soviet Union, whose state-fuelled eruption onto the Olympic scene 10 years earlier had done much to inspire the article in the first place.

There is no doubt the USA, the ultimate nation of pioneering colonials, are the greatest sports nation on earth. If they were to take rugby even half seriously the rest of us may as well go home. But the article acknowledged that the USA, like the Soviet Union, benefited from vast resources, demographically and financially. When a simple per-capita calculation on the arbitrary points system they had arrived at was performed, Australia were catapulted to the top of the charts, their prowess at, among others, cricket, tennis, swimming and golf belying their population then of 10.5 million. Alas, their code of football did not count in *Sports Illustrated*'s calculations, nor did rugby league, or their supremacy would have been even more pronounced. New Zealand were sixth, even with a questionable ranking of only third in rugby, behind South Africa (who led their head-to-head with the All Blacks at that point by 12–8) and France (who trailed 5–1 in theirs but were Five Nations champions at the time). South Africa featured in the exercise only for their rugby, earning them 15th place on the per-capita ranking. Had one calculated their position, though, on the basis of a white population of 3 million from whom the Springboks were selected, they would have toppled Australia from the top spot.

None of it would stand up to much scientific scrutiny, but the findings feel plausible. Determining the best sporting nations can only ever be a contentious exercise. Some sports might be considered more credible than others, rendering any points system a matter for debate. Factoring out resources or the lack of them is another exercise with no recognised methodology. The straightforward per-capita calculation usually deployed might not be fair on the more populous nations. Perhaps, once a certain population is reached, the advantages of numerical superiority tail off – only 15 can ever take to the field in rugby, after all.

Not that any of this should stop people trying. The website greatestsportingnation.com purports to attempt the exercise in as scientific a manner as possible on an annual basis. The USA are fixtures at the top of the unfiltered chart, but Australia are regulars in the top 10, as are Canada (had the IRB accepted British Columbia all those years ago, who knows where Canadian rugby might be now). On the per-capita ranking, proficiency in Nordic or Alpine sports appears to be a great advantage to a nation, but New Zealand are consistently in the top three, with Australia, now relatively populous at 24 million, and Canada (36 million) regulars in the top 10.

These nations are naturally sporty. In the days when sport was purely recreational and less the billion-dollar industry it is today, it should come as no particular surprise that those hardy colonials emerged in rugby's formative years as the teams to beat. Australia may not have taken their place alongside New Zealand and South Africa at the top of the game until the 1980s, but their prowess is no less remarkable given that rugby has operated in the shadow of Australian rules and league for so long – and increasingly soccer. For a modestly sized nation to boast double world champions in their fourth code of football is some achievement.

Countless theories have been proffered over the years, usually to do with system structures or weather, but maybe a process of natural selection is also responsible. When pioneers create a nation, that spirit of adventure, that audacity and strength, is continued in future generations. It makes for damned good sports people. Every white person in a colonial country is descended from folk who, at some point or other, decided to up sticks and start a new life a long way from home. Even today, the decision is not to be taken lightly, but only a few generations ago it was replete with danger too. The long journey to Australia, for example, whether as convict or prospector (neither of whom tend to be stay-at-home types), killed many before they had even arrived. The natural selection inherent in the process led to populations high on boldness and vigour. Retiring types would never make it out there, or even think to go, and so their influence is finessed out. Which is not to say the mother countries cannot produce athletes of a similar calibre – far from it – but the cultures in which they are reared are necessarily shaped to a degree by the sensibilities of the folk who stayed at home. In colonial lands, the radical and proactive are the norm; in the Old World, the conservative and traditional wield great heft.

In Australia, as in the USA, such was the iconoclastic zeal that the rugby way was ripped up almost immediately and another sport formed, Australian rules, which would dilute rugby's strength, before another again, league, was embraced without a thought as soon as it presented itself. New Zealand, the smaller land, seems to have had more respect for the Empire's ways, and perhaps the sparser population mitigated against the establishment of a new sport. Either way, rugby bit quickly there, as it did in South Africa. The Boer War was instrumental, providing a rallying point for the New Zealanders who were sent to fight there, while strangely cementing rugby's place in the white man's culture in the Republic. English South Africans saw the sport as a chance to prove themselves to the mother country, but the game's status as South Africa's football code of choice was secured in the concentration camps to which the British sent the Boers, where the prisoners of war were introduced to the game. When the war ended, they took rugby with them, spreading it into the heartlands. The Afrikaners saw the sport as a chance to defy the British. Both strands of white South African came together through rugby.

All three of rugby's southern-hemisphere 'giants', as they are so routinely referred to, rallied through the Empire games of rugby and cricket, which proved a valuable outlet for young nations to develop their identities, particularly in opposition to the Old World, all the more so through rugby with its accent on confrontation and violence, all the more so when the British had more than enough soccer opponents on their doorstep in Europe. Emerging from populations already hardened by natural selection, their prowess, although remarkable for populations of such size, should come as less of a surprise.

More remarkable is the relentless ingenuity with which the All Blacks maintained their pre-eminence, indeed developed it, despite the gathering arms race of the professional era. That they can credibly claim to be the most dominant team in the history of the world is extraordinary when millions are thrown by far larger countries at the mission just to become the most dominant team in rugby on any given day. They have been the team to beat at all of rugby's World Cups, bar 1991 and 2003.

Much was made by a delighted world of their failures to win one between 1987 and 2011, that they were chokers, but, if by choking we mean freezing under the pressure, their problem was the opposite in most cases. In 1995, they simply lost a titanic battle against a nation for whom more than a rugby match was at stake. The illness that swept through their camp in the build-up may also have played a part, whether through natural means or foul, it matters not. In 1999 and 2007, the years of their two famous defeats to the French, they were the victims of nothing other than their own complacency. In 2007, in particular, they were so far ahead of the field the event was meant to be little more than a procession – an expectation the All Blacks seemed to buy into as much as anyone, never more so than when, 13–0 up in the first half of their fateful quarter-final against France, they started dinking cross-kicks to each other from their own five-metre line. This was not a team feeling the pressure. But the looseness set in, taking hold eventually, until they were no longer in control of it. Their unravelling in the second half – and the mounting horror as they began to realise it was happening – was fascinating to behold.

The closest they came to choking was actually the 2011 World Cup final. That was the match in which they looked terrified under the spotlight, a match – against, once again, the French – they should have lost, their imperious progress up to that point suddenly replaced by a haunted anxiety against a team who had looked a rabble throughout much of the same. But they found a way through, the unfettered brilliance now underpinned by a mental hardness, the fabled ability to 'find a way to win'.

Those two matches against France – in 2007 and 2011 – did much to create the team that would call themselves the most dominant in the history of the world. The All Blacks were traumatised by that 2007 defeat. The mischievous jibes about their inability to win when it mattered had until then perhaps not felt accusations to take seriously, such was their superiority at the time. Just as the 1995 defeat to South Africa created the 1996–7 vintage of All Blacks – a side, featuring Lomu et al, many consider the finest, certainly one of the most entertaining, ever to have played – so 2007 precipitated a hardening of the All Blacks' psyche, without, incredibly, affecting their ability to cut teams up every which way. From 2008 to 2018, they scored more than a fifth of the tries in all Tests between the 10 Tier 1 nations, nearly 50 per cent more than the next most prolific, Australia. Having surrendered their number-one world ranking to South Africa, the eventual winners of the 2007 World Cup, they had it back by the middle of August 2008, midway through the Tri Nations Championship. Other than for a stretch of three and a half months in 2009, they have held it throughout that period and beyond.

In short, they have tightened their grip on the game of rugby, at the very time – in the professional era's second and third decades – all logic suggests they should be overhauled by more powerful organisations now mustering their resources more effectively. What's more, they still retain that special aura previous All Blacks found relatively easy to sustain, appearing on the horizon as they did maybe once or twice a decade. In the age of satellite television, when anyone anywhere can watch them in high definition around 15 times a year, that aura, that lingering sense of mythical creatures from a far-off land dressed in black, is as impressive a mantle to maintain as those endless weeks at the top of the rankings, even when the odd scandal reveals them to be peopled by as many dickheads as the next collection of human beings.

But the landscape beneath them is shifting. In 2005, when it seemed odds on that the 2011 World Cup would be awarded to the bold bid from a new power in Japan, the All Blacks' media officer addressed the press before the third Test of the Lions tour, yet another humiliating imposition of southern superiority after the brief interlude of an English World Cup win in 2003. He appealed to, practically begged, the British media to support New Zealand's bid to host the 2011 World Cup, citing the truth, not entirely obvious at the time, that this was New Zealand's last chance. The World Cup was becoming too big for them to accommodate. Indeed, the assembled knew only too well from the preceding few weeks that the Lions were becoming too big for them too. Whether his appeal to the press made any material difference to New Zealand's bid will remain a moot point, but the equivalent lobbying in the corridors of power certainly did. Again, the old boys' network mobilised, and Japan's bid, a shiny nod to the future, the right choice on so many levels, was overlooked in favour of a homespun nod to the past. New Zealand's bid won. World Rugby took a financial hit by awarding its prized asset to so small and remote a nation. It is not a favour it can afford to extend again. The ensuing three World Cups have all been awarded to economic powerhouses.

New Zealand will almost certainly never host a World Cup again, which is a poignant realisation to arrive at, not a little ominous for them – and only slightly less so for their fellow giants in the southern hemisphere. After New Zealand in 2011, the roster of World Cup hosts reads England, Japan and France; or, after the world's 51st largest economy (according to the IMF's 2018 ranking), the roster reads the fifth,* the third and the sixth. Australia (14th) has a big enough

---

* This ranking is of the UK, as opposed to England, who shared part of the 2015 World Cup with Wales.

economy to expect to host another World Cup at some point, although it might not be for a while. South Africa (31st) was, in an extraordinary feat of contortion, World Rugby's own recommendation to itself for the 2023 vote. When it came to the crunch, though, the delegates followed the euro to France. South Africa will surely be awarded another before long, but expect other countries to start to appeal. Japan has finally become the first 'new' host, and if the USA (first) does not put itself forward sometime soon, World Rugby will practically beg it to. Then there's Argentina (25th) and Italy (eighth), who will want encouraging as the youngest members of Tier 1. By the time they have worked through that lot, who knows where Russia (12th), China (second), India (seventh), Germany (fourth) et al will be on the rugby map.

The jostling for World Cup hosting rights could come to be seen as emblematic of the choices facing rugby globally. World Rugby's executive is set on expanding the game into new regions of the world, but the motivations of those foundation unions, who hold the reins in the background, remain opaque. New Zealand and the aura of that fabled shirt represent most poignantly the face-off between rugby's traditions and the economic realities that, if the history of the world is anything to go by, will sweep away all subtlety and sensibility in favour of crude numbers. Thanks simply to their exceptional ability to play rugby, New Zealand are fighting the good fight with some success at the moment, even as the pressures mount. They have one prized asset over everyone else. It is that shirt and the people who play in it. With it, they make enough to keep the operation afloat and prevent their very best players from following the money to Europe. Wearing the national jersey is important to players the world over, but only one national jersey retains sufficient pull to have stopped its wearers from making economically rational decisions.

Rugby nations reveal a lot about their self-confidence in the rules they draw up surrounding eligibility for the national team. The exodus of a nation's best players, lured elsewhere by the salaries of more lucrative leagues, diminishes that nation's cohesion and status, so some try what is essentially emotional blackmail by denying their players the chance to wear the national shirt if they play elsewhere. France do not have to bother with such rules, because there is so much money in the French game hardly any of their best players go anywhere. England's rules are robust but do allow a player playing his club rugby in another country to be selected under 'exceptional circumstances' – in effect, though, theirs is a blanket ban too. Meanwhile, Australia, South Africa and Wales (dear God, Wales) have twisted themselves into hideously convoluted positions to try to look as if they are making a stand, even while their best players are taking the money elsewhere and still being picked. Only New Zealand have instituted non-negotiable rules that bar any player from wearing the sacred jersey who plays his rugby overseas.

So far, the tactic has proved effective. New Zealand know the value of that prize asset, and they, rightly, have no qualms about maximising its revenue. Their dealings in the sponsorship and media markets have been astute. They organise exhibition matches around the world, over and above the proliferation of international matches since the game turned professional. As the rugby community bemoans the workload of the modern player, the domestic game is normally blamed. Both formats have become far, far more intense to play, but in terms of space taken up in the calendar it is the international game that has ballooned. Of the 600 or so Tests New Zealand have ever played since the first in 1903, more than half have been played in the professional era. In 1994, the All Blacks played six Tests; now they routinely play 14. That equates to an extra two months a year of the most intense rugby the world has to offer, which was not there before.

This is, of course, part of a wider pattern. New Zealand are hardly alone in realising that international rugby is where the money is, which is why the foundation unions are so protective of their annual competitions and why Tier 2 nations are so desperate for more regular inclusion at the top table. And it is why the foundation unions organise as many fixtures as can reasonably be shoehorned into so crowded a calendar, some outside the sanctioned Test windows. But the All Blacks are the only ones who can charge millions of bucks per appearance.

After the cathartic 2015 World Cup win, six All Blacks retired with more than 700 caps' worth of experience between them, including the greatest players of the age, Richie McCaw and Dan Carter. This freed up millions of New Zealand dollars for redistribution among their remaining players. The depreciation of the pound and euro against the NZ dollar over the past 10 years has also helped the New Zealand Rugby Union to keep the salaries they pay their current stars competitive enough against the French and English leagues to hold their first XV together in the face of ever more spectacular offers. But the defections have started to eat into the All Blacks' bench. The tide is lapping against the first XV now. This is the last great battle the All Blacks face – against a foe far more sinister than the mortals they routinely dispatch on the field. Economics has no respect for culture and legend. To overcome that would be New Zealand's greatest victory, and it would be rugby's. Rugby vs The Economy; the All Blacks vs The History of the World. For once, our heroes in black are overwhelmingly the underdogs.

And if they want a glimpse of what can happen to obscenely talented nations stripped bare by the reality of economics they need only look farther out into the Pacific, where so many have been lost to the sprawling wilderness.

The population of Samoa is around 200,000, which is about the only thing the country has in common with Crawley. Samoa have reached two quarter-finals of the World Cup. If Crawley RFC (who play in Sussex 1, level nine of the RFU's league system) were to enter the World Cup, even if we allowed them to select a kind of All Stars XV, taking in the best from East Grinstead (also Sussex 1) and Horley (Surrey 4, level

12), of the same urban area, it is safe to say they would not. In fact, make that Crawley's second XV, what with multiple unavailabilities due to work commitments. And then imagine if countless others of Crawley descent had been lost through migration to Brighton or Croydon in search of a better life. Under those circumstances, it is hard to avoid the conclusion that Crawley would not stand a chance in the World Cup.

And yet they have so much more going for them than the people of Samoa. Situated just off the M23, with excellent rail facilities, even boasting within its boundaries Gatwick Airport, one of the world's busiest, Crawley has infrastructure of a truly 21st-century standard. London is on its doorstep, Europe a hop away. Its economic output runs into the billions. Compare and contrast with Samoa, a Third World archipelago, GDP less than a billion dollars, marooned in the middle of the vastest expanse of water on the planet.

The natives of the Pacific Islands are by some distance the most talented rugby players on earth. We might think New Zealand's prowess is something of a statistical anomaly, or at least that of the white New Zealander, but for the concentration of talent in a tiny pocket of the world's population there is no people to compare with the Pacific Islanders.

Talk about natural selection. At roughly the same time as the Anglo-Saxons were smarting at the audacity of the Vikings for crossing the North Sea in their long boats to pitch up on the shores of Olde England, the Maori were pitching up on the shores of New Zealand, not in anything so cushy as a galleon resplendent with decks and sails, but in some larger-than-average canoes, having traversed a couple of thousand miles of Pacific Ocean in them. But that was a relatively gentle assignment. Their Polynesian ancestors had found their way across vast tracts of hostile wilderness to their respective islands thousands of years before that. They reckon Samoa was first reached by folk hailing from South-east Asia around a thousand years before Christ, and Tonga (population 110,000; think Chesterfield) about the same. Fiji first encountered humans possibly earlier even than that. Indigenous Fijians are ethnically slightly different from the Polynesians, but the net effect on a rugby field is broadly similar – extraordinary physical specimens capable of athletic feats beyond the typical European. Fiji is more populous, getting on for a million inhabitants today, but nearly half are ethnic Indians, who have arrived since the 19th century and tend not to play rugby. The seemingly endless array of Fijian players of terrifying pace and power, not to mention exquisite skill, who light up leagues around the world and thrive so at sevens, is sourced from a population of around half a million. Think Leicester, who might make a fist of it in a World Cup, but less so if we insisted on seeing each player's birth certificate. Certainly, if we tried to send out in their hundreds the most accomplished sons of Leicester to enhance rugby teams around the world we would run out sooner rather than later.

The motivations and condition of those folk who pushed out their canoes into the gaping sea 3000 years ago will never be uncovered, but it is safe to say no one sets out on such perilous journeys into the unknown, let alone survives, without having a bit about them. And there can be no doubt many would not have survived, further sharpening the gene pool of those who did. These are the ancestors of the world's most gifted rugby people. They must have been bold and muscular, united and brave, and over the generations, isolated from the rest of the world and its corrupting ways, those qualities can only have intensified, if the Pacific Island rugby player of the 21st century is anything to go by.

And yet the standing in the world game of these giants on the field is a source of constant controversy, their plight analogous to that of the proud native disenfranchised by the colonial machine. At the 2011 World Cup, Samoa's magnificently undiplomatic centre, Eliota Fuimaono-Sapolu, raged after their defeat to Wales, following a four-day turnaround from their previous match, that the treatment of the

Pacific Islands by the authorities was akin to slavery. As condemned as his comments were – and not just by those authorities – they strike a chord. The bias in the system against not just the Pacific Islanders but any under-resourced nation in relation to the most established is enraging – but it is also inherent. The mismatch in economic power between the foundation unions and the Islanders when combined with a comparable mismatch the other way in physical power on the pitch has led to an ugly system of exploitation akin if not to slavery then to indentured labour. The best Islanders earn huge sums by the standards of their homeland, whither they invariably send the bulk of those earnings, but beneath them hundreds are horse-traded, often left isolated and in dire straits when it does not work out on the field – sometimes even when it does.

It is estimated that nearly a fifth of all professional rugby players are of Island descent. So approximately 0.0034 per cent of the world's population (2.6 million Polynesians and native Fijians worldwide) supplies nearly 20 per cent of its professional rugby players. That means hundreds of Islanders scattered across the globe, some like fish out of water, trying to cope in very different cultures, often for very little money. A few hundred euros a month sounds astronomical in a Tongan village, but it will not stretch far once you are in France, especially if the whole point of your salary is to send money back home. More than $20 million is thought to be sent back to the Pacific Islands each year by their rugby players abroad. Occasionally a tragic tale will make the rugby news, but mostly the Islanders labour on in silence, trying to create a home from home wherever they can find others like them locally. It is a tale of economic exploitation familiar not just to the modern world but the history of humanity, unscrupulous agents and ambitious clubs concerned only with means–end rationality analogous to pimps and capitalists. The initial impulse of sport, let alone rugby, was more Corinthian than that, but when the professional imperative is introduced without any checks and balances sport becomes no different from the rest of the economy.

When professionalism is unleashed on a sport suddenly and so late in the day, that dynamic is even more pronounced.

The struggle to protect Pacific Islanders is likely to prove as endless and shifting as any workers' rights movement, even as breakthroughs are instituted. The welfare of their rugby players is far better publicised a concern than it has ever been, the injustices faced by the Islanders barely acknowledged for the first decade or so of the professional era. As ever, though, meaningful policy change lags well behind political pressure. In 2016 World Rugby created a single vote for Oceania (which technically the Island nations share with New Zealand and Australia, who, of course, already have three votes of their own as Tier 1 nations) before, finally, granting Fiji and Samoa a vote each in 2018. Such developments are steps in the right direction, but in a council now of 50 votes the ability of the Islanders to fight their corner at a political level remains limited. Financially, World Rugby's policies disadvantage them no less. The major unions are compensated handsomely for lost revenues during World Cup years, but no one ever compensates the Pacific Islands for the fact they have no revenues at all. Considering all they supply to those major unions in playing resources, that is an iniquitous state of affairs.

Not that the players are any better served by their own masters. The links between the Island unions and their respective governments are intimate. The Prime Ministers of Fiji and Samoa, for example, are also the heads of their respective national unions. When the Samoan PM claimed his union had gone bankrupt in 2017 he appealed to the people of Samoa to stump up some cash for the team. He did the same before the 2011 World Cup. The good people obliged but the money did not go to the players, who have repeatedly called for changes to the administration. One can understand the reluctance of any organisation to send money into that black hole, but if the RFU, say, was intent on ensuring that any investment in the Islands went to the right areas, it could see to it. World Rugby is doing that now with a proportion of what is left of its funds, once it has paid the Tier 1 nations that 52 per cent of its net revenue. In terms of governance, meanwhile, it had long kept the Island unions at arm's length, insisting they must conform to the relevant criteria before they were admitted to council. None of it is entirely unreasonable, even if concerns about mismanagement might seem as much convenient excuses as anything else.

The real issue is, simply, that of money. There is none. The arrogance of colonialism has given way to the ruthlessness of economics. Either way, the Pacific Islanders are as marooned in the big wide sea as they have ever been. International rugby's revenue-sharing system is inherently balanced in favour of those with Ritchie's precious big stadiums, but when one considers the case of the Islands the disparity becomes sickening. When Fiji or Samoa or Tonga play to a packed house at Twickenham (imagine what sort of attendance the Crawley second XV would draw) they are entitled to nothing of the £10 million of revenue the RFU take on match day. In the autumns of 2016 and 2017, the RFU, under much pressure, made goodwill payments of £75,000 to Fiji and Samoa respectively for their visits to Twickenham, less than 15 percent of the money it paid its own team just to play.

The theory behind the usual revenue arrangement is that the favour is returned the next time Team B get to host Team A and keep all the proceeds, which the southern hemisphere unions have never liked because their stadiums are not as big – and they don't own them, anyway – and/or their fans and corporate guests not as rich. But in the case of the Islanders, whose stadiums and fans are smaller and poorer again, hardly anyone visits at all. New Zealand played a Test match in Samoa for the first time in 2015 – and the match made the Samoan Union a loss. That was not only New Zealand's first Test in Samoa, it was their first in the Pacific. South Africa have never been. England have played Tests in Fiji twice, Australia thrice, the last time in 1984. In the past decade, the only foundation unions to play in the Pacific have been Scotland (twice), Wales and that flying visit by New Zealand.

Economically, it makes sense. It is a long way to go, and there is no money in it, even, it seems, for the hosts. Morally, though, the refusal of Tier 1 nations to offer a meaningful share of match-day revenue to their Island visitors under such circumstances is an injustice to enrage any right-thinking person, whatever their nationality or sport. It is yet another legacy of rugby's century of chauvinism, which has now been sharpened by the sport's propulsion into a professional era for which it had no culture. The contrast between England and Samoa is an extreme one, but that just means it illustrates most vividly and ahead of time the dynamic that unfolds when money is allowed to dictate without regulation. Combined with the imbalance in the game's governance, the outlook is bleak for anyone who harbours dreams of a more inclusive, wide-reaching portfolio for World Rugby. The examples throughout history are rare indeed of an economically powerful body, especially when, as is so often the case, it holds the reins at political level too, willingly giving up even a modest portion of the advantages it holds, so that others might compete more effectively.

There are rugby nations more populous than the Pacific Island nations, but some way shy of the biggest beasts, who have meaningful voices on World Rugby's council. They know only too keenly how quickly their influential positions would be usurped if a parallel universe could be realised in which Fiji, Samoa and Tonga were somehow equal players, equally resourced, equally spoken for, equally prepared. Wales are well acquainted with the sting of defeat to the Islanders, losing to Samoa (known as Western Samoa then) in the 1991 and 1999 World Cups and to Fiji in 2007. But the hurry-ups administered by Island teams with even a modicum of preparation and/or time together, i.e. at World Cups, extends right up to the top. Eventual finalists France lost in the 2011 pool stages to Tonga, who had come within a whisker of beating eventual champions South Africa in 2007 in one of the most extraordinarily magical and impassioned occasions in northern France. Mighty England, in the year of their great triumph, 2003, were trailing to Samoa in their pool match with a little more than 10 minutes to go.

These achievements are astonishing and, pound for pound, surpass those of even the All Blacks. All the more so when almost every international rugby team on earth is or has been enhanced by players of Island heritage, players who, under current regulations, will never play for their homelands.

Even if all the anger surrounding the economic and operational imbalances were to subside, perhaps the most galling injustice facing the Pacific Islands is the mass unavailability of players with the requisite blood coursing through their veins who are tied to other nations, sometimes courtesy of a fleeting appearance for, say, the Junior All Blacks several years earlier. Or, to use World Rugby's favoured terminology on this matter, so poignantly resonant of the slavery analogy, players 'captured' by other nations.

In a perfect world the Island nations would hold on to all their best players, able to match the riches available to them elsewhere, but the reality is they cannot. As in any other economic model, if there are opportunities elsewhere, workers migrate. This reality has applied to the Islanders beyond rugby, Australia and New Zealand, for example, accepting non-white immigrants in the decades after the war, precipitating an exodus independent of anyone's ability on the pitch. Jonah Lomu was the player he was because of his Tongan genes, but he was born and raised in Auckland because his family had moved there, regardless of any rugby talent they may have harboured. When the All Blacks called, it was entirely natural for him to answer. Such tales of economic migration are hardwired into human history.

In the professional era, the migration of rugby players around the world represents nothing more than integration into that wider economic system, unavoidable if less than desirable. Likewise, although a touch more cynical, the offering of scholarships to the Islands' best youngsters by larger nations, the opportunities too exciting to be declined, even if the guarantees of a fulfilling existence thereafter are less than sketchy. Another step again along the spectrum of uneasiness is the establishment by foreign clubs, most notably the French, of academies in Fiji, prospecting like oil rigs for talent that might be whisked away at maturity, or potentially even earlier than that. The welfare of these youngsters is a human responsibility. If rugby is to avoid becoming worse than the laughing stock it already is for the self-righteousness with which it trumpets its value system, ensuring this welfare is non-negotiable.

But, from our far more trivial rugby point of view, the crime here is committed as soon as any one of these players is 'captured'. The capturing nations will argue long and hard about the resources they have invested into the development of these players, as if they have created each one and they alone deserve to benefit. Without doubt, talented players can be turned into great ones by these finishing schools, but no one should be under any illusion about the key ingredient that renders Pacific Island players so valuable in the first place and lends them their unique quality. It is not tailored weights programmes.

These players have become must-have accessories for their 'captors'. The England team in 2018, for example, was significantly the weaker without Billy Vunipola. What a privilege for the English that his Tongan parents chose to settle in Britain in the late 1990s when he and his brother Mako were small (albeit as rugby migrants, their father, an established Tonga international himself, playing professionally for Pontypool, then Pontypridd), because physical specimens like that do not emerge from the islands of the North Atlantic. To integrate them into teams so far from the seat of their gene pool should always feel a form of plunder, even if the modern world increasingly blurs notions of nationhood. One of England's alternatives at number eight, Nathan Hughes, represents a different case, the Fijian qualifying for England through residency, having been signed by Wasps as a 22-year-old.

And so we enter the troubled waters of rugby's international qualification rules. Here the sport reveals itself, as ever, to be intimately wedded to the modern world while utterly bemused by it. The realities of enhanced labour mobility and the global village throw up no end of conundrums for rugby to agonise over, and some of the agonising is straight out of the Victorian age, opinion raging over the alleged cynicism of opportunist mercenaries deemed unworthy of the sacred jersey they have turned up to pull on, courtesy of a granny with the relevant birthplace.

This is a fallacy and at odds with a cosmopolitan world of fluid identities. Many today are the product of more than one country. Some rugby players may feel less allegiance at the outset than others to a country for whom they qualify, but charlatans are few and far between. Rugby players, for all the changes in their sport, still retain a certain hand-to-badge commitment to whatever the cause they throw themselves into at any given time, whether it be new club or new country. It is rare indeed that a rugby player is revealed as indifferent towards their current team, or even less than ferociously dedicated – and in that event they would invariably be dropped anyway.

Without doubt, though, the ease with which they can adopt new flags on the basis of residency is an ugly look. In the case of Hughes and others like him, rugby has long known its three-year qualification for a nation through residency to be inappropriate. The Irish went so far as to incorporate the loophole into their official terminology, inventing the title of the 'project player', whereby they sign an overseas player to one of their provinces with a view to capturing him for the national team three years down the line. At least they are honest enough to give the practice a name. Every other foundation union – and plenty more besides – has indulged in the same, players taking up jobs with clubs then qualifying for the relevant countries three years later, so that their prowess at rugby is in and of itself their qualification to play for the new country. In 2017, World Rugby extended the residency period to five years, with only Ireland and Scotland objecting, and no one should weep if that were to become longer again.

When looking for the real injustice, though, we should follow the language. Qualification for a country is a complicated matter in a modern world where mobility and the interbreeding of nations is so high. Rugby needs to settle hard and fast on a reasonable system, allowing that it will never be perfect. Passports would seem a sensible gauge, whether to establish qualification by residency or to demonstrate the nationality of one's parents or grandparents. But, having established the ground rules, it needs to be acknowledged that many individuals qualify for more than one country.

They should be allowed to play for them, and they should be allowed to change between them. Because the real injustice is the notion of 'capture'. The clue is in the name. There is no reason why players should ever be captured by a nation. Free them all. Only that insistence of a bygone, more rigid age has it so – that one cannot possibly be committed to more than one nation, that to try to represent more is evidence of a flightiness and duplicity unbecoming of a hearty rugby player. On the contrary, the very heartiness of your typical rugby player means they could and would play with every bit as much passion for Wales, say, the land of their father, as they might later for Scotland, that of their mother, or for New Zealand, where they grew up, as for Samoa, where their parents did. The idea that they should be barred from playing for whomever they like, *so long as they qualify,* feels like an infringement of rights – as if they have, indeed, been captured.

Rugby has regressed on this front – and it is difficult not to infer the machinations of petrified foundation unions, spiking the guns of the Pacific Islands. There was a blissful time when players were allowed to play for another country, albeit after a three-year stand-down period. When Samoa beat Wales in the 1999 World Cup, they featured in their side Graeme Bachop and Va'aiga Tuigamala, both of whom had played for the All Blacks. The opportunity for players

73

of such calibre to enhance other nations for whom they qualified was equitable and healthy.

A year later, the whole system was dismantled after a pair of foundation unions, no less, had benefited from its misuse. In 2000, the authorities finally caught up with Wales and Scotland, who had by then wrung a total of 74 caps from three imported players, Shane Howarth and Brett Sinkinson for Wales and Dave Hilton for Scotland. It turned out none was qualified to play for them after all. The scandal was named Grannygate, which was a misnomer anyway, since in all three cases it was a wrongly attributed qualifying grandfather who had caused the bother – Howarth's and Sinkinson's had been born in New Zealand and England respectively, not Wales, and Hilton's was registered as born in England not Scotland. These being foundation unions, no punishment was meted out, in stark contrast to those handed down 18 years later to Tier 2 nations Spain and Romania, which cost Romania a place in the 2019 World Cup and Spain any hope of one, for similar offences, or to Tier 3 Sri Lanka in 2016, who were fined more than 60 per cent of their annual grant from World Rugby for fielding two ineligible Fijians.

All that happened after Grannygate was the institution of a new regulation that prevented players from appearing for more than one country – in other words, a charter for the big nations to start capturing. The motivations for the new regulation were all the more suspicious because it applied only to Howarth, who had been capped by the All Blacks. The issue of playing for more than one country did not apply to the other two, who both played again for their respective countries after they had completed three years of residency.

Inevitably, it was the Tier 2 nations – and the Pacific Islands, in particular – who suffered from the new regulation. By the 2003 World Cup, scores of Pacific Islanders were rendered unavailable because they were either prevented from playing by their clubs or they had played a match or two for another nation – or in the case of Jason

Hammond, who qualified for Fiji, 20 minutes for New Zealand A five years earlier. The lunatic clauses and counter-clauses that became World Rugby's Regulation 8, pertaining to qualification for a nation and the circumstances under which a player was captured or not, made matters still more complicated for those without the legal teams to unpick them. The foundation unions, far from punishing two of their own when Grannygate broke, instead set up the new regulation so that lesser unions further down the line might be compromised by the unavailability of otherwise-eligible players and further clobbered when caught out by the bewildering levels of red tape they could not afford to employ a bureaucrat to wade through. Spain's World Cup dream was ended when it was deemed two of their players had been captured by France, even though France had told them they were not, even though the technicalities in Regulation 8 are convoluted enough to make mad the most patient. Indeed, Spain were praised by the disciplinary panel for successfully demolishing those technicalities at the hearing – to no avail. The episode, just like the notion of capture that underpins it, is as illustrative as any of the double standards that still plague rugby's administration, favouring the old boys' clique over peripheral unions who can easily be made examples of.

This particular injustice would end if the concept of player capture was removed. Global rugby would flourish. Players of international standard no longer required by one country, some of them superstars, would be free to play for any other for which they were eligible. This, by definition – and the definitions are becoming ever more stringent – might not be any at all for a lot of players, but for some it could be just the one other, or in very rare circumstances more (we all have four grandparents, after all). There is no reason, either, why there should be a stand-down period. If a player is left out of the All Blacks squad and he is eligible for Tonga, let him play. Only a misplaced squeamishness about being seen to place your hand on more than one badge argues otherwise. There might be ugly cases occasionally of a bigger union trying to lure from a smaller one a player who qualifies for them too – George North, for example, is as qualified to play for England as he is Wales – but overwhelmingly the direction would be from larger unions to smaller, players no longer required for one country switching instead to that of a dear grandma who used to sing lullabies to them in her Italian, Fijian or Scottish lilt. Who would not be committed to that? International rugby could only benefit from allowing more players to play, rather than languish unused because of this Victorian notion that a person cannot be committed to more than one country. And just as the Pacific Island nations have lost the most to the concept of the captured player, so they would benefit the most were they ever to be freed again.

A loophole has already been opened by rugby's affiliation to the Olympic movement, where qualification for a nation is based on passport. Now players can switch nations again, but only by playing first for their new team at sevens, which operates to a different rhythm from 15s.

The pressure is likely to grow on World Rugby to go further – on this and other issues currently disadvantaging the Pacific Islanders. Theirs is a cause everyone can and does gather behind, essentially that of the underdog, rich in talent but poor of resource and, consequently, of opportunity. New bodies such as Pacific Rugby Players Welfare are increasing the pressure on World Rugby to do the right thing on issues of eligibility, governance and finance.

Meanwhile, rumours constantly swirl concerning the establishment of a professional team on the Islands, or perhaps in New Zealand or Australia, even America – some vehicle at any rate that might mitigate the loss of so many players seeking their fortune elsewhere. Currently, a Fiji international is paid 200 Fijian dollars, around £70, per Test match, which means playing for his country invariably costs each one by the time the outgoings of travel, food and accommodation (which tend to be above the norm for men of such size) are factored in. If World Rugby could ever institute a fairer system of revenue distribution (or, more pertinently, persuade the Tier 1 unions to share more with the rest), so that such players could be paid a meaningful fee per match, the dilemmas so many of them face just to play for their country might also be alleviated.

Ultimately, though, the battle to secure a fairer deal is a battle to force more powerful parties into making economically irrational decisions. Such battles are always uphill, the prospects of meaningful victory slim. The Pacific Islanders are rugby's most miraculous paragons and its guiltiest secret, showing up infinitely more powerful nations by competing with them on the field despite absurd disadvantages and by flagging up neglect off it. The foundation unions, while happy to assimilate their outrageous talents, otherwise behave as if they wish the 'Islander question' would go away. It is the most poignant example of the very many that illustrate rugby's unresolved tension between an imperial system of governance by committee and the sudden unleashing of the forces of demography and economics. The Pacific Island nations never stood a chance once professionalism was admitted. Their exploitation since has been sickening to behold, but it is not an isolated, self-contained phenomenon, like the islands themselves, but a bellwether for the shifting dynamics of rugby around the world.

The economic imperative is insatiable and will not stop in the Pacific.

It is next to impossible to pin down how many rugby players there are in the world, how many in each country. World Rugby records two categories for each nation – total players and registered players. Just a cursory glance reveals evident disparities between how nations count their players. Some, including New Zealand and Wales, enter the same figures in both categories, which means they do not recognise players who are not registered with clubs or schools. Guam, meanwhile, have 1,186 registered players out of a total of 1,211. What it is that stops the Guam 25 from registering is anyone's guess.

A lot of the data feels unreliable. An oft-cited factoid is that England has by far the biggest population of rugby players in the world, courtesy of the figure of 2.1 million recorded by World Rugby in England's column for 'total players'. This dramatic outlier of a figure includes primary-school children who may have touched a rugby ball in PE, as well as a million lapsed players, which the RFU defines as people who have not played for up to two years. The RFU is confident it has half a million regular players, including all formats, from touch to tag to sevens, from children aged six all the way up, 360,000 of whom are registered. The column, then, to take seriously for any given nation in any given year is registered players. Even here, though, one should hesitate to draw conclusions through comparison. At what age does each union start registering players and to what level? And how meticulous are they in doing so?

Accepting that it can never be an exact science, the country that probably has the most rugby players is South Africa, with 530,000 registered in 2017 to England's 360,000. That said, South Africa's figure leapt dramatically from 405,000 in 2016. In 2011, it was 651,000. So, treat with caution. A survey commissioned by the South African Rugby Union in 2013, when World Rugby's figure for the country was 387,000, found there to be approximately 300,000 regular players in the country of full-contact 15-a-side rugby (excluding all other formats, which are included in World Rugby's figures). Those on the ground in South African rugby reckon there are more out there.

In many ways, the story of South Africa and rugby is as remarkable as that of New Zealand or the Pacific Islands, their success predicated upon a population for most of rugby's history not much larger than the former's. And the saga behind the limited reach of that population conforms to any narrative linking rugby with movements of chauvinism and discord. The history of apartheid is a subject that extends far beyond our remit here, its iniquity scarcely needing further iteration in a book about rugby.

Morality aside, the success of South African rugby, second only to that of the All Blacks – and for much of the 20th century at least on a par with it – is quite the achievement, considering the systematic exclusion of more than 80 per cent of the population. How different the story might have been. The whole of South Africa embraced rugby to begin with, black and coloured as much as white. They just were not allowed to play together. It was white South Africa who faced the rest of the rugby world, and white South Africa who dictated, as at governmental level. Not until the 1960s did football become the favoured sport of the majority, rugby by then so inextricably bound up with the hated regime. If it is forgivable to view the tale of apartheid through the prism of rugby alone, the damage done to the sport was incalculable then, because of the sheer number of players lost, and continues to be as the measures to undo it all are pursued with an urgency that creates its own problems.

South Africa are now Tier 1's answer to the Pacific Islands. It is estimated that more than 400 South Africans play professional rugby overseas. As with so much of rugby's demographic, numbers are constantly shifting and almost impossible to pin down with accuracy. At what level of remuneration, for example, does a player call himself professional, at what concentration of blood South African, after how many generations a Pacific Islander? But there are not a lot fewer South Africans servicing the game outside South Africa than there are Pacific Islanders outside the Pacific, allowing for the equally impossible task of precisely drawing out those who have been assimilated by other countries, either through rugby's dreaded policy of capture or through natural migration.

The country those South Africans have left behind is quite suddenly not the rugby power it was, even just a few years ago. As ever, economics has played its part, much of it independent of rugby. The value of the rand has collapsed since the turn of the century, dramatically so since 2010. Against the euro, it has lost around half its value since then, meaning salaries in France are worth twice as much to a South African, as if the salaries in Europe were not big enough already. The developing pattern of a country pulled apart by professionalism differs from that of the Pacific Islands mainly through South Africa's status as a much larger nation with the infrastructure to host Test matches and expect a credible return from them. They also hold the incalculable advantage of being a foundation union. But the storm that has stripped the Pacific Islands bare is the same now setting to work on South Africa and, for slightly different reasons, Australia.

South Africa is both the anchor of southern hemisphere rugby and the loose mooring that could tear it all apart. With a population getting on for 60 million, the country generates most of the television revenue in the southern hemisphere. In 2015, according to a report commissioned by World Rugby, £70 million of rugby's global television revenue came out of South Africa, compared to £31 million from Australia and £30 million from New Zealand. Not many of those 60 million people might account themselves rugby fans, but in their sheer number lies hope, at least – if rugby can win them over, if rugby can bring itself to win them over. South Africa might be seen as a microcosm of World Rugby, the enlightened mission to spread the gospel constantly vying with the interests of those who do not want to lose their grip.

Meanwhile, the white population of South Africa, where rugby has the surest hold, continues to fall. In 2015, it fell below the total population of New Zealand for the first time. The policy of transformation in sport, the attempt to make South Africa's teams more ethnically representative of the country, has created an added dimension with which no other rugby nation contends. Every selection, up and down the system, is lent a political angle that can be twisted this way or that according to one's motives, rendering some changing rooms, right up to the top, poisonous places to be. Even without pull factors powerful enough to do their worst on their own, the push factors in South Africa are unique.

The wider rugby world knows this only too well. Scouts and agents from Europe brazenly pace the touchlines during Craven Week, the famous festival for schoolboy rugby in South Africa, trying to lure away players reportedly as young as 16. To all intents and purposes, theirs is a Pacific Island situation, with voting rights.

The voting rights may soon be all these foundation unions have left to rescue their situation, but votes tend always in the end to follow money. The direction in which rugby's money is heading is clear – 70 per cent of its global revenue is generated in the UK and France, according to that same report. South Africa, though, are situated in an influential position strategically. When the foundation unions are plotted on a map they form a right angle, with South Africa at the crux. To date, they have aligned themselves with their southern hemisphere colleagues several time zones away.

When rugby turned professional, they were the world champions, Australia the team they dethroned, New Zealand the team, regardless of all that, everybody wanted to watch and/or beat. South Africa, moreover, were the team who took the final decision on the way the professional era would organise itself, Francois Pienaar leading his men, and thereafter everyone else, to sign with the unions, to maintain to a degree rugby's link with its past, eschewing Kerry Packer's proposed enterprise, for which everyone else was poised to sign.* Back then, southern hemisphere rugby was where it was at, the north not much more than a sideshow. Professional rugby was basically the southern hemisphere's idea. What a cruel irony if it ends up tearing them apart.

Because, for all the imbalance on the field between north and south, the key metric from 1995 onwards became demography. To borrow from the Americans, it's the economy, stupid. South Africa

---

* The professional era was effectively launched by a face-off between Packer and his fellow Australian media magnate Rupert Murdoch. In 1995, Packer was on the brink of clinching enough signatures to launch his rebel World Rugby Corporation, but a TV deal offered by Murdoch's News Corporation empowered the unions to keep hold of the game's best players.

no longer look from west to east in mutual admiration of their allies in New Zealand and Australia; increasingly they are looking from south to north at the economic powerhouses in Europe, who also happen to reside in much the same time zone. As the Six Nations continues to accumulate wealth and the European leagues throw their money around, the southern hemisphere unions keep tinkering with their systems as the realisation dawns that more powerful forces are at work than the best of them on the playing field. Super Rugby, the provincial tournament of the southern hemisphere, changes its format on almost a yearly basis, taking on a team here, shedding one there, as they frantically try to make it all add up. The Rugby Championship, the competition professionalism gave birth to in its original guise as the Tri Nations, similarly labours, earning less in television rights (£217 million over four years, according to that report for World Rugby of 2015) than either the French domestic league (£226 million) or Europe's Champions Cup (£222 million). Super Rugby (£144 million) earned less than the Premiership (£147 million). And the next round of TV deals saw massive hikes for the English and French.

An instructive moment came with the decision in 2017 to cut three teams from Super Rugby, one from Australia (the Western Force), two from South Africa (the Cheetahs and the Southern Kings). Never have two teams been cut from a competition with less protest than those two South African sides. They practically celebrated and within a month were packed off with a £6 million dowry to join the PRO14 with the Irish, Welsh, Scottish and Italian teams. The Western Force, meanwhile, raged and raged against the dying of their light. With no established alternative for them to head towards, the team from Perth, the most remote city on earth, faced oblivion. The edginess in negotiations between the members of SANZAAR (South Africa, New Zealand, Australia and Argentina Rugby) had become palpable. The following year, the CEO of the South African Rugby Union, Jurie

Roux, and the director of rugby, Rassie Erasmus, quietly joined the board of the PRO14. The bridgehead had been formed.

Nestled in that crux between north and south, South Africa's next move is pivotal. The pull now is overwhelmingly to the north, where so many of their best players play already, whither an overnight flight in business class will see any team or official arrive bright-eyed in much the same time zone. Europe, too, would welcome them, not just for their playing resources but also for that largely untapped population of 60 million. Even the Six Nations might open up its arms for South Africa (certainly, before it is likely to for Georgia or Romania). And so with the removal of South Africa from their current position in the lattice, the Jenga sticks of world rugby come crashing down. Super Rugby and the Rugby Championship have no future. More Australians desert to Europe, until not even the lure of the black jersey can stop the very best Kiwis from doing the same. As the snowball gathers in Europe – and it would end up concentrating round England and France – all other leagues become little more than feeder leagues. International players from countries outside Europe become exotic curiosities to their homelands, welcomed back for whatever Test matches remain sacrosanct in rugby's new calendar. Everyone will have become Pacific Islanders.

That is, *if* the economy is allowed to do its worst, *if* rugby fails to sell itself into new territories with enough heft to counterbalance the black hole that is gathering in England and France. To arrest, or just avert, this gravitation towards a singularity would require radical measures by World Rugby, an organisation that is currently not set up, either structurally or culturally, to be radical.

And would it matter anyway, the free-marketeers would argue? A similar model has evolved in much the same part of the world for The Sibling. The picture shifts according to the times, but football has four, maybe five, big leagues in the world, all in Europe. The others are feeder leagues. The international game is more or less subservient, which is inevitable since it is played less often. For most countries, their best players are indeed exotic curiosities viewed from afar, welcomed back every now and then for the odd significant international, but otherwise a source of pride whose achievements reflect well on their homeland, sometimes from an awfully long way away. They are all Pacific Islanders, with footballs.

And, by and large, the system works. Football is the one genuinely global sport, certainly from a spectator point of view. Others may compare in terms of participation (not much beats the primeval urge to run), but viewership is what has turned football into the current phenomenon. It has long been the world's most practised ball game, which empowered it to take its own slingshot into a new dimension in the 1990s, in this case from simple professionalism to world domination. The RFU may be by far the most powerful player in world rugby, but its revenues are on a par merely with Southampton or West Ham, clubs of middling clout in the top flight of English football. The revenues of the next biggest unions are, well, not in the same league. Unlike rugby, football's concern has never been to convert new demographics to the cause. The breadth of football's base beforehand was such that the sharpening of its top as the sport pushes higher and higher, the distinctive signature of a free-market model, has not compromised the edifice. No matter the gravitation of resources to a few centres of power, be they leagues or clubs within leagues, a sport as intricately woven into the cultures of so many countries across the globe, some highly populous, will withstand any stresses the free market might inflict. Rugby is allowing itself to be shaped now by the same indiscriminate, value-free forces, but rugby does not have those deep, sprawling foundations.

There is an uneasiness about how this will end. Some people want to do something about the current trends; some people are in a position to. Nobody is both.

V

Attention Grab:
Rugby's Would-Like-To-Meets

Every now and then rugby is enlivened by a frisson, an exquisite flicker in revelation of a new future. It happens when a new team breaks into the party. They announce their presence with a ground-breaking win or two, and we thrill that the old order, the roll call of familiar faces, might just be shaken up.

The chances of the upstarts staying tend to depend on how attractive a proposition they are. In the 1980s, it was Romania, but they were not very attractive at all off the field, empowered by Ceauşescu's communist regime – and when the revolution came they ceased to be so even on it. In the 1990s, it was Samoa, with wins over Wales in those two World Cups, and Italy, with a dogged campaign of wins against France, Scotland and Ireland (thrice) in the second half of the decade. One country had a population of tens of millions and a capital city to die for; the other didn't. One was welcomed almost immediately into a Tier 1 competition (having played Scotland and Wales for the first time as late as the mid-1990s); the other wasn't.

Then, in 2007, Argentina announced themselves in glorious fashion, beating France and Ireland (whom they had also beaten in 1999) in the World Cup pool stages, before fairly annihilating France again to finish third. In the same tournament, Fiji beat Wales and came close to defeating eventual champions South Africa in the quarter-final. One had a population of 40 million and a history almost as legendary as Italy's, featuring freedom fighters and Diego Maradona; the other didn't. One was swiftly incorporated into the Tier 1 calendar; the other wasn't.

Such opportunities are of incalculable benefit (and calculable, too). All any Tier 2 country speaks of is the need for regular, meaningful competition against the best. But the experience of Tier 1's newest members is to highlight just how difficult it is to compete against established teams in a sport like rugby, even with those advantages. The failure of Italy, in particular, to make more of the funding and regular competition they have enjoyed since admission to the Six Nations in 2000 and the PRO14 in 2010 continues to perplex – until one remembers it took France more than 40 years to win their first Five Nations. Rugby is not a game conducive to upsets, which is why they conjure that frisson, that flicker of hope, when they do happen. Unlike football, rugby is a territorial game, attritional and brutal – and so is the mission facing any country who wants to break into its inner circle. This is a serious problem for the sport, or at least for the oft-trumpeted ambition to grow it into new regions. Which is why rugby can scarcely afford to lose from that inner circle any of its regular faces, however familiar they may feel.

And then came 2015 and Brighton. This was the biggest upset in the history of rugby union, possibly in all of sport. On the opening weekend of the 2015 World Cup, the bookies gave Japan a 43-point head start for their match against South Africa. On Betfair (an exchange, rather than a traditional bookie), a Japan win was available at 350.00 (349–1) a few minutes before kick-off. With the traditional bookies, South Africa were rated at 1–500. This is bookie-speak for 'it is impossible for B to beat A in this head-to-head'. Leicester's famous triumph over a season in football's Premier League yielded 5000–1, but it is all but inconceivable that any sport has seen an outsider of that magnitude come through in a two-horse race. Certainly, since World Rugby introduced its ranking system in 2003, no side has overcome as large a disparity in ranking points. Tonga's win over France in 2011 is next biggest – the handicap for Tonga that day was 25 points, and their best price 22–1. In the build-up to the 2011 World Cup, Samoa overcame a 21-point handicap to win in Australia. Fiji's victory over Wales in 2007 was despite an 18-point handicap. As upsets, none of them comes close.

In the media centre at Twickenham, 60 miles away, Japan's odds were discussed before kick-off.

'Anyone fancy Japan at 350?'

'I'd rather put £350 on South Africa and get the pound back,' said one of the world's leading experts in rugby.

A couple of hours later, that media centre was bouncing, literally (it was a temporary structure), with the euphoria of professionals whose impartiality is beyond suspicion. The scenes were echoed across the world, when pubs, clubs and living rooms outside South Africa rocked to the feeling that anything was possible. It was not just the unlikeliness of the win, but the manner. Japan had not mugged South Africa with one of rugby's classic upsets, which so often involve the killing of a match in horrible conditions by inferior opponents who stop the favourites playing. In glorious weather on England's south coast, Japan simply outplayed the Springboks. No uninformed observer would have believed that one side were 500–1 on favourites, let alone been able to pick which one.

This felt different, a new team on most people's radars playing rugby as fabulous to watch as it looked impossible to stop. The sight of players from a lumbering foundation union turning this way and that against the new reality seemed symbolic. And yet this was only Japan's second win at a World Cup, despite having played in every one of the previous seven editions. By the end of the 2015 tournament, they would have another two, becoming the first team to fail to qualify for the quarter-finals with three wins. Such are the numbers back home that 25 million people in Japan watched their win over Samoa, nearly a fifth of the population staying up for kick-off at 10.30 on a Saturday night, becoming at a stroke the biggest television audience a single nation has ever mustered for a rugby match – a nigh-on 25 per cent improvement on the previous highest, the 20.7 million in France who had watched England's win over the home nation in the 2007 World Cup semi-final.

These are numbers to conjure with. Could rugby be stirring in a new land big enough to alter the prevailing dynamic, to act as a counterpoint to the gathering monster in England and France? It was lost on no one that Japan were also to host the 2019 World Cup, the first country to do so outside the foundation unions.

Among the missionaries at World Rugby, there are high hopes for Japan. Rugby is not kidding itself that it registers yet in the national consciousness there, but such is the magnitude of the third largest economy in the world it does not have to. Japan represents a future that World Rugby can embrace with gusto. There is rugby there and, most of all, there is vast potential for growth.

Compare and contrast with that other archipelago in the Pacific. Japan and Fiji sit side by side on World Rugby's list for registered players. The figures are ever changing, but in 2017 Fiji actually boasted more, 122,000 to Japan's 109,000. Both are well inside the top 10, ahead of, among others, Ireland, Wales, Italy and Scotland. That figure for Fiji means that more than a tenth of their population plays rugby (and nearly half that population are native Indians, who barely play at all); less than a thousandth of Japan's population does. In Tonga, meanwhile, nearly a quarter of the people are registered players. Whether or not we take these astonishing figures at face value, it is safe to say rugby is at saturation point in the South Pacific, where the economies are minuscule anyway. And so the sport turns its back on the one archipelago, suffused with passion for it and other-worldly talent, in favour of the other who, relatively speaking, could not care less. On a human level, it is a travesty; strategically, it is unanswerable. This is how economics, and thus professionalism, works.

We are at a junction. In one direction Japan shimmers as the symbol of a new future; England and France loom as the destination of the current path. Either way, the implications are profound for all but rugby's most economically robust. It would be naive to imagine rugby could catch hold in a country like Japan and leave everyone else unaffected, let alone better off, but at least it might mean a new centre of gravity to lend an element of balance to the map. For all the crusading zeal of World Rugby's executive, the 2019 World Cup is the first significant step in this direction.

But, again, the old contradictions are poised to clash, the enthusiasm tested of those council members who lurk in the background with all the power. The RFU would no doubt welcome the establishment of rugby in the Far East, so too the Premiership, the Top 14 and, as a result of that, maybe even European Professional Club Rugby, which administers the Champions Cup and the Challenge Cup. But how would the Scottish Rugby Union feel about another monster of 125 million folk joining the party, as well as the double-headed monster they sit alongside already, numbering roughly the same, that is England and France? Or how would the Welsh, the Irish, even the New Zealanders? These are tiny countries already struggling to hold on to their assets. South Africa and Australia are clinging on to theirs every bit as tenuously. And that is half the vote of the council accounted for already.

Commercially, this disconnect is unique to governing bodies in sport (although governing bodies in politics, of all arenas, are similarly structured). Normally in business, an executive works in the interests of the shareholders; the executives of governing bodies in sport, however, are there to service the greater good of the game, while the council is comprised of officers deferring to other bodies whose interests might not be aligned. The independence of those executives is now considered a prerequisite for good governance. This is akin to the divesting of Carling's 57 old farts. Our enthusiastic executives in World Rugby have yet to achieve such independence from a council whose power is disproportionately weighted in favour of the status quo.

We are back to the recurring question. Does rugby really want to grow? This is not posed in a sneering, rhetorical tone. It is a genuinely delicate dilemma. Let us rephrase the motion: *should* rugby strive to grow? Similar questions were swirling before the leap into professionalism. Many back then were uneasy about what professionalism might mean for the sport they loved. Much of the matter in this book bears them out. That tension, between the past and the future, remains unresolved – and maybe that is the way it will always be and should always be.

What would happen if rugby paused to consolidate for a while? Once the Tier 1 nations have been paid off with their 52 per cent, World Rugby distributes its monies around the globe. The strategic dilemmas are manifold. Germany and Tunisia are current projects of priority. China and India always are, the billion-people tipping point making them attractive to speculators, whatever the industry. A glance through numbers 10 to 20 on World Rugby's registered-player list reveals some interesting unions, Sri Lanka, Kenya and China all above 16th-placed Scotland, with Madagascar (for whom rugby is the national sport) one behind on 42,000. Keeping these and so many other pots on the boil is World Rugby's never-ending mission. One line of argument says they should not bother. If the Chinese embrace rugby, great, but let them find their own way. There are enough committed unions in dire need of assistance, not least in the Pacific

Islands, without precious funds diverting to strange new lands who may or may not make anything of them.

Besides, it may well be that World Rugby's expansionist dream has already achieved its decisive breakthrough. Even if they withdraw funding from all but rugby's most faithful nations, interest will likely grow around the world, now that the sport has been welcomed back by Baron de Coubertin's grand old circus. Admittance to the Olympics suddenly makes rugby a very attractive proposition indeed to nations the world over, whatever their background in the sport. And sevens, the format embraced, is a lot easier to play than 15s.

After relentless diplomacy, World Rugby was granted passage to the promised land in late October 2009, when the International Olympic Committee announced that sevens would feature at the 2016 Olympics. Within two years, China, no less, had recruited a professional squad for the women's event. All they had to do was teach them to play. They did not qualify for Rio, but this development alone showed just how seriously rugby might now be taken by countries outside the traditional heartlands.

Sevens is another movement replete with contradictions. Is it rugby's calling card or its nemesis? So easy to understand, so compatible with 21st-century notions of entertainment and frivolity – and, therefore, you do not particularly have to be a cynic to argue, so incompatible with its progenitor.

From the very start, it was born of ambiguous motives. The disgruntled rugby community of the Scottish Borders, as ever exercised by their dismissive overlords in the big cities, came up with sevens as a fundraising vehicle in 1883. They could have had no idea what they were creating.

One aspect was a vehicle through which those of abundant talent might finally achieve success. Fiji, their players brought up on the chaos of impromptu matches back home on uneven turf with unlikely improvised objects for balls, have proved the masters of sevens and duly claimed gold in the men's event of 2016, tearing Great Britain apart in the final with an astonishing performance that seemed to capture the imagination of anyone who appreciated speed, physicality and skill. Which is most people at the Olympics.

Global expansion is far more achievable in sevens than it is in 15s – and far cheaper. Here is a sport that might lay claim to the simplicity that is football's vital edge. Englishman Ben Ryan, who was Fiji's coach, describes how he turned Fiji into Olympic champions with little more than a ball and a rigorous fitness programme. No need for extensive support staff schooled in 15s' arcane procedures, no need for scrum machines or analysts or convoluted game plans or even just the variety of specialist players required to fill the myriad positions in a 15. No need for any particular knowledge or experience. Already, the make-up of the annual World Series leaderboard in the more established men's game reveals a host of unfamiliar names. USA and Kenya are regulars in the top ten; Spain, Portugal and Russia are not far off; Ryan contends that it would require minimal investment to catapult a team such as Uganda into the top ten within a few years. In the women's game, the spread is wider yet, with Spain, Russia and Brazil among those regularly in the top ten, USA and Canada in the top five.

If rugby wants global expansion, sevens is the path of least resistance. No matter how much money is thrown at Uganda they are not going to make the World Cup in 15s in the near or medium future, but in sevens the hierarchy is more fluid. Everything is quicker in sevens, on and off the field.

And so it is easier to watch. As an Olympic sport it is suddenly of strategic interest to some mighty nations, but, even more importantly for its chances of lift-off, no grounding in rugby's esoteric mechanics is required to appreciate sevens. The format, too, is perfect for those who like their entertainment various, undemanding and delivered in bites. The American blueprint of soda, hot dogs, ad breaks and the sense of the game on the field as just one part of the experience is satisfied handsomely by a day at the sevens, with its parade of teams and matches, quarter of an hour each, to be dipped into and out of, as at a festival. Families attend, parties in fancy dress, Mexican waves sweeping round the stadium in beguiling loops.

All of which is anathema to the traditional rugby fan. Mexican waves signify ignorance of the sport, even boredom. No serious rugby crowd engages in them. Kingsholm, Welford Road, Stade Marcel-Michelin and the like would crumble before entertaining such a betrayal of the nuances of what happens on the pitch. Rugby's problem is that those nuances are lost on the vast majority of people. To grow the game would mean overcoming these barriers. Sevens is the friendly entry point into rugby. Strategists see it as the means to an end, but in the modern world means tend to become, like money, the end in themselves, particularly if they are easier to apprehend.

This will become rugby's equivalent of cricket's dilemma with the shortened versions of the five-day match. The former is just so much easier on almost every level – and the sport uses it to try to seduce the uninitiated, which means the uncommitted, into becoming something more than that. The question that is all the more pressing for rugby is whether the leap is realistic between sevens and 15s for the floating sports fan whose interest has been piqued by the shorter game.

At least with cricket the various forms are based around the same fundamental dynamic, one player bowls to another who hits to a field of 11 players and tries with his partner at the time to score runs. The strategies and rhythms of the forms may differ, but if the focus is narrowed sufficiently (and the colour of the outfits ignored) they are indistinguishable on a mechanical level. Should one develop the temperament to appreciate the slower pace, the layers of significance of each player's actions, the prospect of the very human irresolution of a draw at the end of it all, the leap to five-day cricket ought, in theory, to be negotiable. Fifteen-a-side rugby, on the other hand, has the benefit of relative brevity, but requires of a seven-a-side convert that they take on board the mysteries of scrum and lineout, ruck and maul, as well as the regular impasses, however layered, that result from more than twice the number of players on a field the same size.

In both sports, as in so many others labouring in the shadow of football, the struggle is to appeal to an audience reared in the twenty-first century, used to a bombardment of stimuli, indeed expecting it, the attention continually shifting. The audience of traditional sports forms are generally ageing, hence the accent on alternatives that might fit better with the zeitgeist. One of the imponderables is whether spectators will tend to mature into an affinity for the traditional forms of cricket, athletics and the like, or whether we are approaching the end of an age. In other words, will the audience for traditional forms replenish itself, the audience naturally acquiring with age a taste for something more layered, less obvious, after the whirligig of youth in the 21st century? Or will the current audience gradually die out? The next few decades will reveal.

These questions may apply less to rugby, because appreciation of 15s as a spectacle requires knowledge more than it does the investment of time and there is no sign yet of a decline in youngsters immersed in the longer form of the sport, the commercial possibilities of which are easier to harness from week to week than those of the sevens travelling circus. But it is very relevant when it comes to introducing new populations. Should rugby leave such introductions to sevens and the Olympic compulsion, risking that converts never make the leap thence to 15s? There is a real possibility that sevens, far from acting as an ambassador for 15s, simply becomes the dominant form.

All the more so when the country for whom the shortened form seems the perfect fit is already making rapid progress in it, has a renowned appetite for all things Olympian and matches the profile of rugby's ideal Would-Like-To-Meet. If efforts to woo Japan are well under way, the land rugby, like everyone else, really wants to break is America.

*

On a Monday evening in late October 2003, USA and Japan met in the World Cup on the east coast of Australia, 50 miles north of Sydney, in the city of Gosford. The 20,000 who watched an exhilarating match created as raucous a party atmosphere as any rugby can have witnessed, the chants of 'Nippon! Nippon! Nippon!' vying with those of 'USA! USA! USA!', the delighted Aussie locals needing no second invitation to join the riot of noise and colour. It was fresh and exuberant, and just for a moment that frisson at a glimpse of a new future shimmied through the air. If this were to prove the World Cup final in 30 or 40 years' time, there is nothing to fear. The brashness of American crowds may grate around the golf course, but there is nothing like it for denuding rugby fans of any sense of self-consciousness.

It is often said rugby has no chance in America. This is the same line of reasoning that says rugby will never be as big as football. It feels a safe observation to make at this point in history, but it is vacuous. Sports are constantly rising and falling. Speedway was as big as football 70 years ago; now look at it. Greyhound racing too. American football entered one of those periods that make or break a sport at the start of the 20th century with that season of deaths, and cute adjustments maintained the sport's pre-eminence. One could argue it has entered another today, deep into a concussion crisis that rugby is desperate to avoid. The weaponisation of helmets and the head-on-head nature of so many of the collisions have rendered concussion an acute problem for American football. It is telling that some in the sport have already begun to turn to rugby for the refinement of their tackling technique. Should that ever become an established policy, rugby would suddenly have a foothold, even at formative ages.

Rugby is very present in America, as it is. That chart of registered players sees USA at number six with 124,000 in 2017. And the suspicious, but official nevertheless, figure of total players has them second only to England with 1.5 million.

There is every reason to think those numbers could balloon over the coming decades. In theory, rugby was made for the Americans, and they for it. There is a big tick in the colonial box. They boast the biggest economy in the world. Their population is huge and diverse (and includes over a million Polynesians, more than any country), their athletes of correspondingly various types and self-evident calibre. All they have to do now, after the Chinese, is teach them to play rugby.

That process is already under way and making itself felt in sevens in particular, where the pace of Perry Baker, a former American footballer (albeit with a past in rugby), and Carlin Isles, a former sprinter, has helped catapult USA into the highest echelons of the shortened game, coming second to Fiji in the 2019 World Series. Olympic status will only incline more of America's finest – or even just their next finest – to consider rugby as a serious proposition. It is more than conceivable, it is likely, that USA become gold-medal contenders within the next couple of Olympic cycles in the men's event. They already are in the women's.

Fifteen-a-side is a different animal, the prospects of genuine success for anyone who has not played their way to the top the hard way more limited. But if any country could fast-track themselves . . .

American football, the most obviously related of America's games, is the ultimate spectator sport, insofar as it is watched by millions and played beyond college by a tiny few. Those who do not make it as a professional simply stop playing, which means that every year thousands of American footballers drop out of the game as they fail to make it to the next level, or choose not to. Some of them are to all intents and purposes athletes of an elite calibre; all of them would find at least one suitable berth in a rugby team. If USA Rugby could ever mobilise even just a fraction of that pool of talent the results would surely be interesting – and quite quickly so.

Converting college drop-outs, though, would go only so far. The athletic prowess is not in question, but every significant international rugby team today is bursting with athletes of the highest calibre. Unpicking the best defences, à la the All Blacks, comes from more than that. Only immersion in the ways of rugby can achieve it. America would need to develop a deeper culture for the sport.

Anecdotal evidence suggests rugby is already a popular sport, the 124,000 registered players a more than plausible figure, conservative even. But, in typical American fashion, the global picture eludes the signed-up rugby fanatic, oblivious to the country's modest place in rugby's rankings and uninterested in it. The challenge in the medium term so many institutions, from World Rugby to the Premiership to the PRO14, are desperate to meet is to coax American fans, ensconced in their clubs and bars, into looking outwards.

A successful Test team would be a start. The US Eagles are an improving outfit, moving through the teens in World Rugby's ranking system, but still some way adrift of the best. For now, strategic designs focus on world domination in sevens and the women's game. Here, American rugby can see the prospect of success, the kind that will interest their demanding public, on the horizon. A try by Isles to win Olympic gold against Fiji, say, in 2020 is the kind of event to excite any American, whatever their interest in sport. A win against a Tier 1 nation in 15s, on the other hand, even if the All Blacks, does not cut across – and is a much harder directive anyway.

For all the hope rugby holds out for America, predictions of a stirring of the sport stateside have long been made, so far to no avail. The vehicles that have attempted to grow American rugby, and continue to do so, are various. Administration has always been a handicap, with the union, which constantly seems in turmoil, separate from the company that runs the US stop on the world sevens circuit, which is separate from whichever happens to be the latest attempt to break out a professional domestic league, which is separate from the clubs, colleges and schools. The attempts of what is, like so many institutions in rugby, a governing body still organised along amateur lines to administer a sprawling nation of 50 states, each with a rugby presence, constantly break down.

Recent efforts to introduce commercial practice have been a disaster. Doug Schoninger, a Wall Street speculator, tried to institute America's first professional domestic rugby competition, Professional Rugby Organization, and dropped it after a year, claiming foul practice and suing USA Rugby, who were themselves nursing the wounds from Rugby International Marketing, the company they had set up to receive and administer the majority of their revenue. RIM was every bit as much of a disaster, making a loss of around $2 million on the World Cup Sevens they hosted in 2018 and a $4.2 million loss overall. World Rugby bailed it out. As collateral for the loan, World Rugby gained a place on the board of USA Rugby for vice-chairman, Agustín Pichot. If the expansionist dreams of World Rugby's executive clash with the interests of a council dominated by the foundation unions, here the executive has achieved a foothold in the union of the most economically powerful nation on Earth.

World Rugby clearly intends to use it. American rugby is a project of special strategic significance, for all the obvious reasons. Of late, it has conformed to the local tradition of the wild west, peppered with antagonistic land grabs and competing interests. Another classic rugby model, you might say. Should the administration ever be straightened out, the interests aligned, the potential for rugby in America is self-evident. Modest traction as a spectator sport – it would not need to be anywhere near that of the American staples – would put it on a par with rugby in any other country in the world. If anything like the progress The Sibling has managed over the past couple of decades could be achieved, Major League Soccer now playing to average crowds of more than 20,000, more than 40,000 in some places, rugby's map would have realised another new centre of gravity. The accumulation of resources around England and France might be tempered by counterbalances in the East and West. With bases of economic and cultural influence in Japan, America and Europe, rugby could begin to countenance genuine expansion. The implications for the influence of some of those foundation unions would be no less profound, but for the sake of a wider and more various rugby world a relative loss of influence must be considered preferable to the implosion around north-western Europe that seems inevitable if current dynamics are maintained.

After a few false starts, America is committed to growing 15s gradually. Success there and in Japan may yet provide a lifeline for the Oceanic nations, should South Africa ever throw their lot in with Europe. Ventures are constantly discussed to unite Pacific Island rugby with North and South America on the west coast, all a flight away from each other. In the longer term, if powerful American teams could be developed a new Super Rugby might open up around the Pacific, a proposition to rival whatever unfolds in Europe over the next decades.

Major League Rugby is America's latest attempt to establish a professional game domestically. It is a modest venture. If you do not follow rugby closely, you will not have heard of it. One thing the Americans do understand, far better than the Europeans, is the importance of regulation in sport. MLR follows the classic American model. The intention is to grow it from the ground up. The league is a single entity, owning all the clubs. Investors purchase a stake in the league and the rights to administer a franchise within it. No single person can own a club. The highest wage a player can be paid is $40,000. Only five non-Americans are allowed in each team. The league is an acknowledgement of what American rugby is at the moment, a disparate community game scattered across a huge country, and an attempt to unify it. MLR will grow the concern over the next 20 to 30 years and, barring a demise from the sort of political savaging only rugby can conjure, it will remain a balanced product always under control.

These models tend to prove robust, to flourish in time. And thus they are the antithesis of the rugby way.

Part 3
Circling the Black Hole

VI

Laissez-faire:
A French Centre of Gravity

Winning is everything. Win and all else follows, the trophies, the prestige, the justification for existence. They write books about winners, they make films. We are the champions. No time for losers.

The trouble is, we need losers. Can't have winners without them. If you want to assess the health of a sport, ignore the team popping the corks. There can only ever be one of those. Take the pulse, instead, of the teams with their heads bowed.

We will know a competition by its vanquished. Any long-term strategy, be it of a club, union or competition, must be centred on the idea of losing. Only an idiot would see winning as anything more than an occasional treat. Almost everybody in sport, by definition, is a loser.

Within the narrow parameters of a match, of course, no one can afford to think like that. Believe in losing and you will lose. Each competitor has a clear-cut, primeval imperative when it comes to what can be seen at the end of the nose, but when the frenzy is satisfied a more angelic vision is required to appreciate that for all that competitors must be beaten they must also survive for the next instalment. Sporting supremacy is nothing without a healthy and various parade of opponents to beat. This ought to be the founding principle of any competition. The more a winner is allowed to build on each victory, to accumulate resources unchecked, the more that winner becomes the only player in town. The more the losers fall away.

The Americans understand this. The most rampantly capitalist nation on earth, who have never professed to have much time for losers, recognised early the tendency of their own system towards monopoly – and therefore towards a diminishment of the whole. They responded to the emergence of huge monopolies in the 19th and 20th centuries with robust policies of regulation in a range of industries.

In no sector do such theories apply more poignantly than in sport. The Americans were the first to appreciate the need to treat the administration of their sport differently from the playing of it; the one heavily regulated, the other a ferocious exposition of the perfectly competitive. Let the competitors inflict all manner of atrocities in the arena against themselves, the administrators are bound to keep each other strong, the better to fuel the fury of those competitors. To let administrative machinations go unregulated is to invite at best imbalance, at worst a shrinking of numbers, a narrowing of the top. If the sport beneath is large enough (in other words, football), such a dynamic can be tolerated, but, if the aim is to grow a self-sustaining enterprise that might nourish the sport it showcases, a lack of regulation becomes destructive.

This is not an entirely alien concept to rugby. Elements of regulation apply to the major international tournaments, to Super Rugby in the southern hemisphere, to the Heineken Cup in the north (although less so to the latter's successor, the Champions Cup), to the PRO14. The name union here bears encouraging connotations, rather than bitterly ironic, conjuring images of the collective. Solidarity across workers and organisations has a controversial history in political economy, but in sport the virtues of the system, so compelling in theory, have translated into good practice. Generally speaking, in rugby, the greater the power of the unions the more regulated the administration of the competition. The network of tournaments might enjoy stability and prospects were it universal, but, alas, all that is required to tear that network apart is a rogue element or two. It scarcely needs pointing out that in rugby the tigers within are to be found at the centre of the gathering mass in Europe. In rugby the entire, pan-global structure is threatened by the clubs of England and France.

This is a delicate subject, provoking high emotion across the world, mainly among those outside England and France, but also among many within. It is not hard to see why. The picture painted is ugly. Rugby around the world is a fragile ecosystem, beset by threats on all sides, be they rival sports, or just rival leisure activities in this era of bewildering choice, be they health concerns in this era of heightened intensity, be they, simply but most compellingly, those of the bottom line. For the sport merely to hold on to what it has, let alone to grow, a coordination of purpose is required across a nexus of mutually supporting organisations, that delicate lattice of unions and competitions. When an aggressive consortium, let alone two of them, rips through it all from within, because it can, without thought or care for the effect of its actions, furious resentment follows as the night the day, as unrest inequality. The 'union' starts to fall apart. When some of the iconoclasts cannot even keep up with the pace they find themselves so recklessly setting, the anger becomes sharpened with derision and contempt. The rugby family has never exactly laid claim to harmony among its number, but unregulated professionalism has raised antagonism to another level.

The clubs of England's Premiership collectively lost more than £40 million in the 2017–18 season alone. They are the most deeply resented. The orgy of expenditure they have embarked upon looks irresponsible and destructive, ramping up the going rate for player wages, which they themselves self-evidently cannot afford, let alone anybody else. They rail against the international game, the preserve of those angelic unions, refusing to sacrifice fixtures in the face of escalating player-welfare concerns and posturing with borderline desperation at as many sponsors and media executives as they can dance in the lap of. Another ugly, ugly look. To be aggressive is one thing, desperate another; to be both . . .

But they have no choice. There need only be one breach in the system for everyone to get sucked out. The English league represents just such a breach, but they were not the first into the vortex – or at least they are not the ones leading the way. That happens to be the French. Not that it matters. Once the notion of self-interest, the *sine qua non* of the free-market model, has been admitted into the system by just one of its agents, the rest are obliged to follow. The scramble on the field spreads off it, so that just to keep up, or not even that in most cases, those not at the top of the food chain are forced to overextend themselves. The alternative is to accept defeat, and we know from those goings-on on the field that such a mindset is alien to anyone in the sport industry. The moderation of behaviour has to be imposed, as part of a binding collective agreement.

A tendency to boo and hiss at the English and French is natural, but it is pointless. When launched into the professional era, rugby had nothing in place to stop the strongest taking advantage of their strength, so that is, naturally, what the strongest did. To moan about it is to moan about the lion eating the zebra, or the team with a dominant pack opting for another scrum. The club game in England and France is domestic rugby's answer to the Six Nations. It has history, soul and thus an element of prestige, but most of all it is nestled among a population of millions in affluent Europe. It is also played week in, week out. In the long run, if you are a union type devoted to the sporadic international game, let alone a recently created franchise in a rival league, that makes the club game a very dangerous creature indeed.

The sweep from the Atlantic coast through the southern half of France to the Alps, from La Rochelle to Lyon, Biarritz to Toulon, is rugby's centre of gravity. It is the broadest stretch of land, covering the largest population, where rugby is the number-one sport. Football is king in the big, cosmopolitan cities, Marseille, Lyon and the like, but across the parochial heartlands of *La France Profonde*, where each town and village revolves around the local rugby club, who in turn play to *l'esprit de clocher*, the pride that comes from falling within earshot of the community's church bells, rugby remains the sporting religion of choice. The population of the four regions in question is 24 million. This is rugby's largest market, generating significantly more revenue than the next biggest, England, which is more diffuse and difficult to define, pockets of devotion here and there, but unable to lay claim to an entire tract of land like that, bar, perhaps, in the far south-west.

The south-west of France, too, is where rugby first properly bit. As everywhere, the sport was introduced to the country by people of a certain class, which here meant in Paris. Less squeamish than the English about injecting competition into the culture, the French championship was born in 1892, although restricted for its first seven editions to clubs from the capital, a fairly typical example of rugby's chauvinism, which has proved robust and transferable, no matter the culture, no matter the language.

But, as we have found, chauvinism works both ways. The earthier form was quick to take hold in the south-west, *l'esprit de clocher* finding in rugby's brutal, attritional nature a perfect sporting vehicle. A storm was brewing, all the more familiar to a sport so defined by conflict, on and off the field.

Quickly, French rugby became riven by almost exactly the same dynamic as led to the great split in English rugby, only this time rugby union maintained its grip, even if it owed much to a governmental suppression of league that was totalitarian in its ruthlessness. The animosity of the provinces towards Paris was such that they considered themselves virtually different countries, despite attempts to re-establish some pride during an era of crisis in French national confidence. The spread of railways and communications drew France together even as it magnified and aggravated those differences. It meant the provinces had fewer qualms about doing what they wanted when it came to rugby than had been the case in northern England, where ratification by the RFU for the desired changes had at least been sought before refusal left those in the north with no choice. No doubt undermined somewhat by the events of 1789, the confidence of the French governing classes in the face of provincial unrest has never since been as unshakeable as that of the English, a legacy that persists in rugby to this day. The weakness of the French union in relation to the English is the most marked difference between the two current set-ups.

As in England, it turned out the provincials could play a bit, more so even than the aristos. The first time they were admitted to the French championship, in 1899, Bordeaux prevailed in the final over Stade Français, and within a few years the names of Parisian clubs had all but vanished from the Bouclier de Brennus, the legendary, battered trophy of wood and brass the French clubs have played for since that first championship. From 1908 until the revival of Stade Français towards the end of the century, Paris would boast just two titles, both for Racing Club de Paris. The provinces took over. Far from the ivory towers of their notional overlords in Paris, and even further from those of the IRB, they were able to develop their own special culture of remuneration, sometimes brazenly advertising it, usually tucking it into a convenient local job.

And then there was the violence. French rugby has always been famed for it, on and off the field. Its era of crisis (every rugby nation must have one) was the 1930s, brought on by the lawlessness of the

1920s. Amid all the violence, two deaths in the first-class game proved pivotal, one from a collapsed scrum in 1927, one from a tackle in 1930, prompting a local scribe to christen the era *rugby de muerte*.* The latter death came a month after the seething French crowd at a controversial home defeat by Wales, to deny France their first Five Nations title, had caused the English referee to fear for his safety. Rugby in France looked increasingly lawless to those looking in, whether from Britain's IRB or Paris's Fédération Française de Rugby (FFR). After the 1931 championship, France were expelled from the Five Nations for the rest of the decade, the IRB citing violence and the equally abhorrent crime of suspected professionalism.

All of which allowed the culture of rugby as southern France's special pursuit to deepen. Inevitably, links with the clubs of northern England were forged – and for a time league, the sport of rebels, grew rapidly. The nervy FFR chose to throw its lot in with Germany, Italy et al, at the time European rugby's next biggest nations, creating in 1934 the Fédération Internationale de Rugby Amateur, emphasis on the amateur, which is now Rugby Europe and administers the continental game beneath the Six Nations. Chastened, the FFR was readmitted to the Five Nations in 1939, just as the tournament was suspended for the Second World War, which proved propitious for union's eventual supremacy.

The Vichy regime assumed control, and it was closely allied to the FFR. Eager to establish rugby as the French game once and for all, a campaign that, happily, might also impress upon the IRB France's commitment to the 'amateur' way, France's wartime government conducted a purge of league that would set the code back decades. Vichy is one of a few totalitarian regimes to have thoroughly approved of rugby's manly virtues and the amateur ideal. As a result, the FFR

---

* It is not known why Paul Voivenel used the Spanish term *muerte*, but the likeliest explanation is that, having grown up in Gascony, where bull-fighting traditionally involved no bloodshed, he was drawing parallels between Spain's *corrida* and rugby's theatre of violence.

were empowered not only to outlaw league but to seize its assets and players, punishing the latter where necessary. 'The fate of rugby league is clear,' said Vichy minister Jean Ybarnégaray in 1940, as if auditioning for a Bond film. 'Its life is over and it will be quite simply deleted from French sport.'

Rugby, its affinity with totalitarianism as robust as ever, had imposed itself again. When, within a couple more decades, France managed to achieve the consistent success in the Five Nations they had craved for so long, the game's largest market was established for good.

Now the clubs of France have monetised the passion of their constituencies for the sport, they step out into the professional arena as part of the most influential body in the world. The collective annual revenue of the Top 14 clubs (€337 million in 2018, or £295 million) is more than 50 per cent greater than that of the RFU and around three times that of the FFR. It is only £50 million short of World Rugby's revenues in 2015, the year of the most lucrative World Cup at that point. And the Top 14 clubs harvest that sort of figure every year. No other body can rearrange rugby across the world the way the Top 14 can. The past has been based around the unions and the international game. There is terror throughout the rugby world that this dynamic is about to change, if it has not already.

This tipping point was coming the moment the southern hemisphere unions brokered the professional era. The more established a professional sport becomes, the more sway those providing a weekly diet of action will take on. The model was staring rugby in the face all along in the shape of The Sibling, which rugby likes to think itself so different from/superior to. Football is organised the way it is, around clubs rather than associations, not because of some profound cultural difference in the sport itself, but because it was professional and popular for all those decades before rugby ever thought to be. If an organisation offers a product people will pay to see on a weekly basis, that organisation will accumulate more power and influence than one that is restricted to certain windows. The club game becomes the focus inevitably. Rugby was different because for all those years of amateurism its club game had limited ambition or scope to promote itself, leaving the stage clear for the international, which did appeal to many with its quirky, occasional, ritualistic rhythms. In short, rugby's international game had next to no competition. The minute the whistle blew for professionalism the imperative to fill the airspace in between was introduced. A club like Saracens in England, for example, ancient of provenance but with a following in 1995 that numbered in its hundreds, scattered around the edge of a muddy parkland pitch in north London, were bound to rouse themselves into something more urgent. The more populous and affluent the local demographic, the greater the power and influence will grow of those offering a weekly service that interests that demographic. From the start, professional rugby, unregulated professional rugby, was set up for the clubs of England and France to exploit.

Which is not to say the unregulated model works even for those exploiting it. On the contrary. They are no more in control of it than anyone. The instinct to outdo the opposition finds expression, inevitably, through the uncomplicated vector of expenditure. The temptation to take just that next step along it is powerful for as long as that next step presents itself as the key to some important victory or other, until an unsustainable position is arrived at – unsustainable for those furthest along the vector, but also for all those obliged to try to keep up behind. Everyone becomes damaged.

France and England are best placed to lead the march towards self-harm, because they have the largest economies of those countries with a history for rugby, devastatingly so compared to all but Australia. The French economy is merely twice the size of Australia's, but then rugby is merely Australia's fourth most popular code of football. The French economy is nearly eight times bigger than either of South Africa's or Ireland's and nearly 14 times New Zealand's. The English economy is much the same. Unless rugby catches on in America and/or Japan, and soon, professional rugby will continue to concertina around these two.

Even beyond the size of its economy and appetite for rugby, France has further inbuilt advantages. The greatest is that ancient competition of theirs. English rugby, incredibly, did not introduce a cup competition for its clubs until 1972 or a league until 1987, the latter 95 years after the French had introduced theirs. The Bouclier de Brennus had the best part of a century to deepen its reach into the culture of French rugby, before the English thought to try it themselves. It meant the French had a vehicle of great history and soul, which mattered to millions, ready to go when the professional era began. The English then created the Premiership, their answer to football's Premier League, in 1997 and set about drumming up enthusiasm for it. Their success in that regard has been remarkable, but history had already done that work for the French.

They inherited, too, a fleet of purpose-built stadiums. Most clubs in France play in municipal stadiums built and paid for by the local government, which they are free to use as if they own. They receive support from local government and far higher levels of sponsorship, a function of a different corporate culture in France and the simple reality of the size of that market. The financing of the clubs themselves is also unique. Each must draw up a budget at the start of a season and meet it or face draconian punishment, amounting to relegation or worse. Investment by a millionaire is included in this budget *before* the season starts, as cash, not as a loan, and any shortfall at the end similarly met. Each club must have 15 per cent of their budget immediately to hand in the bank at the start of each season. No club is allowed to carry debt. This safeguards against clubs going bust, as happens in England, where the professional arm is dissolved and what is left of the club is sent to the bottom of the system. If the books are not balanced by a club in France, they are relegated to a level their circumstances can afford, but this happens before the club itself is threatened. For all the talk of lavish French spending, they are the only league that refuses to allow clubs to compete if they are insolvent. In England, the arrangement is different. Millionaires cover debts in the shape of loans, so they have a call on their clubs, who are, in turn, dependent on those millionaires. Should support be withdrawn for any reason, the results can be catastrophic.

The French system is a form of regulation, but it is regulation at a level so far out of the reach of most that it stretches the others as if they are coping with free-market conditions. The combined expenditure of the Top 14 clubs for the 2016–17 season (36 per cent of which was player wages) was €363 million (£319 million). This is around 45 per cent more than that of the Premiership clubs in the same season, although there are only 12 of them.

More French regulation developed in the second decade of the 21st century. From 2010 a salary cap was introduced. There are two elements, one the laudable requirement that no club spend more than 50 per cent of their budget on player wages, the other an absolute salary limit that changes from season to season. Very broadly speaking (there are loopholes and exceptions in all of rugby's systems of salary cap), the French limit has held at around 50 per cent more than the playing budgets of the English (although that gap has closed a little) and Irish, and at least twice that of anyone else.

Further measures have been introduced to reduce the number of foreign players in the Top 14. This has been driven partly by the fans, who want to see more local players, partly by some of the owners, who recognise the importance to the sport of a strong national team, and partly, of course, by the FFR, which has also started to offer the clubs sensible recompense for the release of players.

The relationship between the French union and its clubs best represents the economic dynamic that holds the rugby world in thrall, the former terrified of – and not a little compromised by – the gathering strength of the latter. There may be cultural reasons for the relative weakness of the FFR, but the resounding economic reason is the lack of a stadium to call its own. Stadium ownership is the most precious advantage in the professional era for any organisation, be it club or union.

The FFR, whose plans to build a stadium of its own come and go like the form of the national team, conspired with its bid team to secure hosting rights for the 2023 World Cup, proclaiming its economically weighty proposition as the best hope of averting the imminent death of rugby – from *rugby de muerte* to *muerte de rugby* in a little less than a hundred years. It came as no particular surprise when France won, despite World Rugby's own recommendation to itself of the South African bid. The French framed theirs as a chance to wrest back a measure of control from their own clubs, as a chance for the international game to wrest it back. It was a remarkable admission of fear, albeit one that conveniently positioned the FFR as the recipient of rugby's most lucrative windfall. Just as telling was the readiness with which World Rugby's council capitulated into accepting France's bid, in defiance of the board's recommendation.

In concert with the restrictions on overseas players, these developments leave French rugby, where the future of the sport is likely to be determined, poised intriguingly, the clubs showing for the first time an awareness of the repercussions of their rampant acquisition of talent from elsewhere and, even more remarkably, an apparent willingness to reconsider the policy. This is unlikely to help other unions in the struggle to hang on to their prize assets, but it should stem the dispiriting loss of so many of the next best.

The game across the world is in flux, but we should not imagine the scourge is over now the French are showing signs of moderation. Their clubs are debt-free, supported by some very powerful magnates, some of whom claim to have stopped dipping into their pockets for them a while ago. New models of stadium ownership are arising. Racing's new stadium, a joint venture between Jacky Lorenzetti, their owner, and the government, is essentially a music venue where you have to play rugby. It is Wasps' Ricoh Arena and then some. This is a development in the culture of French club rugby, one that is unlikely to weaken it.

The great obstacle to meaningful regulation across a sport is the international dimension. The model works so well in America because their sports are contained, more or less, in a single country, likewise in Australian rules, which makes watertight regulation realistic. But the simple benefit of regulation models, even if pursued individually in countries across a network, is that they slow things down and introduce an element of responsibility to the madness, and of coherent strategy. For the foreseeable future, the French clubs are likely to remain a threat to the equilibrium of rugby in other countries, possibly continuing to be so in their own. The advice of those who advocate regulation is to accept it, not to be disconcerted, and to consolidate within one's own borders. If everyone did it, the frenetic pace of the past 10 years or so, stretching countries and the sport within each into uncomfortable, even dangerous, positions of overreach, would abate. Nothing can be done about the wider fluctuations that pull the world and everything in it this way and that, the rise and fall of economies, currencies and regimes, but at least rugby can give itself a better chance of surviving them by assuming a lighter grip on its own activities.

The French and the English clubs, then, hold the key, as the leading menaces. An element of regulation there may be in French rugby, but there is huge disparity, too, between clubs in the same league. The annual announcement of French budgets on the eve of each season has become a tradition, inviting the world to marvel not only at the astronomical (by rugby's standards) figures but at the size of, say, Stade Français's budget for 2018–19 (€34 million, or £30 million) compared to Agen's (£12 million). A common mistake is to equate these figures to wage bills. These are the budgets for the entirety of each club's operation. The majority of English clubs weighed in at or around the

£20 million mark of expenditure for the 2017–18 season (they do not produce budgets before a season). Apart from Sale (£11.1 million), London Irish (£12.2 million) and Newcastle (£12.4 million) at the bottom and Quins (£30.1 million) and Wasps (£39.2 million, although their financial model incorporates the Ricoh Arena) at the top, most of the clubs punch at a similar weight.

As does the Premiership with the RFU. The dynamic in England is different. In England the union and the clubs are about as influential as each other, or at least they are capable of having an argument more interesting than any contretemps between union and subsidiaries elsewhere. Neither organisation is thought of fondly across the rugby world, but this is about the only contest in which most beyond England side with the RFU. Or wish the RFU would bring those clubs to heel. Wish they had . . .

VII

How Not to Do It:
The Clubs of England

Their detractors like to portray the English clubs as upstarts, eyeballs popping with the cocaine of other people's money, taking it upon themselves to savage noble institutions of history and gravitas, the Lions, the Six Nations, even the RFU itself – especially the RFU. Who do they think they are, bringing our noble game to its knees and their precious Premiership barely 20 years old . . .

This is not entirely fair. The Premiership might be new (roughly the same age as professionalism), but the individual clubs themselves are as historic as any institution in rugby. Of the 13 shareholders in the Premiership, only London Irish (est. 1898) are younger than the Lions (1888), against whom the clubs are so often disparaged as having no respect for history. Indeed, almost all of them came into being as 'Football Clubs'; some of them (Harlequin Football Club, Leicester Football Club, Saracens Football Club) still go by that nomenclature officially. They are from those dusky days when any pursuit with a ball and the use of feet, if only for hacking, considered itself 'football'.

Almost all of them pre-date the big beasts in football's Premier League. Four of them, Sale (1861, the oldest of them all), Bath, Harlequins and Wasps, pre-date the RFU itself, which means they are older than rugby. Exeter and Worcester are the same age.

So they deserve at least some respect. The problem is the century they spent twiddling their thumbs under the strict eye of the RFU, denied a cup until 1972 and a league until 1987, while their counterparts across the water were deepening the gravitas of their club culture with a meaningful competition. But even without that strictly imposed purity there could have been little preparation for the lurch into professionalism. For all the history, the French championship's crowds at the dawn of the professional era were small. There may have been 32 of them, but most of those smalltown clubs in the top flight at the end of the amateur era played to crowds of two or three thousand. In England, newly created league or not, the norm was around 5,000 for the 12 teams of the top flight. Rugby was overwhelmingly centred on the international game, but the love-hate relationship between union and clubs in both countries was poised to unfold as the professional era did.

The two unions have watched, part enthralled by the explosion of interest in their game, part in horror at the gathering power of the clubs. The clubs, meanwhile, steeped in history or not, identified the empty space and set out to fill it. Some were in two minds. Rosslyn Park declined to join the rush, preferring initially to remain an amateur haven for talented players who might not fancy a career in rugby (usually because they already had one in the City and did not want to take a pay cut). Even Harlequins were torn. In the 1980s they were more or less a private club. They didn't want a crowd; they didn't need one. And, sure enough, they didn't have one. In the end, they embraced professionalism because, well, they felt they ought to.

What has happened to clubs like Harlequins since is as persuasive an argument for the viability of rugby as any sell-out crowd for a Test match across the road at Twickenham. If rugby is to grow in its established markets it is not through the saturated international game but the domestic. The clubs of England and France are showing what can be done, even as they represent klaxon warnings for how not to do it. The French championship, then a 24-team affair, had average crowds of fewer than 4,000 in the late 1990s. In 2005, they settled on the 14-club format of today, and the crowds started to pick up, increasing by 25 per cent in that first year. By then, the Premiership (as the first division of 1987's new league had been reconstituted in 1997) had been averaging five figures per game for two seasons, the Top 14 joining them the following year. The average crowds of the two tournaments since have grown together at more or less the same rate, although with slightly different curves, the Top 14's hitting 15,000 in 2011, before treading water at around 14,000, until the Premiership's caught up around 2017. But as a 14-team competition the aggregate attendance in France has always been the greater.

The numbers alone are impressive, but so too the change in atmosphere, ushering in brighter colours and moods. In the 1980s, Harlequins' exclusive audience of a certain class was accommodated in one modest stand and on three grassy knolls. By the start of the professional era one of those knolls had sprouted a temporary stand, which became a shiny new one a year later, and that crowd had taken on some new types to swell to around 3,000 at the turn of the millennium.* Five years later, it had nearly trebled to 8,500. Quins suffered the trauma of relegation then, but for the season of their return their average crowd was well into five figures. By the time they won their first English title, in 2012, it was 14,000 (excluding the 82,000 they attracted that year for the recently introduced Big Game, the fixture they take to Twickenham each Christmas). More than that, the nature of the experience had been transformed. Gone, or at least

---

* The Premiership's official figures had them at more than 4,000, but creative accounting in those days was not confined to the balance sheets.

subsumed, were the Barbours and wellies of the grassy knolls, replaced instead by one of the more raucous experiences the Premiership has to offer. If rugby wants a paragon for how to negotiate the transition from exclusive, blazered past to vibrant, populist future, Harlequins is it.

The same dynamic has been repeated throughout the club game in England and France. Bristol, a city with as rich a heritage for playing rugby as any, could entice only 3,500 to each match in the first season of the Premiership. The trade-off between playing and spectating is delicate for any professional sport. Bristol have had terrible trouble mobilising support in the city, from spectator and sponsor, bouncing up and down between the first and second divisions, but 20 years later, in the season of their fourth return to the top flight, they averaged 16,000.

Across the water, another famous old rugby city, Bordeaux, was riven like so many in the sport's heartlands by hostility between local clubs. Stade Bordelais ruled the roost in the early years, winning the Bouclier de Brennus repeatedly around the turn of the 20th century. Around the turn of the 21st, Bordeaux-Bègles were the ones in the top flight. Their average crowd was 3,000, before they were relegated in 2003. In 2005, the two clubs set aside their differences and merged, returning to the top flight in 2011 with an average crowd of 14,000. Within four more years Union Bordeaux Bègles were the best-supported club in the world with gates of 25,000. Similar tales could be told of La Rochelle, Exeter, Montpellier, Northampton and on and on. Even Bath, titans of English rugby in the 1990s, played to crowds of around 7,000 then; 20 years on, it was to 14,500, a figure constrained by their situation at the heart of a World Heritage city, not to mention their declining fortunes on the field.

Cold numbers these may be, but they tell of an explosion of enthusiasm for rugby in England and France. Cynicism is all too readily (and often rightly) reached for, but if there could be a way of juxtaposing the experience of club rugby in the 20th century with that of today, even the most curmudgeonly would be open-mouthed at the transformation. This is, genuinely, without hint of irony or qualification, a good thing. Anyone who belittles the club game, however ugly its posturing might become, must square their distaste with this surge of fresh energy throughout rugby in these countries, for it represents resources that were not there before but are now. It represents creation.

But there are more numbers, and the trends are in the same direction, not all of them at the same rate. That is lack of regulation for you. At the turn of the millennium, the total expenditure of the Top 16 (as it was then) was €104 million (£70 million at the exchange rate of the time). By 2010, it had grown to €249 million (£214 million), despite the league shedding two teams in 2005. In 2018 the figure was €368 million (£324 million). Once the Top 14 had been established in 2005, French costs outstripped revenues by ever greater margins. The Top 14's operating loss started to balloon, reaching eight figures in 2008–9, where it has remained ever since, dropping below €20 million only twice between 2009 and 2018, surpassing €30 million in 2018.

Accounts of clubs and leagues are notoriously difficult to interpret or compare. The French clubs are audited by the Direction Nationale d'Aide et de Contrôle de Gestion (DNACG), which publishes the accounts of the top two leagues. Nearly half the Top 14's revenues each season, by far the biggest portion, is listed under the category 'Sponsoring'. This figure is impossible to pick apart. For some clubs it represents a portfolio of investments by local businesses, for some it includes the input of a single benefactor, but we can never know the precise breakdown. And does it matter anyway? When is a club a going concern? One supported by a network of local businesses feels a more viable proposition than one supported by a lone sugar daddy, but goodwill payments are goodwill payments. In France the attitude is, if the money is there, it is there. Even before the cumulative deficits of more than €20 million a season, the clubs' budgets include the personal funding of rich men. Contrary to the prevailing view, the club game in France is no more solvent, quite possibly less so, than in England, where the shortfalls in revenue, made good by the owners, are trumpeted loudly as debt.

The professional history of The Sibling should teach us that when it comes to sport the usual rules of business do not apply. Until it became, quite recently, so big it could not fail to make money, football was not a solvent industry either, most of its clubs paying players wages they could not afford, if by afford we mean pay for without going into debt. But falling into debt never seemed to matter particularly, so they *could* afford it. One person's debt is another's investment in the business. As long as there is someone, or some corporation, or some consortium, prepared to cover any shortfalls, a club is a viable proposition. Even when there is not, there are creative options available for survival or rebirth.

None of which is to commend a system that lures clubs, effectively, into daring each other to ever greater heights of expenditure, but it is to caution against assuming the rampant spending of the clubs of England and France is a temporary vulgarity to be endured only until they go bust. It is not difficult to infer that the attitude of many unions, not least those of England and France, has been exactly that, to wait for the clubs to fail, but that confidence is wavering as the balance sheets of everyone else creak just as critically with the attempt to keep up. Which will break first – the clubs or the resistance of a market it is equally easy to infer those clubs are trying to saturate?

Whether either side – the free-marketeers or the unions – is Machiavellian enough to be adopting such a position consciously is a moot point, but the dynamic remains no less provocative for that. The free-marketeers would argue that if the market is strong enough in any given region, appropriate levels of business will be arrived at in the end. They do not believe the market can fail. If the market decides that Australia, say, can support only semi-professional rugby, so it will be, and Australia will just have to send its best players to a market that can support more.

This is the mindset of the club owners, pretty much to a man self-made entrepreneurs with limited experience of corporate culture, who have ducked and dived in a single sector. Instinctively, they have great faith in market forces and a suspicion of regulation and central control, which is another way of saying they don't like being told what to do.

They would point to football as the holy model, but football is the exception, the world's only truly global sport, now that it has broken into China, India and America. Football is so vast and has penetrated so many cultures to their very roots that it can afford to let its elite game fall in on five big leagues, most dominated by one or two clubs, with one overarching super league, the Champions League. No other sport can follow this model successfully. Even the huge American sports understand that their market is too small for them to trust that everything will sort itself out.

The other great advantage football holds, at least over rugby, is its facility for upsets. No matter how much stronger team A is over team B, no matter, even, how dominant they might be on the given day, if the bloody ball won't go in the back of the net, they are vulnerable to an upset. In rugby, the 'goal' stretches right across the length of the pitch. If team A spends long enough camped in team B's territory, the chances are they will force the ball over the line eventually, or at least earn enough chances to kick at an undefended goal to win the match. Team B's chances, conversely, of hoofing the ball down field to snatch the equivalent of an outrageous winning goal are reduced in the territorial warfare of a rugby match.

It has been demonstrated that football can survive a certain level of inequality between its teams. Football even quite likes it. Again, the depth of penetration into local culture helps enormously. Fans brought up adoring West Bromwich Albion will keep turning up whatever the weather and love nothing more than extending a 'welcome' to the stars of Manchester United, dreaming of that occasional upset. But that occasional upset helps enormously too.

Even rugby's free-marketeers accept the need for each team to be able to beat any other 'on their day'. Just as important is to avoid one-sided matches. Rugby's thrashings are ugly, that dimension of violence turning the stomach somehow, in a way a 10–0 rout in football does not. So they introduced a salary cap. It is the one concession to equalisation strategy in English and French club rugby. The English, less confident of the penetration of club rugby into the local culture and losing money at an alarming rate, introduced theirs in 1999, for the third season of the Premiership; the French, more confident, acceded in 2010.

A look at the evolution of the cap is as accurate a gauge as we have of the wage bills of the English clubs. In 1999 the cap was introduced at £1.8 million per club and was at the same sort of level, £2.25 million, nine years later. There is no equivalent of the DNACG in English rugby, so financial results can only be determined by trawling through individual accounts – and sometimes not even by that, since filing detailed accounts was optional for those clubs who qualified as small companies, which was a few of them in the early years. Studying snapshots of available accounts throughout the Premiership's history reveals the sort of surges between profitability and recklessness that are characteristic of unregulated sports markets. In 1998, the first season of the Premiership, before the salary cap, four clubs did not file detailed accounts, including champions Newcastle, but of the eight who did the operating loss after interest was £12 million, an astonishing 44 per cent of their collective revenue of £27 million. If the deficits of the other four could be included (remember that Newcastle team of superstars, remember Richmond?), the figures would be even worse. Hence the salary cap the following year.

But in 2005, midway through that stretch of sensible salary-cap containment, the position was stable. Worcester, Leeds and Sale did not declare, but the cumulative losses of the other nine were just over a million pounds from revenues of nearly £70 million. Four clubs were in profit, Leicester by a million, and Harlequins and London Irish were near as damn it breaking even. Such equilibrium, though, is fragile in this model, the temptation, and freedom, to up the ante on the back of an encouraging outlook all but irresistible.

So the clubs started to spend more on players. In the 2006–7 season, an internal crisis saw around half the Premiership clubs accused of breaking the salary cap. The accusations were never made public and no documents were produced to prove any wrongdoing, but the strains of an unregulated system were starting to show, the teeth of the salary cap proving less than sharp. Far from punishing anyone, the only discernible step was to increase the cap to £4 million for the next season, nearly doubling it in one fell swoop.

Seven years on from our 2005 snapshot, the finances had run away again. In 2012 there was a full house of accounts. The cumulative loss had blown out to £21 million, 18 per cent of the revenues of £117 million. Only Northampton, Gloucester and newly promoted Exeter were in profit – and that only just. Saracens lost nearly £6 million from revenue of less than £8 million.

Consolidation after a second salary-cap scandal, this the rather more public one relating to the 2013–14 season, saw improved results again in 2015. The overstretched London Welsh did not file accounts, but the revenues of the other 11 that season had risen in three years from £117 million (for 12) to £156 million, and losses had fallen to £13.6 million (9 per cent of revenue). Four clubs were in profit, and Quins only half a million in deficit. Saracens and Wasps were still knee deep in deficits, but they now owned their own stadiums. Saracens' revenue in 2015 was double what it was in 2012 on the back of a home of their own, Wasps' more than treble.

Cue another frenzy. In the following two years to 2018, revenue (of the 12) had risen by more than a third in three years to £210 million on the back of a new TV deal, but the salary cap had escalated again from 2014's £4.5 million with a marquee player excluded (let's call it

£5 million) to 2018's £7 million with two marquee players (so *c.* £8 million). The operating losses of the group had blown out to well over £40 million (20 per cent of the revenue). And so the madness will continue.

The Premiership salary cap of £7 million with two marquee players is set to stay until at least 2020. Expect consolidation again before another leap forward, inevitably driven by the strong. Within these figures are the stories of the individual clubs, the established itching to push on, even before they are ready but certainly before the rest are. Everyone has lost money, bar the admirably solvent Exeter who joined the Premiership party in 2010, although their cause was aided no end by the sale to developers of the County Ground, which helped finance the construction of Sandy Park, their current home.

In these incoherent surges between hope and recklessness, hope and recklessness, we see an organisation lost, admitting in the form of that salary cap that they need to be protected from themselves but not respecting the problem enough to draw up any regulatory measures that bite. A salary cap is a key plank of any regulated system, but on its own it is weak.

In 2015, the Premiership investigated that alleged breach of the salary cap by two unnamed clubs in the 2013–14 season, the difference from the breaches of the decade before being the production by a whistleblower of documented proof. The anger and resentment that swept throughout those who considered themselves innocent was palpable. In a sort of inverse parody of the 'I'm Spartacus' scene, clubs came out one by one and declared they had not been investigated, as the public held their breath to see who would be left undeclared. Alas, as many as four remained silent: Saracens, Bath, Leicester and Newcastle, the latter sufficiently modest to be beyond suspicion. Bath had the temerity to announce they were within the cap for the 2014–15 season, glossing over the fact the breaches under investigation had occurred the season before.

The identity of the offenders has become one of the more open secrets in rugby, even if it is not legally sensible to declare in print. But legal considerations were what held sway. Salary caps are next to worthless without a legally binding collective bargaining agreement. The two clubs knew this and indeed pointed to the breaches the previous decade that had resulted in little more than an amnesty. Had the matter been taken to court, the offending clubs would have won at a canter, so the breaches, once again, were dealt with in-house and, needless to say, in a rather gentle manner. Such was the anger, though, inside and out, the Premiership announced that thenceforth, definitely this time, the salary cap would be really, really enforceable.

So they keep saying, now and throughout the cap's history, but to make it so would require degrees of regulation far beyond those the clubs' owners are prepared to countenance. Even if there were not countless ways to make the salary-cap police's job more difficult through the convenient employment of family members or other benefits in kind, without a collective bargaining agreement offending clubs will always be able to shrug their shoulders when caught and point to the section marked 'restraint of trade' in the statute books. And even if you were an enthusiastic proponent of regulation, which the Premiership clubs self-evidently are not, the negotiation of a collective bargaining agreement is a horribly, horribly complicated business, the process, as well as the results, enough to make any entrepreneur weep. The collective bargaining agreement (CBA) of the National Basketball Association in America is 600 pages long and not written by Tolstoy. Ice hockey's is more than 500, baseball's 400, American football's 300.

It is worth it. Whether the aim is a closely contested competition that could be won by anyone or a reliable programme for growth or simply stability, regulated systems in sport are demonstrably successful.

Australia's National Rugby League (CBA 300 pages) is the flag-bearer for competitiveness. In 2018, four teams out of 16 finished the regular season level at the top of the ladder, with the next four level two points behind – that's half the teams finishing within a win of each other. This represents, even by NRL standards, exceptionally close competition, but since the current league was inaugurated in 1998, 12 of the 16 teams that contest it have been crowned champions. None have successfully defended their title.

If disproportionate levels of interest and growth is the aim, then the Australian Football League (CBA a trifling 124 pages) is a shining light. The cumulative population of the Australian states where AFL is king is barely 11 million, and yet it is the league with the world's fourth highest average gate, its 37,000 in 2018 less than a couple of thousand shy of the Premier League, which is third behind the NFL (67,000) and Bundesliga (45,000). Unsurprisingly, it seems to have reached saturation, that attendance figure having levelled out this century, but from the institution of its CBA in 1990 the AFL's average attendance rose from 25,000 to 36,000 in eight years. It took 12 years for the Top 14 to grow its average attendance by the same amount – and that from the base of a mere 4,000 in 1999 with a population of 24 million in its heartlands. The AFL has opened new teams in new markets, its independent management structure allowing strategic decisions to be taken beyond the warring heads of the individual clubs themselves.

Pre-CBA, South Melbourne relocated to Sydney in 1982, initiating an attempt by the sport to break into league's heartlands. In 1997, the AFL merged two further teams to form the Brisbane Lions, before adding, when it felt ready, a further team in each of New South Wales and Queensland this century, projects with timescales of 20 to 30 years. As with any business, fortunes have ebbed and flowed, but, with a coherent strategy beyond those of the individual clubs vying with each other on the field and strict terms determining the rules of engagement for those clubs, the AFL is in a stronger position to negotiate the hazards. In 2015 they signed a six-year TV deal for AU$2.5 billion (£1.4 billion) – compare with French rugby's ground-breaking four-year deal of €388 million (£345 million), signed in 2016 for the start of the 2019–20 season. And 40 per cent of that goes to ProD2, the French second division.

America and Australia are not only the world's best sporting nations, they lead, perhaps inevitably, in the administration of those sports. The accompanying table overleaf lays out the typical equalisation policies of a regulated system and which of them a selection of leagues uses.

The first observation to note is the obvious difference in culture between administration in the big American and Australian sports and those in Europe. The former deploy all of the measures in most leagues, while European rugby's three leading domestic leagues, the Super League of rugby league and football's Premier League use hardly any. The Premiership, Top 14 and Super League have a salary cap, the PRO14 is a closed league (i.e. without relegation) and the Premier League operates a fixed squad size. And that is it for the key equalisation measures in these leagues.

The other observation to make is that either you are signed up for equalisation, or you are not. The more policies deployed, the more they reinforce each other. A salary cap on its own, as we have seen, is barely worth the paper it may or may not be written on. And, if one of the objects is a competitive league, there is not much point in a salary cap if some are way short of it, hence the importance of a salary collar (which enforces a minimum spend on player wages). And there is not much point in a collar if some clubs cannot afford it, hence the importance of differential funding, sending resources to those teams and/or markets that may need extra help at any given time to establish themselves and/or grow.

And so the interconnectedness of the policies goes on. Underpinning it all, though, is the collective bargaining agreement, as well as a strong independent governing board – not, for example, the Premiership's arrangement until recently of hauling out a couple of suits from their own clubs to fill the chair and vice-chair. Self-interest cannot be circumvented under such a system, nor a broad vision realised for the

	NFL	NBA	MLB	NHL	AFL
CBA	yes	yes	yes	yes	yes
Salary cap	yes	*partial*	no	yes	yes
Salary collar	yes	yes	no	yes	yes
Min. individual wage	yes	yes	yes	yes	yes
Closed league	yes	yes	yes	yes	yes
Player draft	yes	yes	yes	yes	yes
Fixed squad size	yes	yes	yes	yes	yes
Independent governance	yes	yes	yes	yes	yes
Differential funding	yes	yes	yes	yes	yes
Prize money	no	no	no	no	no

long-term benefit of the game and all the participants in it, a vision beyond the week-to-week striving for an edge over each other that necessarily consumes the clubs individually.

The prospects of such a system being instituted where rugby needs it most – in the Premiership and Top 14 – are not healthy. The barriers to setting one up are significant, particularly if a free-market model has already been established. And then there is the ferocity of the disputes between clubs and player collectives. Player collectives in America and Australia are legally obliged to be independent from the governing bodies they negotiate with – and are ferociously so. When proper collective bargaining agreements are being hammered out, industrial action, including lock-outs, is common. The negotiations are a necessary evil, but each agreement provides a framework that lasts for years.

There would have to be a compelling will among the clubs to set one up. We are back to the recurrent question of motive in rugby. Do the rugby clubs of England and France really want the game to grow? They want their audience to grow, and their power, but do they want the game to? One former chief executive of a Premiership club visited the club owners of the time to drum up support for the establishment

NRL	EPL	Prem	T14	P14	SuperLge
yes	no	no	no	no	no
yes	no	**yes**	**yes**	no	**yes**
yes	no	no	no	no	no
yes	no	no	no	no	no
yes	no	no	no	**yes**	no
no	no	no	no	no	no
yes	**yes**	no	no	no	no
partial	no	no	no	no	no
no	no	no	no	no	no
no	**yes**	*cups*	*cups*	*cups*	*cups*

of just such a reorganisation of the governance model and was told by one of the millionaires: 'I couldn't give a fuck about the good of the game.' That may be an extreme view, not necessarily representative of the majority, but there is more at stake for these men than the success or otherwise of the Dragons or the Waratahs in keeping abreast with the pace set, or even that of rivals within the same league.

With the clubs, the emphasis of the question is slightly different from the one we might level at the Tier 1 unions. Could the owners countenance a loosening of control over the destiny of the organisations they have each invested so heavily in? Is it even reasonable to expect them to? The irony is that a system of regulation helps everyone, including the clubs being held back, because when everyone grows together not only is the platform more stable, the strategies more coherent, but the end result so much more attractive, witness that TV deal for the AFL, whose 18 clubs netted collective revenues of a billion Australian dollars in 2017 (£590 million).

This goes back to the dawn of the professional era. And that in turn goes back to that century of posturing and fiddling. As other sports at various points over the past couple of hundred years took the decision to introduce remuneration for their players, rugby held out and held out, the elastic stretching ever tighter, until, right at the end of the 20th century, rugby let go. There was neither the time, will nor framework to manage the slingshot into the professional era. The bickering between the RFU and English clubs in the late 1990s is already the stuff of legend, even though there was not actually as much as there should have been, since the main problem was a complete lack of communication. Which, of course, left the clubs and their owners free to fill the void. The RFU, the ultimate custodian of the amateur ideal rugby had guarded so closely for a century, did not want to know. History will not judge it kindly for that, but there is little it could have done anyway.

The network of clubs with a past was, as in France, extensive, established and ready to go. They represented the path of least resistance. The alternative was to create an intermediary level of entities between club and country, administered by the union, around which to build a coherent model for professional rugby – and to create it from scratch. This was not a realistic proposition for the relatively weak FFR in the face of its agitating clubs, but even the RFU, nowhere near as powerful then as it is now, faced formidable obstacles. In the 1980s, it had introduced just such a conceit, the divisional championship, based around four arbitrary sections of England – the North, the Midlands, the South-West, and London and the South-East. The intention on the field was to bridge the gap between the club and international game, and the new level of competition was indeed credited by many with the England team's resurgence in the late 1980s – although the clubs might just as powerfully attribute that to the establishment of a league in 1987. But the championship was not designed as a commercial proposition. Divisional rugby did not survive into the professional era.

Something like it was the most coherent alternative supplied by an RFU torn apart by internal tensions as the surge into the professional era stressed every tradition the old organisation held dear. Far less encumbered by tradition were the rich men who immediately moved in on the clubs, some acquisitively, some because they were invited, none with a view to being lectured by an organisation that did not know what it wanted – and at the time was deeply in debt, a long way from the commercial enterprise it is now. Cliff Brittle, chairman of the RFU board, staunchly advocated a regional franchise system, not dissimilar to the models so productive in America and Australia, nor even that in Ireland now, but he was isolated in the unwieldy system and the clubs seized control. By the time the RFU had become commercially fit for purpose, the terms of the impasse were set.

These were the cultural barriers against anything other than a system based around the club game in rugby's two heavyweight countries, England and France. There is an argument the RFU should at least have moved to secure the contracts of their leading players, rendering them the exclusive property of the England team, but an international player without a club to call his own seems almost as bereft as a club player barred from playing for his country, a scenario perennially hanging over the current system. Central contracts are still mooted as a solution to the management of England's leading players.

The model that has evolved in England sees the RFU pay the Premiership an annual sum for access to the players. Just how much that sum should be is always open to debate, but the principle of the arrangement is sound. The RFU has all its players at professional clubs, receiving professional coaching. Most of the players' salaries are paid by those clubs. The England coach has access to his squad regularly throughout the season and for unbroken stretches during the autumn and Six Nations. All for around 15 per cent of the RFU's annual turnover. Once England and age-group costs are factored in, the funding of elite rugby tends to cost the RFU between 30 and 40 per cent of its revenue. The alternative model, attractive for different reasons, sees the Irish Rugby Football Union spend nearly two-thirds of its annual revenue (€54 million out of €86 million in 2018) on the elite game, supporting four provinces, which it also underwrites. One is relatively cheap, but the downside is a loss of control; the other sees the union exercise absolute control over its resources, but the system requires more investment, financial and otherwise, with accompanying vulnerability to market conditions.

Central contracts, even if they were possible to effect now that the clubs own and, crucially, produce the players, would do nothing to cool the ardour of those clubs in England and France to dominate the landscape. They are best placed to do just that through sheer weight of numbers and the mandate to provide a weekly diet of action. But they cannot be controlled – even by themselves it sometimes seems – careering on to who knows what destination.

If only that remained their problem alone. The current model stretches rugby around the world into deeply uncomfortable positions, certain players, coaches and their agents the only stakeholders to have significantly improved their financial position – but at what cost holistically when the only hope to begin to meet their costs is to make them play more matches? A regulated system, with a head able to adopt an independent position above the component parts of the body, armed with that precious collective bargaining agreement, would introduce an element of control.

Assuming all 12 Premiership clubs make full use of the salary cap and none sneak more payments over it (both unrealistic assumptions, but at least it gives us an idea), the English clubs currently pay around £96 million in player wages. They also lose (in 2018) well over £45 million. Which means they pay roughly double the wages they can afford. Or they need to reduce the wage bill by half. Or increase revenue by a quarter, which is not impossible within a few years. Regulation across a league would allow such realisations to be arrived at and appropriate policies to be implemented. And stay implemented.

The Premiership's game plan, insofar as there is one, is to wait for the revenues to catch up, but experience suggests wages will accelerate away again as soon as they do. Nothing has changed that might avert that.

Longer term, the game plan is the creation of value. In 1995, Nigel Wray paid £2 million for a stake in Saracens at the dawn of the professional era and has invested tens of millions more since, which begs the question why. In his case, undoubtedly, love has played its part, for rugby and Saracens, but in the late 1990s he used to speak excitedly too about the potential for 'the brand'. Saracens had a distinctive emblem and a location-neutral name, for which he saw great potential. Words like 'brand' have tended to rile rugby folk as much as they have confused, but only now, as big finance starts to flirt with the Premiership, do we begin to sense what the clubs might have been creating all the while. This is essentially what has happened in football, the creation of value, or the cumulative prices people are prepared to pay for individual clubs, even as those clubs lose money, more than compensating for the annual losses. The bet rugby's investors are making is that the value of, in the English case, the Premiership is similarly on the rise. And who is to say they are wrong?

The paradox is that, although regulation might calm the brinkmanship and allow the regulated league to breathe, the evidence suggests it would also empower the league to grow in an efficient, cost-effective manner and to do so far more quickly than a market-led approach. Regulation in the mid-to-long term ought to make the French and English leagues stronger more quickly. Which hardly solves the problem for everyone else. Regulation models, alas, are much harder to apply beyond a single competition or league. Without the self-contained element enjoyed by the big American sports, rugby could establish an effective global model only if individual leagues came to appreciate the importance of the sport's health in other regions, the notion of a rising tide floating all boats. The realisation does not feel imminent, but meaningful policy changes internally would represent a start. The hope is that the moderate behaviour introduced into the system by the regulation of individual leagues might give all the chance to find a similar equilibrium for themselves, to grow more confidently and to plan more coherently.

Because there are examples of coherent administration in rugby. One of them is holding its own quite nicely on the fringes of the European main.

VIII

Poised on the Edge:
The Celtic Fringe

In the late 1990s, there was a . . . what is the collective noun for sports administrators? . . . a crusade of sports administrators who used to meet for a drink every now and then in London. One of their favourite ways to pass the time was to sit around musing over their dream assignment. If you could pick a sport to turn round anywhere in the world, which would it be? There was just one rule. You weren't allowed to choose rugby in Dublin. Because that would be too fucking easy.

Ireland is the biggest country in Europe with no professional football, and Dublin the biggest city (this is how sports administrators see the world). Football is the biggest participation sport in Ireland, as it is in most places, but Irish football fans tend to support the big clubs of northern England or Glasgow, taking the boat over on match day. Dublin is a city of a million people, with another million in the surrounding areas, and it is, relatively speaking, a sporting desert. It had no professional sports team, full stop, until rugby turned. And it had no winter sport, full stop – to watch at any rate. The local staples of Gaelic football and hurling, which are huge spectator sports, are still amateur (officially at least) and they are played in the summer. Professional rugby in Ireland was an open goal.

They have taken it. Another classic pub conversation, not just for those curious folk in sports administration, is which country has come out of the first couple of decades of professional rugby in the best shape. If the measure is progress made, the winner, clearly, is Ireland. Even if it is not, one look at the Irish set-up must be enough to make green with envy most of the unions in the world.

There should be no surprise that it is the system of all the rugby nations' that most closely resembles the sort of regulated arrangement outlined above, one body in control, able to take a detached view and implement strategic decisions, four professional teams among which resources can be allocated according to requirement, significant investment in player development beneath those four teams – but most of all a system whose component parts from top to bottom service the whole. The Irish model cannot be accounted an American-style set-up because it does not constitute a self-contained league and is exposed to external factors it cannot control, but the Irish model represents yet another persuasive argument for the virtues of not leaving everything to chance.

At risk of belittling Irish rugby's achievements unfairly, there was a further inbuilt advantage. While every other Tier 1 union, certainly in Europe, agonised over how best to structure professional rugby, Ireland had a ready-made solution. The four provinces are absolutely perfect for the transmission of professional rugby in a country of Ireland's size. Not only do they transcend the cities, towns and villages that supply any country with its clubs, thus sitting neatly between the club and international games, not only are they owned by the unions – or rather simply 'branches' thereof – but they are ancient kingdoms unto themselves, actual kingdoms through various periods of history, with which their inhabitants connect profoundly. People have gone to war for the provinces of Ireland. The same cannot be said, at least in a literal sense, of the Neath-Swansea Ospreys, or of London and the south-east. While Saracens wrestle with the conundrum of allegiance to the brand, Ireland can galvanise their rugby folk around provinces that have existed in some form or another since the Dark Ages.

All of which is not to suggest professional rugby has been a picnic for Ireland, but the preconditions have facilitated the establishment of the ideal system, and Ireland have wrought that adroitly in their favour to show those unions still caught in a no-man's-land of administration just what can be achieved.

Irish rugby was a mess when the game turned professional. Indeed, for all the legendary players to have emerged from Ireland, results-wise they had been the poor relations of the original Five Nations, with just the one grand slam in the 20th century. There were no signs of that changing either side of the leap to professionalism. In the 1990s, Ireland mustered eight wins in the Five Nations, fewer than one a year. In the first four championships of the professional era, they occupied or shared last place every year. In 1999, they were eliminated from the World Cup by Argentina, still very much a Tier 2 nation back then. There were no hints either of the glory to come from their provinces, until Ulster became European champions in 1999, the year the English clubs did not take part. Even without the English, Leinster came bottom of their pool that season, fewer than 5,000 turning up for two of their three matches. Hence, those jibes among our carousing sports administrators.

Who is to say another union in the Irish position would not have panicked by the year 2000 and ripped it all up. For anyone in rugby with a memory, the early years of professional domestic rugby in the Celtic nations are agony to recall. Let us not dwell on them more than we have to. Depressing attendances (Connacht regularly played to 500 in the first season of the Celtic League), depressing arguments, depressing apathy. Competitions rose and fell with ugly hybrid titles, the Welsh rebel this, the Welsh–Scottish that, until the Celtic League was settled upon. Teams came and went, the Welsh and the Scottish trying frantically to make the past add up to a coherent, or even just viable, future: Border Reivers, Caledonia Reds, Celtic Warriors, here one day, gone the next.

The Irish, meanwhile, held their nerve. Relief was on its way in the shape of a golden generation, led by the northern hemisphere's player of the 21st century, Brian O'Driscoll, who burst onto the scene in 2000. Unless it was a coincidence, the new Irish system had already set to work, unbeknown to those mischievous sports administrators. Even if it was a coincidence, the new structures provided that generation with the optimum conditions in which to thrive.

All else followed. Ulster and Munster attracted respectable crowds in the early years, but Leinster were swift to join the rush, as the crowds of the three provinces rose vertiginously in the mid-2000s, averaging well into five figures, at times nudging 20,000 in Leinster's case (when their annual PRO14 match at the Aviva Stadium is included). No other teams in the PRO14 come close. After Ulster's early triumph, Munster were next to inspire with a series of heroic near-misses in Europe until they attained catharsis with the titles of 2006 and 2008.

Then came Leinster, who dominated the next decade. There are 73 rugby clubs in Leinster, the most of Ireland's four provinces. That is just two more than in the English county of Surrey. And still the Ireland internationals and Lions keep coming, often enough of them at the same time to fill a 15.

All of Ireland's international players are played exactly when and as much as the union wants, the subsequent success of the national team fuelling that of the provinces and vice versa. If any player is short of game time in any given season, they can be moved to another province, according to player and/or province requirements. There are regulations pertaining to the number of non-Ireland-qualified players per province, far stricter and easier to enforce than in Europe's other countries. Even Connacht, the smallest province by a long way, won the PRO14 in 2016, completing the Irish set of winners. And all that on union revenues that are much, much lower than that of the RFU or the English clubs, still less those in France, less even than the Welsh union's turnover.

If only everyone else were as under control. Their system has enabled the Irish to punch above their weight, without the numbers of the English or French, or the rugby-centric cultures of New Zealand, South Africa or Wales, but they remain vulnerable to developments across the water like the rest of the world – just not quite as much.

The change in organisation of what was the Heineken Cup, now the Champions Cup, is illustrative of a dynamic inevitable without regulation enshrined into the constitution. The Heineken Cup was a union-led competition and thus subject to significant equalisation strategies, albeit incidental rather than central to any strategy. Revenues were split six ways, the weaker unions with fewer competitors receiving the same basic amounts as the stronger with more. Another effect was the rather less exacting qualification procedure for the Celtic and Italian teams. All but one of the 12 who would end up (from 2010) constituting the Pro12 were waved gently through, while the English and French tore into each other for the right to qualify from their respective leagues. The arrangement amounted to a redistribution of resources, the powerful English and French clubs receiving as much for participating in the tournament, through their unions, as, for example, the Italians, with a mere two teams, invariably the weakest in the tournament, sometimes embarrassingly so, who got to play every year, come what may.

The failure of Italian rugby to take advantage of the privileges extended to it by admittance to the big European competitions, both at international and club level, is undeniably puzzling. They have enjoyed huge levels of support, the kind a Pacific Island nation or one developing in eastern Europe could only dream of. But for a period of promise between 2005 and 2007, they have next to nothing to show for it from 20 years of trying. Another classic impasse between the amateur factions among their administration and the requirements of the new era is usually blamed by those who know, a chronic neglect of player development the result, but there are hopes that this has been addressed. If rugby in Italy (population 60 million; economy number eight on the IMF's 2018 list) ever becomes more than a cult sport in the north-east of the country, we might have another contender with which to reckon. In equalisation terms, that disproportionate funding, however much it might gall those more deserving of it, would then be accounted progressive investment.

So far it has not had the desired results, in Italy at least – and, anyway, the Heineken Cup was not a consciously regulated competition, so the money was just sent off to the six corners of Europe without conditions or investment plans. No strategic vision was ever set down. Certainly, the clubs of England and France saw no reason why they should be, effectively, subsidising the Pro12 teams. Resentment developed, most of it towards the Irish, with Munster and Leinster victorious in five of the seven editions of the Heineken Cup between 2006 and 2012. So the English and French pulled rank after Leinster won a second consecutive title in 2012. They were sick of the Pro12 teams waltzing into the tournament every year; they particularly resented the way the Irish, and to a lesser extent the Welsh, could pick and choose when they played their best players, who were rare sights indeed for long stretches of the Pro12 season, even outside the international windows. O'Driscoll played nearly twice as many Test matches as he did league matches for Leinster. Paul O'Connell and Sam Warburton, the other Lions captains of the era, likewise finished their careers with more appearances for their country than for their domestic teams in the various guises of the PRO14. Some called it sound management; the English and French reckoned it was unfair advantage.

Their walkout, which led to a more streamlined, more cut-throat tournament, the Champions Cup, two years later, was an ugly sight, eliciting just as much resentment the other way. Again, it took little or no imagination to portray the clubs as irresponsible brats, splurging money they could ill afford on everybody else's players, complaining when it did not bring them the success they craved, then demanding more money because they desperately needed it. Equally easy was the counterargument. The English and French brought the most eyeballs and so the most money, and yet their 26 clubs received the same level of basic funding from the competition as the four of Italy and Scotland, or the eight of Ireland and Wales. Meanwhile, only one of those Pro12 teams would miss out on Europe in any given year; none of them would have to worry about relegation; few even seemed to care about the league at all, regularly fielding weakened teams because, well, it didn't matter. The Irish and Welsh were able to focus all their energy on Europe and then have a bonus tilt at the Pro12 in the remaining weeks of the season if they happened to be within range. If a level playing field is what you were after, it was patently unfair.

But sport is unfair. It's not fair, either, that there is so much more money in England and France than there is in Scotland and Ireland, or that rugby is so much more central to Welsh culture than it is to Italian. The American response would be to try to smooth out the differences in strength, to level the playing field as far as possible, with coherent equalisation strategies. The Heineken Cup's disproportionate funding was an example of that – except it was not, because it was not the result of any coherent planning or principles enshrined in a constitution. There just happened to be six unions who shared the money between themselves.

The clubs resolved to take it off them. The English and French gave notice they were breaking away. The move effectively meant the end of the competition for everyone, a state of affairs the clubs considered vindication of their economic power, their right to a better deal.

The shift from union to club, from subsidised peripheries to an intense core, is consistent with the conclusion towards which any unregulated system tends. The Italian case is illustrative. They were guaranteed two places under the old regime, but the leap from their domestic league, the Super 10, to the Heineken Cup, both technically and economically, felt too great, so they joined the Celtic League, which became the Pro12, in 2010. Unwittingly, they had paved the way for what was to come, the loss of their guaranteed place among Europe's elite. Where they had qualified for Europe separately, now the Italians could be lumped in with the other three unions, reducing the feeder leagues from four to three. Apart from the fact their fortunes in Europe, never exactly healthy, deteriorated further when they joined the Pro12, they were now vulnerable as part of the third league, the target for English and French reforms. Their guaranteed two places were reduced to one in 2014 for the new Champions Cup, then, following further reform, none. The 2018–19 edition was the first to feature no Italian team. The free-marketeer view would be, good, it is up to the Italians to prove themselves worthy of inclusion. The American view (how absurd to consider them alternatives) would be, bad, you have lost numbers from your competition and the prospects for growth in the applicable region are compromised.

The arguments raged on both sides and, as ever, were well matched. Those accusations of bad management and bad temper levelled against the clubs were reasonable, as was their insistence that the competition's structure mitigated against them. Regardless, only one side prevailed. The clubs won, which means the market won, as it always does without regulation, which means the sport contracted. The new competition was heralded by its advocates, who insisted, mostly with English accents, that everyone would be better off under the new regime because everyone's revenue would increase. What was not to like?

Even allowing for the fact a sudden deterioration of the sponsorship market meant the promised uplift was not immediately forthcoming, lesson one of any economics class tells us that if we become richer but our peers richer still, we become, in fact, poorer. There is no other way to dress the shift from Heineken to Champions Cup than as a loss for the Celtic nations, a loss for the relatively weak, potentially crippling for them in the long run. There are fewer teams in the new competition, all of the losses suffered by the weakest league.

Now none of the Celtic or Italian unions is guaranteed a team in the Champions Cup, with the Italians for now the most obviously vulnerable. It is true they have supplied limited highlights in the first 20 years or so of European club competition, but one thing is truer: the chances of their fortunes improving would be next to nothing with their exclusion altogether. Where will it stop? The Welsh and Scottish have never won Europe either, and they hardly generate millions. How long will their presence be suffered?

In a rather sinister flourish of mafia-speak, one unnamed owner of an English club told the *Rugby Paper* when the new arrangement was finalised: 'The Welsh regions stood solidly with us . . . That's something we shall not forget.'

Don't you believe it. If rugby ever needs reminding that the usual dynamics are still powering the machine, confirmation is to be found in throwaway comments like this. Political alliances still work fundamental changes, but overarching them all, inevitably, is the economic imperative. The Welsh would be naive indeed to think their decision to follow the coins to the English side will be remembered should they ever find themselves between those English and more coins. For all their history in the game, for all the prestige their legends have earned, Wales remains a tiny country, riven by all the same internal tensions that have rendered the English and French models so contentious, as caught between history and the future as they are. But Welsh rugby does not enjoy the heft to prevail regardless. If, spiritually, we are all Pacific Islanders, the Welsh, like the Scottish, are the closest geographically to the singularity pulling global rugby apart. Whether that proves a blessing or curse remains to be seen.

The history of rugby has special places reserved for Wales and Scotland. If rugby is an Empire game, Wales and Scotland complete the nations that make up imperial Britain.

Scotland – or at least Scottish rugby types – guarded this status closely, hence the furious face-off with England in the 1880s over whether a try had been scored, over how a sport should be governed. Scotland and rugby established much the same relationship as England and rugby had, which is to say transmitted through the ruling classes.

Wales, on the other hand, embraced rugby from the bottom up, the enthusiasm of the working class for the sport insinuating it into the national culture as nowhere else bar New Zealand. Pound for pound they are by far the most successful of the Four, Five then Six Nations, another reminder that penetration into a culture remains a precious advantage in any sport's arms race. This is undoubtedly a function of numbers, but also of intangibles such as working-class hunger (figurative if not literal), toughness and the lack of a sense of entitlement. There are coaches at the highest level who have publicly acknowledged their consideration of such personal circumstances in selection strategy. Whether this approach is right may remain a point of debate, but the affinity of a working-class lad or lass for the rough and tumble of the rugby field seems a more than plausible inference. It may or may not be a coincidence that England's greatest team (the 2003 World Cup winners) was the one with the highest proportion of state-educated players (10 out of 15, six out of eight in the pack).

The parallels between Wales and the north of England are obvious, as was the hardened locals' aptitude for a collision sport with a ball. For a while, those parallels threatened to derail Welsh rugby altogether, when the propensity of league to lure working-class Welshmen to their clubs reached a peak in the 1980s. As in Ireland, rugby in Wales was looking bereft when the game prepared to upgrade to professionalism. In the 1990s, Wales finished the Five Nations last or joint last six times. By that measure, Welsh rugby would appear to have been invigorated by professionalism, three grand slams between 2005 and 2012, and another in 2018, as many as Wales secured in even the glorious 1970s. But the picture beneath the national team is more complicated.

The reverse applied to Scotland. The 1980s and 1990s were Scotland's best years, accounting for two of their three grand slams, as well as a few near-misses. The Five Nations culminated with the 20th century in the greatest championship of them all, 1999, won by a Scotland team playing the rugby of the gods. How they slumped thereafter.

Rugby in Scotland and Wales, so intimately bound up with the sport's history, shares many similarities, for all that the former has radiated more than a whiff of the elite about it, while the latter has not. Both populations are modest, 5 million and 3 million, respectively. Nearly twice as populous it may be, but that class dynamic has restricted Scotland's tally on World Rugby's registered-players list (to be treated with caution, of course) to half that of Wales's (47,000 to 94,000). Nevertheless, both nations found themselves contemplating at the dawn of the professional era the same club culture as England and France, with populations more in line with Ireland – but, crucially, without the provinces of the latter.

So they set about trying to manufacture some. The results were not pretty. As ever, population was the fundamental driver – population and culture.

The Scottish Borders, for example, is one of the most famous rugby regions in the world with a profound culture for the sport. This is where Scottish rugby can claim to be the people's game. If anywhere were deserving of a provincial team in the brave new world of professional rugby, it is the Borders. So they gave them one. The trouble is, game of the people though rugby may be in the Borders, there are only 115,000 of those people. Chesterfield, in other words. Except that in the Borders the 115,000 are scattered across the mighty countryside – some of the most beautiful country known to humanity, but sprawling and empty nonetheless. The Scottish Borders council area is nearly 2,000 square miles, the size of neighbouring Northumberland, which also happens to be England's most sparsely populated county with 165 people per square mile. The Borders has 60.

They are hardy folk, descended from those in the front line of the endless warring between England and Scotland, those whose constant attentions inclined the Romans to build a wall. They have given the sport some of its greatest players, perhaps not as prolific per capita as the Pacific Islands but certainly the most prolific region of the North Atlantic islands. Hawick has produced more Scotland internationals than any other club; Hawick is the throbbing metropolis at the heart of the region; Hawick has 15,000 people. Melrose, as evocative a name as any in rugby history, birthplace of sevens, home of Jim Telfer, Doddie Weir and Craig Chalmers, has barely 2,000. Size-wise, it's a village, albeit part of the Borders' largest urban sprawl, the 22,000 of Galashiels and its surrounds. That's the population of Horley, satellite town of Crawley. In the Borders council area there are 15 rugby clubs, of any size, which is actually quite a lot for a population of that size, but not a lot if you are trying to establish a professional rugby team for the area. Even if you extend the region west to Dumfries, you pick up only another five.

Demographics again. For all the rugby culture of the Borders, for all the achievement and talent, there are just not enough people. Until they revived the Victorian network in 2015, there was not even a railway service. The Scottish Rugby Union tried twice to institute a professional Borders team, as well as (once) a team, the Caledonia Reds, servicing the vast tract of land (20,000 square miles) that extended north beyond Edinburgh and Glasgow. Two years into the professional era, it merged both districts into Edinburgh and Glasgow respectively, but with the creation of the Celtic League the Scottish union gave the Borders another shot in 2002. The first year saw crowds of four or five thousand, actually quite the achievement – one in 25 people of a far-flung region. But by the time of the Borders' second closing, in 2007, these had fallen to one or two thousand, sometimes not even that.

We had another Pacific Islands situation. However devoted to the sport the Borders are, however many players to the game they have supplied, the economics demand that rugby in Scotland be based around the two big cities, Glasgow and Edinburgh, where rugby barely registers in the public consciousness. In Glasgow, particularly, rugby is so far behind football as to be almost invisible, but there does not have to be a very high take-up from the population of half a million to make Glasgow Warriors viable. Helped by on-field success, Glasgow were selling out Scotstoun (capacity 7,500) every game by 2018 and were ready to expand.

By then, Scottish rugby looked stronger than at any time in the professional era – Edinburgh reached the semi-final of Europe in 2012, Glasgow won the Pro12 in 2015, a few months before Scotland were moments away from a World Cup semi-final. But how connected to it do the folk in the Borders feel? This is the way professional sport tends, away from the local and passionate, towards the big towns and cities, where the passion is diluted across vast populations, whose very size is what gives professional sport in them a chance. The same dynamic applies in the end, of course, across nations.

Studying rugby in Britain reveals certain preconditions that tend to give a professional club a chance. You need a population centre of around 100,000, with another half a million or so in the surrounding areas, and no other dominant code of football (Exeter, Gloucester, Bath, Northampton, Worcester). If you have another dominant code of football, the numbers have to be much higher (Leicester, Newcastle, Bristol, Harlequins, Saracens, Wasps). If you are the third-choice code of football, don't bother. Sale (in the second largest conurbation in the UK) are the only example in the English Premiership of the latter, and theirs is the most consistent struggle.

Wales have the conurbations of Cardiff (population of half a million), Swansea and Newport (both 300,000), around which they have attempted to build a coherent framework for professional rugby. Further west, Llanelli, whose franchise, the Scarlets, has basically been granted rights to the rest of Wales, is smaller (50,000) but without the distraction of football.

The Welsh model, though, has suffered particularly from another hindrance to the strategic creation of entities above club level – parochialism. The Welsh Rugby Union, not unreasonably, hoped the myriad clubs that had sprung up through the communities of the south might coalesce around the new franchises. But so deep does the rugby culture run throughout Wales that those clubs harboured an enmity towards each other they were not prepared to transcend in order to support whichever franchise happened to be closest to them. The franchise that became the Dragons was supposed to unite Newport with the whole of Gwent, but the patrons of the valleys had no time for those from the big city, and they would not come. The ill-fated Celtic Warriors were supposed to unite the people of Pontypridd and Bridgend – no chance. They were closed down after a year. So then they wanted Pontypridd to get behind Cardiff. Ha! Neath and Swansea? The All Blacks and the All Whites?

Wales have based their professional model around these regions, which were set up in 2003 for the third season of the Celtic League. Among some of the rugby folk old enough to remember, a certain cynicism remains to this day, harking back to a golden age when the old stadiums creaked with locals passionate about their ancient clubs. The passion is not in question but, beyond perhaps the odd festival fixture, the numbers, the week-to-week numbers, do not bear scrutiny. Newport and Cardiff were the best supported in the first two seasons of the Celtic League, with gates of around 7,000, before the former managed to effect an actual drop in attendances, which has yet to be made up, when they combined with the rest of Gwent. Otherwise, the individual clubs had inadequate support to sustain a level of professional rugby that might hope to compete with the big beasts in Europe. However passionate the following, there were too many clubs, the local population spread too thinly. In theory, though, if they could be combined into franchises . . .

Historic sports clubs, soulful and embedded into local culture as they are, do not do theory – and they are none too keen on shiny franchises. The arc of the Welsh regions' average gates has been loosely wedded to their success on the field, which has been limited, particularly in Europe. Only the Cardiff Blues have managed to break 10,000, in the seasons of 2009–10 and 2010–11 when they played at the Cardiff City Stadium. The strategists of Welsh rugby, desperate for change, dreaming up conceits with names like Project Reset, are now more or less reduced to waiting for the emergence of new generations, who are not as defined by ancient rivalries, who know only the Ospreys, the Blues, the Scarlets and Dragons. In which case, what will become of the smaller clubs they will have transcended?

We are back again to the conflict between amateur and professional, the past and the future. Rugby in too many of its heartlands is hamstrung by this tension. The Welsh regions, unlike the Irish and Scottish equivalents, started life as privately owned, independent of the union, an awkward hybrid between the English and Irish models. They have had to grow new histories and identities almost from scratch because of the very depth to the roots of the sport they have been built upon – or over, as the cynics would have it. It goes without saying that the early history of professional rugby in Wales and Scotland is riddled with arguments, civil wars and coups of an almost insanely unreasonable intensity. Such antagonism is a function of love for the old ways, a function of what many consider sport to mean, the notion of a recreation to bind people together at a close-quarter, meaningful level. The guardians of tradition are suspicious of the idea of sport as entertainment, sport as megastore.

But this is the pact rugby entered into when the game went open. Professionalism – and not the kind, long familiar to Welsh rugby, that meant money appearing in the bottom of the kit bag after a game – is not compatible with the local. Professionalism can and does mean extensive connections with the community, but they must be new and they must be extended from higher up and they must service the directive of a business to grow. In so doing, the new sports-club-as-megastore becomes susceptible to charges of opportunism and soullessness from those who just want things to stay the way they are. And, like megastores, the new businesses have a profound impact on the local infrastructure they supersede. Things are, indeed, never the same again.

Part 4

On a Rocket to Somewhere

IX

Progress and Destruction:
Saracens and London Welsh

One cold Monday evening in November 1995, 350 locals elbowed their way into the pavilion of the rugby club they held so dear. It was a massive turnout for an extraordinary general meeting. The players had been let out of training early to attend. Nobody knew what it was about, only that if they cared about the future of their beloved club they had to be there. The dirty walls creaked as members jostled for standing room. The bar could barely keep up. Scores of dusty photos stared dumbly at the scene, each one a year more faded than its neighbour, a chain stretching back beyond a century. This was a home to everyone present, modest, ramshackle and all the richer for that in soul.

A hush washed over the throng when the tall, elegant president of the club finally rose to address the room. The club had a decision to make. They had survived until then on takings of about £250,000 a year, just about enough to keep the floodlights flickering, the bar stocked, the showers occasionally warm. Now there was a gentleman in the wings prepared to invest rather more, enough in fact to transform the very nature of the club's existence. The members looked around at each other, some eyes sparkling with excitement at the possibility of a brave new world, some narrowed with wariness about what this would mean for the way things are and always have been.

Progress they call it, the ones with the sparkling eyes. And who is to say they are wrong? It is all too easy to condemn those sharp of suit as all about the money and the future, no feel for history or heart. They know the price of everything and the value of nothing, etc, etc. Then again, what about those with their backs turned on tomorrow, wallowing in the familiar, obstructive of progress. If it were left to them we'd still be in the trees, etc, etc.

Both dynamics are vital to humanity's story, the former moving us forward, the latter colouring things in as we go, but they remain in opposition to each other, a creative tension whose net result is the trail humans have cut through the wilderness. Rugby, certainly in the land of its birth – and therefore, indirectly, throughout the world – had been shaped by an imbalance between the two, skewed for so long by its fascination with tradition, when suddenly, in that year of 1995, the progressives were allowed to burst in.

The scenes in our humble clubhouse represent an apt distillation of the dilemma sweeping throughout the game, particularly in Britain. As ever in these situations, the wary insisted on guarantees and vetoes, which were granted, so that when the vote came their hands slowly followed those of the excited, which were thrust in the air without hesitation. But, deep down, they would have known such concessions are only ever temporary. There is no meeting progress halfway.

This being England and our investor of a certain manner, the takeover was conducted in the best possible taste. Nigel Wray was almost apologetic as he offered the Saracens membership £2 million for their club, whose tangible assets his accountant had valued at nothing more than £100,000. He assured them a veto of 51 per cent. 'The last thing I want is anyone saying, "Rich bugger takes over Saracens,"' he said.

'I want to join the Saracens team.' And he would have meant it. Of all the investors who swept into rugby, he was the one most steeped in the sport's ways. Were progress as refined as Nigel Wray, tradition might stand a chance. At the very least, he was to prove himself devoted to his new club in the decades that followed.

He never expected to make any money from Saracens, but neither did he expect the venture to cost him the tens of millions of pounds he has invested since. Once progress is admitted, without regulation, everyone becomes caught up in the momentum. Other investors were less sensitive to rugby's past. Sir John Hall, Ashley Levett. English rugby embarked upon a frenzy of spending. A memo from the time of that EGM reveals the level of expenditure Saracens had hoped to get away with, a pair of big signings (in their case, Michael Lynagh and Philippe Sella) on a couple of hundred grand and the rest of the squad on retainers and/or match fees that would come in at something less than another hundred. It proved hopelessly naive. Saracens ended up leaping into the fray with as much gusto and wallet as the next club. They had to. Within a couple of years, that 51 per cent veto had been revoked as the stakes grew ever higher and the worst fears of the wary were realised. Saracens' first team moved, first to Enfield, then to Watford, then to Barnet, as they tried to make the sums add up, or just not yawn destructively. The squad stayed initially at the old pavilion on Bramley Road in Southgate during the week, the facilities revamped as far as they would go to satisfy the training requirements, until even Bramley Road was left behind.

Rugby still does not know what to make of Saracens. They have been despised and ridiculed for what was for years fruitless spending, none of it remotely justified by a fan base that, although in no time roughly 10 times that of the Bramley Road years, numbered itself still in only four figures a couple of decades later. And yet the benefits of the venture, not just to English rugby but the communities of north London, cannot be denied.

Even before professionalism, Saracens were renowned as a nursery for talent. In the old days, that talent would invariably move on – Jason Leonard, Dean Ryan, Ben Clarke – but before 1995 was out Saracens were empowered to offer contracts to their latest young stars, Tony Diprose and Richard Hill, and to focus on producing more. For all the ill-feeling since over their perceived extravagance, that production line has never let up, so that big-name signings these days merely fit in and around the talent already there, the retention of which has become Saracens' biggest financial headache.

From the whistle for professionalism, they were market leaders in developing links with the community. One of their most important signings was the late Peter Deakin, schooled in the American art of sports marketing, who worked a transformation in the crowds of Bradford Bulls before doing the same with Saracens. Perhaps influenced by the American notion of a league of competitors working together, he invited all the clubs of the Premiership to seminars revealing how he and his team had in one season worked an increase in Saracens' average gate from 3,000 to 9,500, including the surreal scene at the time of 20,000 for one home match. And so the rest of the Premiership went out to preach the same gospel.

There was cynicism, of course, that Saracens' raison d'être was less missionary work in the community, more the drumming up of enthusiasm for their activities on the pitch, but this is where professional sport and its economic imperative can be a genuine force for good. Revenue maximisation and social provision need not be alternatives – indeed, they can be mutually reinforcing. Saracens have always set great store in it, even when their project appeared to stutter in the first decade of the 21st century, until in 2018 they became the first sporting enterprise to open a mainstream secondary school, in one of the most deprived areas of Barnet.

That came towards the end of a decade when the club started to succeed, too, in those activities on the pitch. Their domination of English rugby in that time has been predicated upon a policy of personal development for the players that, like their community work in the 1990s, was ahead of its time. The idea that more rounded people make for more rounded players marked a step change from the early years of professionalism, when the focus on all things rugby was ferocious. Saracens were the first to invest in the preparation of their players for the world beyond.

All of which cannot be accounted anything other than pioneering, transformational and, in direct opposition to the stereotype of the professional enterprise, actively noble.

But it does cost an awful lot of money. This is where the resentment comes in. The first to feel such was a majority of those crammed into the old pavilion. At the 1997 AGM, by which time Saracens had already moved to Enfield, before moving again to Vicarage Road in Watford, which they were to fill with that 20,000 within a year, a lady stood up and told Wray that in one year he had singlehandedly ruined a club that had been around since 1876. She and her husband had been devoted to Saracens, their local community centre, for decades. Now it was gone.

The feelings of such people are always the first casualty when progress sets to work. The next casualty, in this case certainly, is the anticipated economics. In the same memo from November 1995 that proposed the rather modest player budget, a projected curve of Saracens' near future was also set out. The aim was to achieve an average gate of 10,000 by year five (in the end they would achieve 9,200, having managed 9,300 by year two) and turnover of £2 million (actually £4.6 million), by which time profit might be £1.5 million (nowhere near). That level of economics was to be blown sky high by the expenditure free-for-all of the ensuing years. In year five (2001), Saracens made a £1.6 million loss, actually their best performance up to that point, for accumulated losses of £10.9 million. By 2018, the 22nd year, their accumulated losses were £70 million (40 per cent of their accumulated turnover of £173 million). No matter what they had achieved – the good works, the players, the culture, all of it to impeccable standards, yielding by then trophy after trophy – the venture was, is, hopelessly unsustainable. Without Wray and a handful of other investors he convinced to join him, it would not exist. Which begs the question, how much of a rugby club is the new Saracens, and how much the gift of one man to the world?

Football is well acquainted with this quandary. The relationship between fan and club is a curious one at the best of times, the former deriving not just pleasure but a sense of personal worth from the success of the latter, as if to support a team that is winning somehow means the fan is winning too, their stock having risen with the club's, each reflecting well upon the other. But what happens if their club achieves success because it is bought for them? Any sense of the organic growth of fan with club is surely erased. Some Chelsea fans felt Roman Abramovich took their club away when he wrote them a cheque for the first time in 2003. Others could not believe their luck as the stars and trophies rolled in. Regardless, it was not Chelsea FC, historic club of middling success and stature, who achieved what followed, so much as one man and his money. Any fan who thought hard enough about it might well feel it was no longer their club.

So, a certain amount of resentment there. But then there is the resentment of everyone else. The landscape is changed when a club achieves success it has not generated itself. The rest are forced into unnatural positions, too, if they want to keep up. Some call it financial doping, others investment in the game. For all the debts Chelsea and those in their wake started to rack up, the value of the collective product, the Premier League, was growing all the while so quickly that the investment does not seem so gratuitous any more. Rugby in England is hoping for similar.*

---

* The purchase in December 2018 of a 27 per cent stake in Premier Rugby by CVC, the private equity firm that transformed the value of Formula One, has been hailed by some as a first step along this path. The £230 million sum they paid is a welcome cash injection for the clubs, some of whom were looking in serious trouble, but the implied valuation of £852 million relates to central revenue and ignores the cumulative debt of the 13 clubs of Premier Rugby. That central revenue will now fall for each of them by 27 per cent. The deal will pay off in the long term if CVC can work the sort of upturn in media rights they effected for Formula One.

In the meantime, England's best-supported rugby club, Leicester, have sustained themselves for the most part. Theirs was the first decade and a half of the 21st century, in which they won eight English titles and two European. In those first 22 years of professionalism they accumulated losses of just £3 million (1 per cent of a turnover of more than £300 million). From 2000 to 2015, they were in the black for all but three years, accumulating profit of £1.6 million. But they have not won the Premiership since 2013, and they racked up £2.5 million of that £3 million deficit in the last three years of the period, from 2016 to 2018. In 2019, Leicester were put up for sale. How they resent being forced into the red just to stay within touching distance of a club, however well run, who have not earned the financial resources available to them. As for other clubs, less well run, who spend just as far beyond their means without any success to speak of, the resentment towards them is leavened with contempt.

This is how it must be in an unregulated system, ill-feeling running as high as costs, clubs forcing each other into precarious positions, the patience, not to mention finances, of investors stretched to the limit – and often beyond. The early years of professionalism in England saw several clubs of great history and prestige collapse, West Hartlepool and Orrell of the north, Richmond and London Scottish of the south just some of the more noted examples. In the year 2000, Richmond and London Scottish had to re-join the English league system at the bottom. They are now back among other famous names, just off the highest level. In Richmond's case, there is no appetite to re-enter the fray of professionalism. They know what promotion to the Premiership can do to a club not equipped for it, as the subsequent demise in 2017 of neighbouring London Welsh reminded them. The game of chicken is continually escalating as the clubs outspend each other. And so the gap between the top flight and everyone else is expanding, until crossing it becomes a treacherous undertaking – not only for those going up.

There is one classic equalisation measure the Premiership clubs have always wanted to take from the regulated model. Wray, for example, has invested tens of millions of pounds into Saracens and, by extension, English rugby. He feels, not unreasonably, he has earned the right to guarantee his club a place at the top table. Like most of the investors in English club rugby, Wray wants the Premiership to become a closed league.

Some arguments are so finely balanced, they never go away. The debate surrounding promotion and relegation to the Premiership is as old as professionalism.

From the moment he invested his first couple of million in Saracens, Wray has argued strenuously that the sensible construction of a business is impossible with the perpetual threat of removal from the marketplace should the lottery of results on the field fall against you. As it happens, he knows the feeling of relegation, if not the reality. No sooner had he signed his first cheque than the Saracens team that was about to be transcended started to lose on the muddy park at Bramley Road. On the last day of the 1995–6 season, Saracens lost at Gloucester, which meant relegation.

Off the field the diplomatic machinations kicked in. A one-year moratorium had been set when rugby went open, so that teams could prepare. It was unacceptable, the argument ran, to expect a club to put new structures in place for the professional era, and an investor new money, only to take away their seat at the top table when the old amateur set-up failed on the field. Besides, Michael Lynagh and Philippe Sella were on their way. Could the Premiership really afford to pass up on such attractions in its first season as a money-making enterprise? Already, the concept of a professional top flight was beginning to separate itself from that of the rest of English rugby.

That year, the argument against relegation won. Saracens and bottom club, West Hartlepool, stayed up for the first season of professionalism, joined by Northampton and London Irish from the league below. Bar one flirtation in 2002–3, Saracens have never come close to relegation since, but other clubs have handled the trauma with greater or lesser success. Some have bounced back to become champions (Harlequins and Northampton); others have lost despairing chairmen (Worcester, Bristol); others again have fallen away into the quiet life (Bedford, Leeds, Rotherham).

And then there was London Welsh. One of the great names in rugby, they might have sat handsomely among the others of the Premiership, certainly if history were anything to go by. Nevertheless, they play their rugby on the outfield of a cricket pitch in Kew. They are a throwback to another time, when the following of club rugby, no matter how legendary that club, was flattered even by the description of 'cult'. In 2012, somehow, they played their way to the brink of the Premiership. There was a complicated play-off system at that time in the Championship, the league below. London Welsh proved themselves the fourth best team in the league over the normal season, then, consistent with that assessment, came second in their play-off pool. Which was when, from somewhere, they summoned the form of their lives, to negotiate two two-legged play-off rounds and win hypothetical promotion.

But they did well to attract a thousand people to a typical home match on the edge of that cricket pitch, and the grandees of the Premiership, now used to gates well into five figures, were desperate to stop them coming up. What is more, for all Welsh's heroics in the play-offs, they were not the best team in the league. The Championship clubs had dreamed up the complicated play-off system to determine their winners – and, like any play-off system, it was primarily designed to maximise revenue. The Premiership could just about handle the idea of the best team coming up from the Championship, but the fourth best . . .

There are minimum-standards criteria for clubs who want promotion, mainly relating to their stadium, which had denied Rotherham a few years earlier. Welsh's home was as far from qualifying as it is possible to imagine, so they needed to find a new one – and quick. They alighted on the Kassam Stadium in Oxford, in much the same way as a blindfolded child pins the tail on the donkey. They missed the deadline for submitting their proposal in the event of promotion, a failing that was dismissed in the subsequent appeal as a technicality. It should have been rated rather more than that. In short, London Welsh were nowhere near prepared for a season in the Premiership.

Their cause became an ideological crusade for romantics everywhere. This is the magic of sport, the underpowered defying all logic to make it to the promised land. How cynical to try to stop them.

The contention here remains the crux of the argument over promotion and relegation, which boils down to a face-off between amateurism and professionalism, between romance and business. It is the same debate that was waged before rugby went open. The case for the professional way won that time – and quite comprehensively – but for a newly professional sport to make the most of its circumstances there can be no half measures. The unwieldy mass of rugby's history means the break from amateurism has never been clean. Every time a debate goes against the prevailing culture, the picture is complicated, the outcomes messier.

Welsh made a decent fist of their first season up, guided expertly by the wily Lyn Jones, but off the field there was chaos as an understaffed admin team tried to keep up. Errors of judgement were made, documents falsified, careers ruined, points deducted. After relegation and the accompanying 'parachute' payment, they were promoted again, and this time, in the 2014–15 season, the results on the field were hideous too. Twenty-two matches, 22 defeats by an *average* scoreline of 46–10. If rugby is disadvantaged by the rarity of its upsets, neither is it helped by the ugliness of its massacres. Their average gate in Oxford was 3,300. The team broke up and, then, in 2017, so did the club, unable to pay their debts. The professional arm was liquidated, and the amateur club returned, à la Richmond and London Scottish, to the bottom of the English league system to start again.

The minimum-standards criteria receive a lot of bad press – and Welsh's legal team, led by their chairman, Bleddyn Phillips, who happened to be one of Britain's foremost lawyers, managed to convince the appeal panel that the decision to deny them promotion in 2012 should be overturned. But rugby in England is so far from being an established concern it can barely afford to carry any passengers. The London Welsh affair was a disaster – not just for London Welsh. The last thing a fledgling industry like the Premiership needed was to lose its only base in the far north-east (Newcastle, who would be relegated) and be forced to replace it with a third team from London trying to spread the gospel into a saturated Thames Valley, where London Irish (Reading) and Wasps (High Wycombe) were already fighting for each other's fans. Everyone knew that, but it still cost millions of pounds, scores of jobs, three wasted years and the humiliation and decline of one of the game's most famous clubs to have it confirmed. Romantic it most certainly was not.

More prejudicial against ambitious teams in the Championship than the minimum-standards criteria is the system of shareholdings the Premiership clubs set up in 2005, whereby they earn the right to more of a share of broadcasting revenues according to how long they have served in the top flight. London Welsh received £1.5 million from central revenues in each of their two seasons in the Premiership, compared to the sums of between £3 million and £4 million for everyone else. Each time they came up, the team who went down also received more. This arrangement has attracted the interest of Members of Parliament. Motions have been tabled in the House of Commons accusing the Premiership clubs of operating a cartel.

The clubs have denied the accusation, citing the access through promotion that remains available to their league, unlike so many others in rugby and sports around the world. But, in effect, operating a cartel is what they are doing. How can it be otherwise when an association of clubs invests millions to further a professional enterprise, while those who might theoretically join them at some point do not? The leap from one modus operandi to the next becomes ever greater. There are 13 holders of the all-important P-shares, distributed thus because at the time (2005) Harlequins, an established Premiership club, were outside the top flight. It is an ungainly number and, of course, one more than the 12 that have constituted the Premiership for most of the professional era. When a promoted club have spent two consecutive years in the Premiership they earn the right to buy the P share from one of the two clubs necessarily outside it at that point. Exeter are the only team to have done this, buying Leeds's share in 2012. In theory, anyone else could do the same, but Exeter are the exception who prove the truth that this is a next-to-impossible circle to break into. To all intents and purposes, it is a cartel. No one has deliberately set it up this way, but it is the result of the peculiar circumstances these clubs found themselves in, hurled into a professional era from very humble beginnings. They, or their chairmen, invested millions of pounds, which built the value of the Premiership, all the while conveying it further and further away from the pyramid of leagues below. Those who had invested the money wanted some kind of security on it, hence the shareholding arrangement.

When one of the boys, Harlequins, were relegated, the realisation dawned that a) none of them were safe and b) Quins' immediate return was ardently to be wished for. The Premiership could not afford to be without one of its biggest clubs for long. When Quins did return and, what is more, win the title within six years – just as Northampton would a couple of years later on exactly the same cycle – the fear of relegation actually subsided, but each time an established club goes down people lose their jobs, millions are squandered and time is wasted. In 2019, Leicester (average gate 20,000) nearly went down; Ealing (1,000) were not a million miles away from replacing them. Newcastle did go down, the only representatives in the north-east of England lost to the Premiership again, just after the city had staged that season's European finals to uplifting effect.

So much for the business argument. Sport, even when it has turned professional, is meant to be about more than that. Without 'the dream', what is the point? This is why so many were against rugby's turning professional in the first place, even if the notion it could be avoided was unrealistic. Romantic, you might say. Leicester City are usually cited when questions of romance come up, but the idea they won the Premier League in 2016 as a band of happy-go-lucky upstarts, rather than a multimillion-pound business in an established multibillion-pound industry, is no more than a part of that industry's folklore – or hype, as folklore becomes when billion-pound industries get hold of it.

English rugby's equivalent 'industry' is those 13 clubs. An awkward parody of musical chairs has developed, whereby one of the 13 take a season out, doing nothing more than tread water while they wait to see which of the others are next to have a turn wasting time and money on the sidelines. From the onset of the shareholding arrangement in 2005 until 2018, the relegated team have returned to the Premiership at the first attempt 10 times out of 13. The only interlopers into the ritual have been London Welsh, who were ruined by it, and Exeter.

The latter's success has become the leading exhibit of the case for promotion and relegation. Exeter are a superbly well-run club, who, in contrast to London Welsh, spent years and millions mustering a credible package. Of all those who disapproved of the London Welsh episode, none were more critical than Exeter, who knew what it took – and how long – to do things properly. If there were other Exeters out there, we would be able to see them coming. There are none. But not even Exeter's success would have been possible without the

£12 million windfall they received from the sale of their previous ground to developers in 2005, empowering them to build Sandy Park, their stadium and conference facility on the M5. Nor could they have thrived so well without their situation in England's only region, the far south-west, where rugby dominates. If the Premiership were able to make strategic decisions as a collective and had wanted to take on an addition to their number, they could not have chosen a site with much more potential than Exeter.

We return to the idea of a regulated system. A closed league is one of its classic features. This does not mean the end of expansion, or the exclusion of those who dream big, but it does mean taking control of when and where such developments take place. The models in America and Australia are illustrative. In the 1950s, the NFL was a competition of 12 teams, 10 of them packed into the north-east corner of the USA. In the 1960s they vied with the newly formed American Football League, squandering resources as they tried to outbid each other, until the leagues merged in 1970 and grew at their own pace to form the 32 teams of today, spread round the country. Major League Soccer has grown from 10 teams on its inception in 1996 to 23 today, with further expansion planned. In Australian rules football, the 11 clubs of the Victorian Football League in the 1980s have grown into the 18 of the Australian Football League today. In each case, the governing body of the competition, independent from its individual clubs or franchises, adopts a long-term view, assessing when and where new teams might be viable, then diverting funds towards those areas to help the establishment of the new team, the timescale for each of which is mapped out 10 or 20 years into the future. Thus new teams in the league are actively helped by the others, as opposed to discriminated against and resented.

Such expansion is not only possible within a regulated system, it is impossible without. Under the current system, the barriers against entry to the Premiership are enormous, regardless of the shareholding arrangement, which is, in essence, a half-baked attempt, conceived on the go, to achieve the growth and security that a properly regulated system would achieve anyway – and on legally surer ground. The struggles of a club such as Bristol to break into the Premiership tell their own story. Bristol have everything going for them, a P share, a metropolitan population of a million and as strong a culture for rugby as any city in the world, not to mention the support of by far the richest chairman in English rugby, whose fortune runs into the billions. Their turbulent first couple of decades of the century trying to make it work ought to put into perspective the ambitions of anyone else on the outside considering the leap from amateur to professional.

The argument over a closed or open league has been delicately balanced indeed, but the further we venture into the professional era the more the case for continuing with the open system weakens. Not that an end to promotion and relegation would fix everything. Like the salary cap, it is but one equalisation measure and on its own of only so much effectiveness. As a condition for stability, it is 'necessary but not sufficient', as a logician might put it, just one dimension of a strategy whose measures reinforce each other.

But it is not only the elite who would benefit. Perhaps the most cogent argument for an end to the yo-yo-ing madness of 13 clubs striving for 12 places is how little the elite has in common, or should have in common, with the sprawling mass of English rugby's pyramid below, with the community game. The professional game in any sport, but especially a physically contentious one such as rugby, should be sealed off from the amateur. This is standard practice in every other sport in the world. Bar one.

Football's model, as ever, is the dangerous paragon, beguiling its sibling into thinking it can be the same, when football, by its sheer scale and its profound insinuation into cultures around the world, is unique in the sporting universe. Rugby's portfolio is far more limited. France can just about sustain two divisions of professional rugby;

England can manage one; the rest of the Tier 1 nations have long since known they must buddy up with other countries to sustain their professional domestic game.*

From the community game's point of view, a seamless structure from top to bottom is poisonous. Because the professional ethos does not end where the money ends, and the money does not end where the elite game does. Professionalism seeps throughout a seamless structure and transforms the nature of the sport, permeating every level, even the most 'grassroots', with the insidious ethic of striving to be the best one can be, when the best one can be is never going to be that good, so why not just relax and take yourself a little less seriously? If the health of a sport is measured by the vitality of its community game – and when a sport turns professional one could argue that it is not – the first few decades of the open era have had a debilitating effect on rugby.

---

* New Zealand and South Africa do sustain historic and very modestly remunerated professional leagues below and separate from Super Rugby, but they are also separate from the amateur game below them.

X

From Beer to Protein Shake:
A Withering in the Community

It might not be fair to blame all of this on the professional ethic. Professionalism gets hold of everything in the end, it is true, but the causality is harder to draw out. Is professionalism an independent force that humanity has unleashed upon itself, dragging us along whether we like it or not, Frankenstein's monster out of control? Or is human progress, that instinct to reach for the stars, the unanswerable dynamic here, which professionalism merely accompanies? Either way, the journey is the same, driven by the pursuit of excellence – at the expense, in the end, of recreation. This is a human dilemma. Our right to reach for the stars is non-negotiable, but so too is the right to relax and enjoy ourselves from time to time, leaving interstellar travel to other people, those who want it. If only it were so simple. In time, the one impulse tends to squeeze out room for the other.

Professionalism has been unleashed on rugby, but rugby was beginning to turn anyway – indeed, had so quite decisively in some parts of the world. This is not a question of money, necessarily, more of culture, an attitude.

The professional way is a particularly alienating energy for a collision sport. When professionalism takes hold of one of those, the aping of the elite game renders the levels below not just undesirable for the typical recreational player of the amateur era but dangerous. This tendency towards a more unforgiving environment may not be a result of the seamless game alone, but the notion that the elite level is theoretically accessible to all, no more than the end point of any ambition to move through the system, is likely to frame the mindsets of at least a few of those competing. And a few is all that is needed. The Premiership may not seem a realistic goal to a team in level eight, but it might to a team in level two, the methods directly relevant, which will have knock-on implications for those in level three, and so on down.

Some, normally those who hark after an amateur age when tackling was less confrontational, object to the categorisation of rugby as a collision sport, but, if collision sport is a legitimate category, rugby clearly qualifies. One might even go so far as to say that The Sibling's other great edge, besides the early adoption of, well, professionalism and a league system, is its nature as merely a contact sport. This leaves it lighter, more supple, better equipped to keep the lifeblood of participation flowing, even when standards are raised as humanity continues to improve itself.

A key difference between football and rugby is that, in the former, a player running with the ball can be stopped without being touched. In rugby the only way to stop that player is by what is, essentially, physical assault, even if it need not be particularly violent. This is because the player who runs with the ball in rugby has it in the hands, not loose at the feet. And because of that, the nature of the tackle in rugby poses all sorts of questions about what should happen next. From the fact the ball is 'attached' to the player in possession are derived most of rugby's arcane rituals, its rucks and mauls and thence its scrums and lineouts. Perhaps whoever first ran with the ball in his hands really did strike upon the key feature of rugby, paving the way for all the others. Thus rugby became the more complicated game (although others, like league and sevens, have shown it could be a whole lot simpler too).

But it also became much the more violent. This is its appeal to many, and it is not superficial. The transition of the higher number than ever of young children who play rugby now from the tag version to the full-contact is fascinating to behold. Long before health and safety will allow it, kids will entreat, practically beg, their coaches: 'Can we do some tackling now? Pleeeeeaaase!' Sometimes the barely continent plaintiffs are the smallest. There is some sort of instinct for colliding with others rooted in, if not all of us, enough to make rugby a deeply attractive proposition to a lot of people. And for those who fancy it less there is the equally addictive prospect of evading the same. No wonder the game appeals. Before dismissing rugby as 'not as popular' as football, it is worth noting that, if we aggregate all the countries that have come to be dominated by the oval branch of the family, the sport gains the not inconsiderable markets of America and Australia.

That very lust for contact, though, metamorphoses into something increasingly apocalyptic as we reach ever further for the stars in a collision sport. There comes a point when participants enter a pact that requires greater commitment just to remain involved, to survive. Inevitably, as real life catches up with those eager youngsters, not least the requirement to meet it without physical injury, the invitation to collide with others is passed up.

There are a lot of developments feeding into the fall in rugby's playing numbers, which is more or less established as fact around the world, despite the bold figures World Rugby massages into existence, alongside hopeful hashtags and exclamation marks. More or less established, as opposed to actually established, only because there are no reliable figures from the amateur era and the tales of desolate fields where once thousands ran free are anecdotal and can never be properly tested. No doubt they are exaggerated as much as the official line is, but the refrain seems consistent that the number of adults playing rugby for love has plummeted since professionalism.

It is impossible to take the pulse of the community game around the world, or to reach conclusions about the community game anywhere that are not generalisations. For reasons of geographic convenience and personal knowledge, we shall focus on the community game in England and hope that the issues it faces are broadly those faced everywhere. *Unholy Union* has conducted a survey among more than 350 of England's clubs, taken evenly across the country and throughout the levels of its pyramid of leagues.

When asked how many men's teams they fielded in the mid-1990s who would hope to play on a weekly basis, 48 per cent of our clubs said four or more; when asked how many now, the figure was 15 per cent. Conversely, 16 per cent said they fielded only one or two back then, compared to the 50 per cent who do now. Judging by the content of more than 200 supplementary comments from the survey, it appears many clubs count a team as playing weekly if it is regularly available to play, but the cancellation of fixtures for second and third teams is a continual refrain. So the reality is likely worse than these figures suggest.

No one, not even the RFU, tries to deny that playing numbers in the men's game in England have declined significantly since rugby turned professional. There are any number of reasons put forward for this. Indeed, in the 1990s themselves, the lament often went up for a halcyon time when the fields were full of matches of all standards and the bars rang out late into the night. Nostalgia is a constant condition for the human who can remember far enough back – and not always to be trusted. Allowing for that, 54 per cent of our clubs claimed that in the mid-1990s the last drinks at their clubhouse would be served at some time after 10 p.m.; only 30 per cent could say the same now. In the mid-1990s, 11 per cent were shut by 8 p.m., compared to 38 per cent now.

Society is constantly changing. This was so in the 1990s as much as it is now, but the pace is accelerating. Social media has transformed the way people socialise, or at least organise their social lives (20 per cent cited social change as the biggest impact on their club in the past 30 years). The walls of the clubhouse are no longer as far as the post-match drinker can see, nor the team-mates within them the only friends. People make plans and leave early. An increasing number do not drink at all. The beer is more expensive than it used to be. Bars close early and make less money. Or, to mitigate the pressures on finance, they are rented out for functions to keep revenue coming in and close early because of that. Either way, the status of the club as a social centre is affected.

The rise of individual sports – indeed, individualism, full stop – is another drain on the men's game. For most of the 20th century, if a man played sport he slung a kit bag over his shoulder and pitched up at a clubhouse, where he might expect to spend the rest of the day, at some point during which he would run around a field for an hour and a half or so. Now sport is likelier to mean a personal journey, waged between a pair of headphones, in the gym, on the bike, on the road, in the pool, perhaps all four. There are government guidelines these days regarding the amount of sport each of us should find time for, usually measured out in minutes across a week. Eighty minutes on a Saturday is not ruled out, but thoughts among the health-conscious tend to turn instead to a regular diet of individual pursuits to be fitted in and around busy lives. Some may even consider a pounding on the rugby field actively unhealthy.

Notions of health become increasingly scientific and rigorous the further we trespass into the future. We might call it the professionalisation of living – everything more efficient, more urgent. The reaction tends to polarise, all or nothing, gym or sofa. Likely candidates for men's rugby, i.e. between the ages of 18 and 35, face further pressures, which women might be said to have felt keenly for longer, perhaps best articulated by the journalist Mark Simpson, with his formulation in the 1990s of the concept of the metrosexual. This, loosely, refers to the idea of a more self-conscious masculine ideal, which means spending the time (and money) to make the most of one's appearance, with the right treatments and accessories. Recently, in the 2010s, Simpson has declared the metrosexual dead, transcended by the spornosexual, whereby the ideal has morphed into looking like a sport or porn star. The must-have accessory for the 21st-century male has become the body itself, the more athletic and musclebound the better. This has been interpreted as a fusion between the metrosexual attention to appearance and the more traditional ideal of the man as conqueror and protector. In short, it means the gym, and lots of it. In extreme cases, it can mean steroids. Rugby is by no means incompatible with any of the above, but these developments alter the cultural background. Those who still want to play are delivered to the game by society as different physical propositions from the average club rugby player of the 20th century, before we have even considered the effects of the professionalisation of community rugby, the tightening of slack not just in the muscles of the competing physiques but in the training regimes, in the attitudes.

In our survey, 18 per cent of the clubs placed little or no emphasis on training in the mid-1990s, compared to 5 per cent now. A modest 27 per cent considered training to be very important or vital (i.e. compulsory) in the mid-1990s; now 46 per cent of the clubs do, and this in a survey taken across every level of England's community game. Clubs up and down the league system take their rugby more seriously than ever.

How can that be criticised? How can it even be avoided? It fits into wider patterns of society, which in turn dovetail with that human lust to 'improve' oneself, all admirable traits. Results tend to take over. The only way to prove improvement is by pointing to those dimensions that can be measured, the quantifiable ones. They tend to drag all other dimensions along with them, regardless of the effects they may have on the qualitative aspects it is harder to measure. Schools are susceptible to this process, as are so many industries – retail, catering, entertainment, media, publishing, and so on. What is left behind is a harsher, less forgiving landscape.

Sports clubs are susceptible, too. If rugby's participation levels in the men's game have fallen since the 20th century, it is no more than symptomatic of those changes in society. Team sports are not in fashion across the board. According to Sport England's Active People Survey, the number of rugby players over the age of 16 who play once a week (any form of the game, including touch) has fluctuated since the records began in 2006. A major campaign by the RFU, 'Go Play Rugby', which included a trailer before every showing of *The Bourne Ultimatum* on the first two weekends of its screening in England in the summer of 2007, helped effect a rise from 185,600 in 2006 to 230,300 in 2008. Then followed a relentless fall to 159,800 in 2013. In the middle of that decline, Sport England cut its funding for the RFU by £1 million for failing to hit participation targets. Cue more relentless campaigning by the RFU – and a home World Cup in 2015 – such that the numbers climbed again to 199,000 in 2016. On it goes, campaign after campaign, each with a different name ('The Game of Our Lives' was 2017's offering, 'We Play Rugby' 2019's) but all with the same urgent aim, to increase participation – or just to keep it from falling. The Premiership conducts a suite of programmes too.

The work is never-ending, and much of the success has been achieved through the women's game and other initiatives, such as touch rugby. That 7 per cent rise in numbers over 10 years (from 2006 to 2016, notwithstanding the rise and fall *c.* 2011) actually puts rugby in England in a better place than most other team sports. All of England's major team sports were down over the same period (cricket's fell by 19 per cent, rugby league's by 39 per cent), with the notable exception of netball, whose numbers surged by 61 per cent. Women's participation in all sports is soaring across the world, and rugby is enjoying the benefits of that movement as much as any. From 2006 to 2018, the number of registered women and girls playing rugby in England rose from 7,000 to 34,000. If they all played regularly (which, it should be said, they probably did not), that would more than account for the 13,400 rise in playing numbers detailed in Sport England's survey. But keeping participation numbers up these days is a constant struggle, requiring higher levels than ever of funding and energy from the RFU.

These longer-term figures are suffering from the short-term numbers that determine a club's culture – the PBs in the gym and on the track, the results on the field. All levels are infiltrated. This cultural shift cannot be measured so easily, but the anecdotes of a new attitude and new physical realities in community rugby have come thick and fast in the professional era. Injuries are up, with 66 per cent of our respondents agreeing that they are more frequent now than in the mid-1990s and 28 per cent considering them a problem, including 3 per cent who rate them as a threat to their club's viability. In the multiple surveys the RFU have conducted in the professional era, two of the three reasons that recur consistently for people who give up the game are injuries and the fear of them.

As for any attitude, anecdotes are all we have. One personal example, illustrative of a more austere culture, dates back to 1999 and a second XV match between two clubs in London Division Two South (level six of the English system). The visiting team had just the 15 players, three of whom went off injured in the first half. The hosts, a town club, started to cut loose against the remaining 12. They would not offer the visitors any of their substitutes, who watched from the touchline in matching tracksuits. When the referee suggested, after the 50th point had been registered in the second half, they call it a day, the hosts refused, pointing out that they had been denied the previous season's second XV title on points difference and so wanted to rack up as many tries as possible.

The visitors that day, who delivered the customary three cheers with some irony at the end of an 80–20 drubbing, were from a club called the Old Blues, derived from Christ's Hospital School. None of them knew there was even such a thing as a second XV title, let alone believed anyone should be bothered about winning it, but times were changing.

These old-boys clubs are classic representations of rugby's crisis of identity. Some are ancient of provenance (the Old Blues date back to 1873), but the mere presence of the word 'Old' in their titles reeks of rugby's association with the public school, even if many were formed from state schools, even if all went 'open' long ago, accepting any player they can rope in, regardless of where they went to school. They also represent a certain ideal, that of the Corinthian amateur, which is just as ambiguous, admirable in its accent on playing over competing, recreation over ambition, but vulnerable to accusations of dilettantism, even arrogance. Town sides love nothing more than to rip into them.

The Old Blues used to be among the leading clubs in the country. Their fixture list between the wars included Bath, Harlequins, Gloucester and Leicester. They fielded as many as 10 teams. But open clubs are able to mobilise a far larger parish than old-boys clubs. As they get their act together – begin to professionalise, you might say – they tend to pull away. The drift from old boys to town represents that from amateur to professional. The Old Blues went open, i.e. started to welcome players who had not gone to Christ's Hospital, in 1968, but even by 1999 they resolutely refused to train during the week, which made them very attractive to a certain sort of recreational player. In 2002, though, under strain on the field against better organised teams, they admitted defeat. Midweek training was initiated at last, a player-coach employed. At the same time, a generation of classy players, good enough to mix it in level six of the English system with clubs who trained twice a week, happened to retire in one fell swoop. Midway through the second of two subsequent horror seasons, in 2004, the Old Blues were forced to pull out of the London leagues and drop down two levels. Times are happier now. All they have ever wanted is to play rugby and drink beer, which these days they achieve through two teams, the firsts in Surrey Two, which is level 10.

Such tales dismay some people, telling of the decline of a cavalier spirit, where the game, and all the trappings round it, the playing and the revelry, is everything. Not the graft and not the result. Others are irritated by the lack of diligence and welcome the greater structure and work ethic of the 'professional' way. It does not matter which camp a player – or a club, or a sport – falls into, the latter mindset will out, because it is more ruthless and ambitious, because it is defined by results, which end up judging us all. This process is constant. The landscape has been changing for decades, as evidenced by the experience of a club like the Old Blues, but the onset of the professional era has not only legitimised the trends in rugby, it has accelerated them ferociously.

Even without the prevailing energies in society, as well as community rugby, the calibre of player, or at least of athlete, produced by the sport is unrecognisable from that of the amateur era. In the first decade of the century, the academies of the Premiership started to take in hundreds of players each. Harlequins, for example, would welcome 250 kids each year, sourced from south London, Surrey and Sussex, to fill their U14 intake. That might not mean much more than a T-shirt and a few training sessions, but if the kids had reached that level a majority would likely continue to play into adulthood. At U18, four or five of them would be offered terms with the club. The other 245 would, at various stages, be released back into the wild, so to speak. If 13 other academies (the 13 Premiership shareholders and Yorkshire Carnegie, formerly Leeds, have RFU academy licences) were doing similar, that is around 3,500 kids in academy programmes per year. Times that by 10, say, for a 10-year playing career, and you have 35,000 adults this decade who have a recognised and nurtured aptitude for the game. It means they can play. It means they have all been in the gym since the age of 14. Even allowing for drop-outs (and our survey suggests there are a lot of those), that is more than enough to populate the first few levels of the English pyramid – of which there are only 12, or 10 in the North and Midlands divisions. You wouldn't want to be rocking up to the clubhouse with last week's muddy kit slung over your shoulder and a week's worth of after-work drinks in your belly to take on that lot.

Which leaves you with a choice – join them in their training programmes or drop down the system. Or out of it altogether.

Professionalism and league systems are intimately associated with each other, hence the RFU's aversion to them for so many decades. When they were first introduced into the English game in 1987, it was as clear an indication as the introduction of the World Cup in the same year that profound changes were afoot. When asked what has had the biggest impact on their club in the past 30 years, the most common answer in our survey was not professionalism (18 per cent) but the introduction of the league system (36 per cent).

The leagues represent another paradox. Hardwired into them is the notion of competition, which aligns all teams on the vector of results and self-assessment. They are popular. Not one of our respondents rated the leagues as anything less than important to them, a crucial source of motivation. But they are unforgiving, too. The last thing you want to be is caught in a league you are not equipped for, particularly in a sport like rugby where heavy defeats come with a twist of visceral humiliation. Motivation levels spiral. Suddenly, that two-hour trip to Thanet feels like one to miss.

The league system has been a constant source of stress for the RFU (maybe its predecessors were right to avoid them for so long). And the administrative costs of playing in a league are a constant source of stress for clubs – the travel expenses, the ever-escalating health-and-safety requirements (further exacerbated by the ever-increasing athleticism of the participants), physiotherapy costs, the larger squads required, the need to source quality coaches just to survive, the upkeep of facilities. All of it means rising expenditure, which is not offset by membership subs and certainly not by increased takings in the clubhouse.

So the RFU has tried to address these concerns. From 2012 to 2014 it conducted a competitions review and found that, among other measures, a restructuring of the league system below level three was in order, to mitigate travel requirements and ease the pressure on player welfare. Under a seamless structure, player burnout is not just a concern at the top level. Like the professional ethic – indeed, hand in hand with it – player burnout permeates all levels of the system, but at the lower levels there are no club psychologists and/or healthy salaries to support the players. At these levels, they just stop playing. Our survey did not address that, but club after club volunteered the observation anyway that players are retiring from the community game earlier than ever, rarely playing much beyond 30.

In the report for the competitions review, the RFU illustrated the collapse in playing numbers by pulling out the examples of two clubs, Morpeth in the north and Harrow in the south. It charted the number of arranged fixtures of both clubs from the 1982–3 season to the present at 10-yearly intervals. In 1982–3, Morpeth played 187 fixtures across six 15s, their sixths playing 25 times; Harrow played 181, their sixths playing 17. Ten years later, both teams still fielded six, although Morpeths sixth XV played only once. Harrow's played 15. Ten years later again, the eighth season of the professional era, both were reduced to four teams, Morpeth playing a total of 108 fixtures, Harrow 115. In 2012–13, the respective figures were 86 across four teams and 56 across two.

Having compiled surveys and listened to focus groups from clubs and players around the country, the RFU, keen to address such a steep decline, proposed a 'flatter' pyramid in 2014, which meant introducing regionalism higher up the structure. Instead of the first four levels (the Premiership being level one, the Championship two, and so on) constituting national leagues, the system would split into regions at level four, then the regions split into four leagues each at level five, and so on. The effect would have been to increase the teams in each tier – and therefore reduce the travel and fixture load – from level four downwards.

The response was uproar among the clubs in the higher levels – tellingly from administrators rather than the players whose views had fed the review – particularly a group of them in the north, who suffer from the extra pressure of competition from rugby league. Under the proposals, each league would lose at least two clubs from its number, which would reduce fixtures and thus income from home games. In an embarrassing climbdown, the RFU was forced to shelve the findings of its investigation, said to have cost £200,000.

The rebellion against the proposed restructure had coalesced around an official from Vale of Lune RUFC in Lancashire. A couple of years later, in 2018, 20 clubs from, ironically enough, Lancashire broke away from the RFU system to form their own mini-leagues, citing the unmanageable costs of travel around the north and a desire to keep things local.

The incompatible energies keep warring. The tensions between player welfare and revenue are not restricted to the elite game. Here we had at amateur level an impasse familiar to the elite, a welfare-led proposal rebuffed because of worries about revenue. Income pressures are impossible to avoid. Victories for money over player welfare are always ugly, but the reality is too often overlooked by critics that revenue is the necessary evil keeping the whole enterprise afloat. 'Making a quick buck' is the usual complaint, but precious few rugby clubs are making any bucks at all, and that is true at all levels of the game.

In the case of those higher up the leagues a further concern was that the intensity of competition would be diluted, the risk of ugly mismatches heightened, with 336 clubs planned in levels four to six, compared with the current 200, each level augmented by clubs brought up from the one below. In other words, those serious about their rugby did not want fewer games against weaker opponents.

The fixture shortfall is an issue, but league fixtures need not account for all of a club's matches in any given season. The observation was regularly offered in our survey (usually by clubs in the lower leagues) that the demands of the league system are relentless. These clubs yearned instead for the flexibility of more friendlies, to be organised by themselves with old foes. Playing more local games helps all clubs in rugby's age-old mission of conviviality. Mismatches might well occur in the short term from a restructuring of the league, but the localisation of a fixture list increases enthusiasm in the community.

Fylde and Preston Grasshoppers, two mighty old foes of the north, found themselves in the same league in the 2018–19 season for the first time in eight years, Fylde coming down and Grasshoppers up. A thousand people attended their fixture. Dings Crusaders' promotion to National League Two South landed them in the same league as fellow Bristolians Clifton and Old Redcliffians, with similarly invigorating results. Does it matter if standards level out a bit when local rivalries are kept aflame and friendships revived? And yet it seems the popular wish is for the current steeper pyramid of competition, with ambition hardwired into its circuitry, no matter what the effect on participation.

The RFU identified two categories of player in its review, or poles on a spectrum – 'ambition' players and 'enjoyment' players. The former strove to be the best they could be, prioritising rugby over other life issues; the latter knew they would never be the best, but liked to play, accepting that sometimes life might get in the way.

The two energies are next to impossible to accommodate in the same system without strife, particularly in a collision sport. It is poignant, but absolutely inevitable, that the RFU initiated its investigation and arrived at its recommendations according to the spirit of enjoyment, only for it to be denied by the spirit of ambition. There is no mantra holier in the 21st century, and not just in rugby, than 'to be the best one can be'. At the elite level, striving to that end is a moral duty, but beyond that such dedication becomes a trickier energy. To criticise or deny it seems absurd, even an affront to a person's rights, but the implications for everyone else – and for the health of the sport, if by health we mean participation – are plain to see.

Easier to criticise, however, is the ambition of clubs themselves, the kind driven by administrators rather than players. This is where the seamless structure starts to feel toxic. Irresponsible administration is at the heart of it. Clubs aim ever higher. They recruit players and pay them. The motivations are bewildering. Do they harbour ambitions to play in the Premiership? If so, why? If not (and surely they cannot all), what are they ambitious for?

To have a group of players who have grown together strive to make the best of themselves, to move up the table and beyond, is admirable; the trouble starts when a club tries to manufacture such success, recruiting players unnaturally with financial inducements. Just like those elite clubs goading each other on to ever-higher levels of expenditure, all it takes is one or two to decide they want promotion and everyone else feels obliged to do the same, sometimes just to hold on to their own players, sometimes to bring in better. One club from level four, close enough to the Premiership to feel the heat, volunteered the following to our survey: 'We are a rugby club, as in we have a list of players who turn up, play the game and leave straight after. Over the last 30 years, the social aspect of playing rugby seems to have been lost. In the 1990s you would get five senior teams out and everyone would stay after and mingle with away teams. Now, you are lucky if an away team stay more than an hour after the final whistle.'

This echoes a familiar refrain. A club recruits and pays new players (for unfathomable reasons, presumably to do with ambition); existing players resent it, pushed out of the first team, or just not paid as much as their new team-mates; and no one stays to drink beer. The question of what the club is actually for hangs over the empty bar. The typical model here is to set up a new company to pay the first-team players. These rugby clubs are community centres, which means they cannot pay players and qualify for grants. So they separate the first team from the rest, set up an independent company through which to pay them and use the other branch, the original club, to collect handouts from such bodies as the RFU.

It has become possible in England to be a mediocre player and make a living out of rugby, a dangerous living, because your wage will be nowhere near enough to retire on and could end at any time with the next injury, but enough to get by. When in the system, a player knows who is paying what. Sometimes he might move down a level to a club who are paying well. It is a rootless existence, which can corrupt, too, the roots of the clubs these players pass through, reminiscent of a prize fighter or, that dreaded term, the mercenary. In a full-time professional environment, such nomadism is inevitable and justified by reasonable salaries; at community levels it seems nonsensical.

The RFU has had more success passing legislation to tackle this. As from the 2018–19 season, the equivalent of a salary cap for the community game has been introduced. It is not illegal to break it, but to do so is to lose rights to RFU funding. Thresholds for gross payments to players have been set for each of levels three (£275,000), four (£157,500) and five (£65,000). Modest allowances are made for player-coaches, and these extend to all levels beneath level five, where no other payments to players are permitted at all.

The measures, effectively, are a directive from the RFU that rugby should be an amateur game below level five. Why it should not be so at levels three to five as well is anyone's guess. The gap between a playing budget of £275,000 and a Premiership club's £8 million is a good deal wider than one level of a league structure might suggest, wide enough indeed to render pointless, even dangerous, any thoughts of traversing it. Allowing a policy of payment to linger below the elite like this, tailing off into the amateur game like a frayed rope, is as messy a state of irresolution as any rugby has contrived, but the community salary cap is a step in the right direction.

The conclusion is difficult to avoid that the next step is a clean break from any notion of professionalism beneath the Championship, then a reconsideration of the Championship itself, which is no less an apocalypse of clubs overreaching themselves, with all the cultural implications, than anywhere else in the pyramid, despite the fact a majority have no ambition to play in the Premiership. The argument then becomes ever more insistent to seal off the Premiership, contain the professional game, and establish relationships between Premiership and Championship clubs more formal than they already are for the sharing of squad players otherwise starved of game time.

In this way the community game might be returned to the community. Might be. At adult level, the concern is that collision sports tend naturally anyway towards a wastage in participation figures. If there were a spectrum of collision sports, with fitness at one end and extremes of body type at the other, the only one further towards the latter than rugby is American football. League, Australian rules and ice hockey have more of an aerobic component, but American football has virtually none, being all about short, ferociously intense bursts of activity between long breaks. To make such a pastime realistic for the likes of you and me would require levels of funding and administration so exacting that American football does not even try to pretend it can meet them. Their model is stark, with no community game at all – at least not for the game as practised by the professionals. If you are an adult beyond college and not a professional, you do not play. Even at college, you are a professional in all but remuneration.

Which begs the question, does any of this matter for a professional sport? Even if adults stopped playing rugby altogether outside the elite, the elite would continue – indeed it might benefit from the increase in potential spectators available on a Saturday afternoon. American football is completely transparent about its priorities. It is a spectator sport – and the biggest in the world by average attendance. As long as there is a steady flow of players supplied to the elite by the junior game and an audience to watch them, it works.

Rugby union sits more or less side by side with league on the collision spectrum. If it has not suffered the fall in participation that league has of late in England, we can put that down largely to the millions of pounds the RFU invests in the community game each year. Rugby has a profound culture as a participation sport, so much so it seems inconceivable it should ever become like American football, certainly any time soon, but that is the direction in which it is tending. In England, without the sustained campaigns of the RFU, who knows where playing numbers would be now. For as long as protein shakes are drunk more readily than beer, there will remain an austerity in community rugby that would sit more comfortably in a professional environment. But without any financial rewards to speak of.

This is a matter close to the RFU's heart. It is, like every union around the world, the custodian of the community game, typically investing a fifth of its considerable revenues each year trying to keep the English game healthy beneath the top flight, more than any other union. It is a thankless task, as evidenced by the league restructure that was thrown back in its face, just as much as by the perennial complaints of those whose clubs might have been overlooked in recent rounds of funding, casting envious glances at the new 4G pitch their local rivals have just had installed, or the smart new clubhouse. In our survey, 78 per cent of respondents considered themselves on their own within the seamless structure, with only 7 per cent seeing themselves as part of one mutually sup- portive family showcased by the elite. This situation is unlikely to improve in the short term as the RFU struggles to balance the costs of funding the elite game and the community.

When rugby turned professional, a new class of player was created at the top end who needed paying, but the need to service the game at the lower levels would be no less pressing than before. If anything, it would be more so. Here was a new tension for rugby to contend with. What to do with the new money?

XI

Fuelling the Shoots:
Kids and Drugs

The debate concerning funding strategies is as old as professional sport – how much should go to the community game, how much to performance, how much to facilities and promotions? For participation sports (such as swimming or athletics, with high numbers taking part relative to watching), the balance is less delicate and funding questions are usually answered by the state and club membership. Other sports with a significant market of spectators but low costs of performance, popular amateur sports such as the Gaelic games in Ireland or college football and basketball in America, also have relatively straightforward decisions to make. In America, coaches in college sport are highly rewarded, but otherwise funds from TV and sponsorship are invested into facilities and the community. Rugby used to be the same. With no players to pay, an extensive community game could be supported and the great cathedrals of rugby – Twickenham, Murrayfield, Lansdowne Road, Cardiff Arms Park – built without a penny of public money.

Fuelling the Shoots: Kids and Drugs

As soon as rugby turned professional, a cadre of professionals needed paying. In France and England, the responsibility for the majority of that falls to the clubs; in others, where administration is centralised, the union bears more of the brunt. Either way, there is a delicate balance to be struck between the elite and the community – and the implications of mishandling it can be damaging.

It is often argued, for example, that rugby in Australia has suffered through an overemphasis on the elite game, forced into trying to compete with European salaries while devoting further attention and resources to trying to grow the game beyond the traditional heartlands of New South Wales and Queensland. The opportunity cost is a neglect of, or at least compromised investment in, the community game. This is the top-down model favoured by John O'Neill (CEO of the Australian union for 14 of the early years of the professional era), a belief that the success of the show teams is everything, that the health of the community game will follow from that. It places an awful lot of pressure on those show teams. You can't be world champions all the time. The alternative is the bottom-up model that a group of influential figures in Australian rugby advocate, whereby a healthy community game will supply the player base for a successful elite. Which is fine, but try being the head coach of a national team at the top of an underfunded elite game; try being the union.

The debates over this are never-ending, the success or otherwise difficult to prove. In 2017 a well-publicised report by Roy Morgan, the Australian market research company, claimed that the number of those over the age of 16 in Australia who played rugby regularly had collapsed by 63 per cent since 2001 to 55,000, making it Australia's 26th most popular sport, one place below ballroom dancing. Rugby Australia immediately refuted the findings, claiming that the numbers (of those who had had more than five 'rugby involvements' in 2016) exceeded 270,000 and had actually gone up. And so the search for the truth regarding participation goes on, beyond the anecdotes of angry or crusading folk.

The RFU, meanwhile, enjoys by far the fullest revenue streams and is absolved of financing England's professional club game. It does, of course, have to foot the bill for the international game at all levels, and it pays handsomely for the right to have access to the clubs' international players, a sort of compensation package for the use of assets that do not 'belong' to it. Then again, if we trace the provenance of each player, we would be led back not to Harlequins or Sale or Northampton but to a wide range of humble community clubs and schools.

This is where it all starts. This is why the RFU, no less than anyone else, needs to balance carefully the funds it diverts to performance and the community. This is why it does not like seeing clubs benefit from the new facilities and resources its grants help establish, only for them to spend money needlessly on paying players. It messes with the balance when clubs lose sight of their primary role as community centres through which as many people as possible might fall in love with rugby. For these clubs, there should not be a balance to strike at all between 'performance' and community, because they *are* the community.

If the RFU has its way, that culture for first-XV ambition will be curbed, however hard it may be to regulate its new policy regarding payments to players. It is important to try. Because where the community game in England remains vital – and is thriving – is the resource it provides for women and children. Why anyone would want to jeopardise that by overreaching themselves in a next-to-pointless charge up the leagues is a troubling question.

When asked to rate the health of their club now against 30 years ago, our respondents were split almost exactly in thirds as better off, the same and worse. But the comments section qualified this finding by alerting us to the changing model by which many clubs operate, whereby diversifying to provide different services to the community was key to their survival. If we had asked clubs to rate the health of their men's section, the response would not have been so even. Overwhelmingly now, clubs owe their health to the minis and juniors. Time and again, respondents to our survey described the men's section of their club as supported by the children, with the rise of women's rugby breathing yet new life into the system (16 per cent of our clubs had a women's section in the mid-1990s, compared to 43 per cent now). For all the fluctuating energies in modern rugby, the more barren landscape, here is the colourful counter-revolution. English rugby may be nostalgic for the days when the fields teemed with people who just wanted to play, but that idyll is still realised on a weekly basis, albeit generally on a Sunday morning rather than Saturday afternoon. For the most reassuring sense that everything in rugby is going to be OK, it pays to stand in a wide field during a mini-rugby festival and marvel at the shifting masses of children of different ages and both sexes.

This is a new energy surging in the professional era, just as those of the adult game ebb. Undoubtedly, those same movements in wider society contribute. The professionalisation of parenting urges that one's children partake in a range of activities, for fear of future obesity or the addiction to screens. But so too does the increased investment of a governing body mobilised by the exigencies of the professional era to become better parents themselves to the sport they oversee. The average age of English rugby's playing population is falling – or rather getting younger, rejuvenating. This will have implications for the adult game, but from the coldly strategic point of view of a professional sport it is better than the reverse. Rugby might lose what is left of its soul if the community men's game were to wither away to extinction, but the professional arm could still thrive without it, à la American football. It could not survive without a steady supply of blood from the junior game.

The more wholesome values of which rugby is so proud can be found here, the importance of playing over winning, the endless enthusiasm of volunteers, the incorporation of all types – of body, class, race and gender. And the tills ring, the griddles hiss. Everyone wins.

The darker side of the 'w' word, though, is never entirely absent, even in the early years. Again, this is hardly rugby's problem alone. The concept of the aggressive parent or coach is well established in any number of sports, as is that of the overwrought child. The RFU's taste for a survey extends to regular updates about the views of its younger members. It is clear from the line of questioning that the RFU is particularly concerned about the kind of win-at-all-costs mentality, as manifested by the classic pushy parent or coach, that has wreaked such damage on the community game at adult level.

By the time your average youngster has transitioned out of mini rugby to youth, at around the age of 13, familiar pressures are starting to be exerted, quite ferociously so if that youngster shows any promise. No one speaks with any confidence about the degree to which the greater number of children introduced to rugby as early as the age of six translates into a swelling of the ranks of adult players. Many are sceptical. Another regular refrain from our survey was that, after 10 to 12 years of it, many kids are "rugbied out" by the time they reach 18. They certainly feel the usual pull of the attractions and obligations of a young adult – university, travel, work, girls, boys.

Some are picked up in the early teens by those Premiership academies, creating further tensions between player and native club. Several clubs in our survey complained about the influence of the academies (or Developing Player Programmes), the system dazzling their youngsters just by virtue of the association with the big time, only to return them disillusioned when they do not 'make it', often disinclined to continue playing. Then there is the question of availability. Tales abound of academies withholding players, when those players might be better served just playing for their local club. The local club would certainly be better served by it.

Schools are another drain on clubs past minis level. There is nothing new about this, but what is new this century is the professionalisation of schools rugby. Academies tend to work more closely with schools, knowing that the ever-more-focused set-up at certainly the most renowned of the rugby institutions, but even elsewhere, will take care of much of the day-to-day conditioning and coaching of the players. Invariably, such schools are private, which leaves rugby in this respect still open to the infamous charge that it is elitist.

This is only partly fair. The contention that rugby judges people by their background should be roundly dismissed, but the ancient association with the English public school (which in Britain, for no obvious reason, means private) is still strong. Rugby is yet to crack the conundrum that is the state sector. Evidence is forever conflicting here. The RFU and the Premiership clubs will trumpet each and every initiative of theirs to stimulate rugby in the state sector, some with evident success, but one never has to go far to hear lamentations on the dearth of working-class kids coming through. Much of this is undoubtedly a result of the ongoing reality that rugby is at its strongest in the public schools, and the perception created by it. That reality is a question of culture, but also of resources. It is harder for state schools to invest in the necessary equipment or recruit the necessary coaches, still more the necessary participants. At any given time, the background of the England team is analysed. Usually, a majority are from public schools, but to an extent this is a self-fulfilling prophecy, because so many of the best players from the state sector are offered scholarships by these places. Inevitably, further attention and resources are thus channelled to them, and so the culture is perpetuated.

The notion of school as academy is well established in New Zealand and South Africa, who have always led the rugby world in no small part because of it. Here rugby comes close to aping the American system, school rugby in these countries registering in the national conscience, attracting five-figure crowds and television deals. In South Africa, a first XV player at a strong rugby school has access to the same sort of resources a Super Rugby player does – gym, coaching, dietary advice and so on. That in itself places pressure on the players. The schools feel it too. All too many measure their worth by the results of the first XV. Inevitably, the same dynamics that one might expect, even disapprove of, at professional level begin to emerge at schoolboy level. Schools around the world have long offered places to pupils on the basis of their aptitude in any number of disciplines, but the distinction between awarding scholarships and actively recruiting is fine. In 2018, a coalition of Auckland schools moved to ostracise one of their number for its aggressive acquisition of first XV players from other schools around the country.

In the same year, *The Times* of London reported the surreal phenomenon of the Welsh complaining about English schools luring 'their' Tongan kids away with lucrative scholarships, apparently unaware that the Tongan families were in Wales in the first place because they had been lured away from their homelands by the relative riches on offer. In professionalism, money is the only metric, and there will always be someone richer than you. The same article ran the following quote from a source in the English public-school system: 'Schools now are so keen to win. One school rang me and said, "We can't compete. Our ranking as a rugby school is dropping and that will affect our intake. We need some Tongans."'

Rarely can quite so much of what is wrong with rugby, and indeed the world, have been distilled into a single quote – the indiscriminate tyranny of results, the appropriation of other people's resources and, in this case, the leaching of such processes into what a right-thinking society might consider sacrosanct, the education of its children.

None of this is new in the wider world, but it is new in rugby, thrust into the wider world so suddenly and without mediation at the end of the 20th century. As recently as the 1980s schools rugby in England was a quaint pursuit, a teacher, even in some of the most prestigious rugby schools, hauled from out of the classroom to impart any expertise they might have known to the first XV, who generally milled around in tracksuits only vaguely matching, if at all, not a school crest or sponsor's name in sight. In 1987, that seminal year for rugby competitions, the RFU introduced a 15-a-side schools cup at U15 level for the first time, then at U18 in 1990. Within a few years the finals were being held at Twickenham and more and more schools were becoming very keen indeed to win them. Now the leading schools come armed with not only a squad of unnaturally acquired players but a corps of specialist coaches, a van full of cameras, drones and technology for the accurate analysis of performance and, according to anecdote, more than occasionally a certain aggression of attitude that might sit more comfortably indeed in a professional – and adult – environment.

And so the conditions exist for the sin that dare not speak its name.

Performance-enhancing drugs are an established reality in adult community rugby. Here, again, anecdotes are rife, but every now and then unarguable evidence is presented quietly to the world in the shape of a press release and the registration of a name in the records. Of all the sports on the hit list of the world's various anti-doping bodies, rugby features as highly as any. In the UK, it is by some distance the sport with the most cases of guilty verdicts for the use of banned substances. Whenever you choose to peruse UK Anti-Doping's list of current bans, you can be sure rugby will be top. On a randomly selected date in December 2018, 25 of the 70 UK athletes serving a ban at the time were from rugby. The sport with the next highest number was league with 12 (so the two codes accounted for more than half the cases), followed by weightlifting with eight. Cycling had six. Cycling. Six. The sport with the most famous doping problem of all has a problem, in the UK at least, less than a quarter the size of rugby's.

It is also important to note that this, again, is not necessarily a problem with rugby per se. Many of the cases are those of amateur players nowhere near the top flight, driven by motives other than proficiency in the sport. Some are – or were before they were caught – semi-professional. All of the rumours and evidence suggest there is little or no culture of doping in the elite game in the UK, certainly at an institutional level. It would be next to impossible for a club or national team to organise a programme of doping for its players without at least whispers percolating through, or cases emerging from the regular testing all players are subject to at the highest levels. Which is not to say no elite rugby player has ever taken performance-enhancing drugs. It is just that, if any have, they would have done so as youngsters coming through the ranks, when careers were still to be made or lost, when eyes were a little less prying.

As talk turns to drugs in rugby, the words South Africa and south Wales are rarely far from the conversation. The latter is thought to be particularly susceptible to the most common form of drug abuse, what might be termed that of the spornosexual. Perma-tanned and bulging with muscles, ready to whip off a tight-fitting T-shirt whenever the situation demands, many Welsh gym-goers also happen to love playing rugby. Steroid use is little less than an open secret in the lower levels of Welsh rugby. It is perhaps no surprise that local reports hold the community game in Wales to be as desolate a wasteland as any of rugby's traditional playgrounds. Very average players these new creatures may be, but 18 stones is 18 stones. When forged in the gym for hours on end, they represent a health hazard on the field, no matter how limited their offloading game. Those who take their rugby and/or conditioning less seriously will tend to steer clear.

Of those 25 rugby players serving bans in the UK at the end of 2018, nine were from Wales, more than a third, which is a disproportionate number given the populations involved. All of them were in the top two leagues of the Welsh club game, where players are good enough to be of interest to the testers, but a way shy of the highest levels. In Wales, testing is more vigorous relative to population size than elsewhere in the UK. Still the elite returns a clean record.

The country with the highest incidence of positive tests in the elite game is South Africa. Around half of these cases are South African – and some of the rest involve cocaine, which can be performance-enhancing but is usually taken for recreational purposes, or cannabis, which is decidedly recreational. Legend has it that many a mighty South African was reared on a diet of 'steak and steroids' in the apartheid years. Since then, the culture has had to become more light-footed. Nobody tries to deny that drugs are a serious problem in South Africa. But, as in Wales, when a country knows it has a problem, its efforts tend to increase in the field of detection. South Africa were the first to investigate the use of drugs in the area many others have dared not look. South Africa have been turning up positive cases among their schools.

It would be naive of any rugby-playing nation to think their schools were free of the same. Again, anecdotes abound of unnaturally large boys in the school first XV, their aggression running away with them not only on the field but about the school. Now research is starting to investigate the phenomenon. The RFU, in conjunction with Leeds Beckett University, conducted a survey of 771 schoolboys across the country and 135 teachers and coaches. Of the boys, just over half of whom played rugby, 58 per cent considered the use of performance-enhancing drugs to be a serious issue in schools, with nearly 50 per cent of the teachers and coaches acknowledging the same. More than a third admitted to taking protein supplements, the classic introduction to the harder stuff, within the previous three months. As a result, the RFU is establishing education programmes targeting those between the ages of 14 and 18. In England, testing at this level, as in the community game, is limited and based on intelligence and whistle-blowing.

The South Africans, meanwhile, are less circumspect. In 2014 the South African Institute for Drug-Free Sport launched its Schools Testing Protocol, which initiated unscheduled testing for steroids in schools. It secured dispensation from the World Anti-Doping Agency to do so, the practice technically falling foul of the latter's code relating to minors. Any child at any level of sport can be tested, from first XV to U14E. Then, in 2017, New Zealand introduced random tests for those players of the four first XVs in the finals of the national championship.

And so rugby finds itself in a dystopian future, appalling to any who still value the amateur ideals. When children are being investigated, on reasonable grounds, for the sort of practices that adults can only be shamed into confessing, acutely dangerous to themselves and the other children with whom they take to the field, a sickening feeling comes on that the sport has morphed into something from which it is no wonder the common human is turning away.

To blame rugby entirely for its own culture is unfair. It is no more than a part of the wider world. Even to blame professionalism for the austere vice that grips the sport, seemingly throughout its structures, is only half the story. Had rugby somehow succeeded in defying the wider world on the question of remuneration and remained amateur, the likelihood is this state of affairs was on its way regardless. What is particular about rugby's case is that it has an affinity for performance-enhancing drugs, their benefits self-evident for a game that values power so highly. The cheating element, which enrages so many when the 'd' word is mentioned, is almost a side issue here. The reality is simply that the use of steroids and other such drugs is on the increase in society, which means it is on the increase in rugby – and, in a sport like rugby, their infiltration has repercussions for everyone.

In South Africa, positive drugs tests have been returned at every Craven Week, the annual festival for provincial schoolboy rugby, since 2009. In 2018 they returned the highest number yet, six out of 122 tests. And those are just the ones so untutored in the practice they failed to render themselves 'clean' during the one week they know they might be tested. How many more sophisticated users evaded detection altogether? Some of those caught were described as on a 'cocktail' of different drugs. One of them, it is said, had been injected by his mother.

South Africa have long been in the vanguard of the fight against performance-enhancing drugs. At the very least, other countries can expect to feel the same sort of pressures percolating through their own systems in the near future, if not already. The Sharks, Durban's Super Rugby franchise, run a community programme called SharkSmart through their medical department. In 2011 SharkSmart conducted a survey of more than 12,000 pupils from the ages of 13 to 18 across schools in the region. Via an anonymous questionnaire, the survey covered a range of wellness issues for adolescents, only one of which was steroid use. Of the respondents, 9,824 were male. From those boys, 9.5 per cent of the 18-year-olds admitted they had taken steroids at some point in their lives, 5.7 per cent in the previous 12 months. The respective figures across all the age groups were 4.6 per cent and 2.7 per cent (among the 2,639 girls, they were 1.2 per cent and 0.8 per cent). Nearly two-thirds (63 per cent) of the boys who admitted taking steroids in their lifetimes said they did so for aesthetic reasons and 30 per cent for performance. This tallies broadly with the findings of the National Image and Performance Enhancing Drugs Info Survey of 2016 in the UK, which found the figures to be 56 per cent and 27 per cent respectively among adult users across England, Scotland and Wales.

Steroid use, it seems safe to say, is a significant presence in cultures across the world in the early 21st century. Only 48.8 per cent of the users in the SharkSmart survey thought it was 'cheating' to use them. That figure takes in everyone, including those who are motivated by image rather than performance, but it does suggest that some youngsters grow up thinking it normal to be on steroids. If they felt pressure in a sporting context, they were two and a half times likelier to have taken steroids than if they did not, but if they had taken cannabis that odds ratio rose to 5.5 and, if harder recreational drugs, to 7.2. In other words, steroids are now a part of that age-old culture of revelry that sees young males on a dancefloor or at a party prospecting for the attention of others.

Most people take them because they want to look good. Rugby's problem is that a guy who is a bristling ball of muscle because he wants to look good is still a bristling ball of muscle. He is a better rugby player because of it, or at least a more formidable physical proposition, and anyone who wants to compete needs to make their own decisions about how far they will go and how. When you are on the cusp of selection and the coach delivers that old chestnut about your not being quite big enough, all sorts of further questions are raised in the mind, especially if you see, or even just think you see, others use illicit substances to achieve the same effect. Of the users in the SharkSmart survey, 11 per cent cited pressure from their coach as a motivation; 9 per cent cited pressure from their parents. More worryingly still, 14 per cent said they sourced the drugs from members of staff and 7 per cent from their parents. Under the tyranny of results, everyone feels the pressure, even those whose role is to protect. Dr Glen Hagemann, medical advisor to the Sharks, remembers sitting on a tribunal for the South African Institute for Drug-Free Sport in which a parent testified that he had injected his son with steroids without his son knowing. He told him it was a vitamin supplement.

Such vignettes of seeming derangement, however extreme and unrepresentative, are the sort to enrage those who sit outside the environment, and even most of those within it. But that environment is key. There is a simple, value-free spectrum that defines rugby, now that it is part of the modern world – and that is the pursuit of results, or professionalism. People see cheating – and certainly pharmaceutical cheating – as somehow removed from that, qualitatively different, on another spectrum. It is not. Cheating is merely what lies on the other side of an arbitrary boundary determined by lawmakers and enforced only as effectively as it is easy to detect. But it is most assuredly fixed on the same spectrum of self-improvement along which we progress according to how badly we want or need to win.

Steroids improve performance in power-based sports. If they were legal (and safe), their use in those sports would be a simple, logical choice, no more difficult a decision to arrive at than to run in the latest footwear or to ride on the latest bike. But they are not legal (or safe, which surely accounts for 'most' of their illegality), so those hellbent on travelling as far along the spectrum of self-improvement as they can will eventually bump up against this barrier, which marks the furthest reach of legality. With entreaties screaming through their heads, be they from parents, coaches, fans or, most often, their own selves, they must consider the worth or otherwise of crossing the Rubicon. Most (hopefully) still stop short of that line, but the decision of those who do not ought to be placed in the context of an ever-changing environment, more brutally quantitative within and outside rugby, where qualitative sensibilities are increasingly hard to discern. The instinct to judge, while the prerogative and duty of disciplinary committees, ought not to be so feral among the rest of us. The very ardour with which athletes are urged on to ever greater heights of achievement by the outside world and themselves is the same compulsion that drives some across the line of legality, a migration that tends to gather momentum as more and more choose to bolt. To blame those athletes alone, as if each decision were taken in splendid isolation and motivated by pure evil, is to disregard the part played by a culture that places such value on achievement and results. We should not be surprised, then, if the transgressions continue – indeed, increase.

All of which places rugby in an invidious position. The repercussions of this process of self-improvement, even if cheating were taken out of it, are particularly severe for so physical a sport, further complicated by its much-treasured code of the team, of breaking into it, but also of not letting it down. And then there is the simple question of having to survive, an increasingly perilous directive. It is no wonder the casual players are leaving in their droves, further sharpening the edge of those who remain. It is difficult to know how this can be undone. We are back to the right of anyone to improve themselves as far as they can. There may be measures the community game could take, but they amount to trying to tell people to stop being so serious about a pastime, to be less competitive, to consider themselves separate from the elite game, which may well be their inspiration, which some may well harbour ambition to attain. They amount to a renunciation of the professional way.

Meanwhile, that professional arena grows ever more analogous to the Colosseum. Its players are on a conveyor taking them towards an uncertain future, which some indeed are already labelling a dystopia. Rugby is beginning to apprehend the seriousness of the situation. And rugby, not without cause, is terrified of it.

Part 5

The Invincible Mortals

XII

New Sport, Old School

First, a few truths. We take a risk every second we live. Most of the time, the risk is minimal, but it increases whenever we leave the house, cross the road, get into the car, on a plane or train, whenever we climb a cliff face. There are people out there who measure these risks as best they can and plot them on graphs with designated regions for acceptable, tolerable and unacceptable levels. These different categories of risk are society's way of acknowledging that nothing is perfect, we could each die any moment, but it would be ridiculous not to do anything for fear of that. Moreover, sometimes a few risks need to be taken. Within reason.

Countries measure levels of risk differently. A common standard is the likely number of fatalities arising from a pursuit or occupation per 100,000 people exposed to it. In America, they tend to consider that risk over the course of a lifetime; in the UK it tends to be over a year. For example, the Health and Safety Executive (HSE) in the UK reckons that a mortality rate of 100 per 100,000 per year is the top end of the tolerable level when it comes to the exposure of employees to risks in the workplace. Should your oil rig or construction company start to rack up a mortality rate approaching that figure, your practices would come under intense scrutiny, but the point is that only at 100 and above would they become unacceptable. HSE also posits a risk of 2 per 100,000 per year as the threshold between tolerable and acceptable and 0.1 as that between acceptable and negligible. In other words, everything at 0.1 and below is absolutely fine, God willing, and no steps need be taken at all to mitigate risk. According to a study in 2008, the risk of dying from a lightning strike in the UK is 0.01 per 100,000 per year, although that fate is considerably likelier in more rural, stormy parts of the world. The global estimate for lightning's annual mortality rate is 0.6 per 100,000.

The UK is not just a propitious place for avoiding lightning strikes. The country is one of the world leaders for road safety, its 3.1 fatalities per 100,000 per year in 2016, according to the World Health Organization (WHO), putting it neck and neck with those paragons of good practice, Sweden, Switzerland and Norway. The rate for Europe overall was 9.3, for the world 18.2. South Africa's was 25.9. Drive a motorbike, though, and the risk shot up to 50.6 in the UK, according to the Department of Transport's figures.

In 2017, according to the Office for National Statistics, the rate for alcohol-specific death, i.e. from a disease specific to alcohol use, in the UK was 12.2 per 100,000 of the country's drinkers. The rate for alcohol-attributable death, though, was 46, but that is per 100,000 of the entire population of 66 million, on the basis that anyone in theory could die from an alcohol-generated accident. If you were one of the UK's 29 million drinkers, that rate, impossible to calculate precisely, would likely double. Figures supplied by the Global Burden of Disease Study of 2016 produce a rate of 24 for alcohol-attributable deaths worldwide among the young (aged 15 to 49) – again, using the entire population of the world in that age group as denominator, regardless of whether they drink. The average annual risk between 2014 and 2016 of dying from cancer before the age of 34 was 4.6 per 100,000 in the UK (Cancer Research UK), and at any age it was 252.

It's a dangerous game, this life.

The risk of playing sport can be plotted on the same scale. There are problems with this, as there are with some of the above figures, the main one relating to a determination of the size of the population exposed. The WHO's figure for road mortality rates was calculated simply by dividing the number of fatalities by population size, since, as with alcohol, we are all theoretically subject to the risk of death by road. The motorcycle figure was arrived at by a more complicated calculation based upon miles on a motorbike, as driver or passenger, per person per year. They are all, necessarily, estimates.

The same issues pertain to sport. What population should be deemed appropriate for calculating the risk of, say, rugby? It is not possible to know the average number of minutes played by a player across all age groups, standards and countries. It is hard enough to know the number who have simply played at all. The same problems apply for this calculation. Dr Colin Fuller has conducted some of the most valuable research into the risk level of playing rugby. His 2008 study, 'Catastrophic Injury in Rugby Union: Is the level of risk acceptable?', investigated the rate of catastrophic injury in England and other countries, registering 'fatalities and brain/spinal cord injuries resulting in significant permanent neurological deficit and which were a direct consequence of playing rugby union'. This excludes cardiovascular events, which might occur during any form of exercise. He took as his population an estimate of the average annual number of school and club players in England over the period 1992–2002, finessing out mini-rugby players who are not exposed to the same risk of injury through contact. He arrived at a figure of 490,000, which allowed him to calculate the catastrophic injury rate for rugby in England over the 10 years in question as 0.8. The fatality rate would have been lower.

A reliable, up-to-date fatality rate for rugby is hard to come by, not least because of the population question. So too is the actual fatality count. South Africa, New Zealand and England are the most transparent. In 2008, the South African Rugby Union began a safety programme called BokSmart, which has recorded catastrophic injuries in South African rugby ever since. The population of rugby players in South Africa as supplied by World Rugby is one of those subject to dramatic fluctuations, and so not to be trusted, but a survey commissioned by the South African Rugby Union in 2013 arrived at a playing population of 291,940. This figure was for full-contact 15-a-side rugby, excluding all other formats. One of its authors, Dr James Brown, concedes that it might not be entirely exhaustive, so we could work with reasonable accuracy, though perhaps a tad conservative, from a population of 300,000 exposed to the risks of contact rugby in South Africa, 230,000 of which are youth. Excluding cardiovascular events, there were 19 fatalities in South African rugby from 2008 to 2018, inclusive, generating an annual mortality rate of 0.6 per 100,000.

New Zealand releases its figures through the insurance company that covers the nation's sports injuries and through the government's statistics. In the same period, 2008–18, there were five fatalities in New Zealand in rugby union (and one other in league). World Rugby's figure for New Zealand's playing population is one of those that has remained steady throughout and thus has a feeling of authenticity about it, rising from 140,000 to 150,000 in that timeframe, around 120,000 of which are youth. This generates a fatality rate of 0.3, but it is unclear how many of that population play non-contact forms of the sport, so the real rate could be higher.

The latest figures from the Injured Player Foundation in England suggest the catastrophic injury rate since Fuller's study has remained much the same (exactly the same if we adopt the population he used of 490,000). There were two fatalities directly related to rugby over the 10 years from 2008, which generates a fatality rate of 0.07 per 100,000 from another conservative population estimate of 300,000 playing contact rugby. This is an exceptional figure, well within the HSE's range for negligible risk and attributable as much as anything to the facilities of an affluent country.

Mortality rates in rugby, just as in any other activity, vary considerably according to country. World Rugby's official figure for rugby's mortality rate worldwide is 0.6. So, the old proverb about an unlikely death could be applied literally to rugby. Allowing for the estimated nature of the figures, the chances of dying in a rugby match would seem, indeed, to be roughly those of dying from a lightning strike.

There is, though, significant variance between age groups – a theme repeated across all studies. When it comes to fatalities, youth sport is much safer than adult. The rates in South African rugby are 0.2 and 1.9 respectively; in New Zealand, they are 0.2 and 0.7. South Africa's adult rate rose by 0.5 over the last three years of the period, because of seven deaths from 2016 to 2018, of which more later.

In 2018, the rugby world was rocked by four deaths in France. This felt an outlandish series of tragedies for the game to contend with, and not just in France. World Rugby lists the total number of players in France as 604,000, but as ever there must be some doubt how many of those actually play and in what format of the game. The figure it holds for registered players has fluctuated wildly in recent years between 273,000 (2017) and 542,000 (2016). A 2016 study into cervical spine injuries took the playing population of France to be 274,000, based on the numbers registered with the FFR, but one of the four victims (whose date of death fell in 2019 after an induced coma) was not registered with the FFR, along with many others who play nevertheless. If we were to adopt for France the same (conservative) estimate we have for England and South Africa of 300,000 people playing contact rugby with some regularity, we can see that, even in that terrible year, rugby's mortality rate in France was around 1.3 per 100,000, well within what would be deemed acceptable by HSE in the UK. According to Eurostat, France's mortality rate for accidents in the workplace, across all employment, including office-based, was 2.6 per 100,000 employees in 2015.

As much as we might try to place the risk of playing rugby into some sort of context, it really, along with all sports, belongs in a different bracket from the rest of the perils that beset us in everyday life. For a start, we choose to play, which means avoiding the risk is as easy as to choose not to. And we do not play nine-to-five or 24/7 – for good reason. All we can say with the above statistics is that in any given year of our lives, these are the odds of our dying from an activity should we choose to pursue it. Rugby, in the grand scheme of things, does not rate highly. Nor should it, because it is just a game.

But the question of choice is important, too. Some interests we do not have to pursue, but we do anyway, despite the risks. Society frowns on a lot of them because of the dangers, perceived or otherwise, and then wrestles with the urge to stop/help those who insist on playing with fire. Freedom of choice usually prevails. Alcohol, as we have seen, is significantly more dangerous than rugby – and not just to those drinking. Smoking is much, much more so. In 2016, the worldwide mortality rate was 630 per 100,000 of the world's 1 billion smokers, according to the Global Burden of Disease Study. Another 884,000 died of second-hand smoke, 11.8 per 100,000 of the 7.5 billion of us on the planet. In the UK, the mortality rate is more than a thousand per 100,000 of Britain and Northern Ireland's 7.4 million smokers (Office for National Statistics). There are no redeeming features to either of these leisure practices, bar the nebulous sense that a lot of us rather enjoy them, for reasons we cannot always delineate. There are, though, many, many reasons not to partake, most of them blindingly obvious, pertaining to health, nuisance level and out-and-out danger to the partaker and others. Yet they persevere in our culture. Indeed, intoxication is as old as society itself. It has earned its right to stay.

Rugby has not. So rugby, especially now that it has become geared up on the amphetamine of professionalism, needs to watch its step.

In the hierarchy of sports, it is undoubtedly one of the riskier, but by no means the riskiest. A pair of studies in the early years of this century, for example, presented figures that produced a fatality rate in horse racing for the latter years of the 20th century of 25 per 100,000 per year in Great Britain and 28 in the US. In France the figure, skewed by 11 deaths in jump racing from 1980 to 2001, was 51.

Again, we are comparing pursuits of a different dynamic, even if both are in the realm of sport. The population of race jockeys is small (barely a thousand in Great Britain), but each can race hundreds of times a year. Rugby players are much more numerous, but they do not expose themselves to their sport's risks anything like as often (not yet anyway). For a jockey to ride in a race is probably about as 'dangerous' as for a rugby player to play in a match, but over a given year they race so often a jockey's lot becomes significantly more so.

Which brings us on to the question of perception – as ever, one of rugby's biggest problems. A youngster, or a youngster's parents, contemplating a career in horse racing will just see humans riding wild and free on a steed. The activity itself looks nothing other than exhilarating. The only way to die from it, the observer will note, is to fall from your horse, which might be perceived as to make a mistake, or to 'play badly' in rugby parlance. 'That's fine,' our would-be jockey might surmise, 'I'll just make sure I don't fall off. And even if I do the chances are . . .'

Rugby, on the other hand, has a degree of violence hardwired into it. The observer need only watch for a few minutes to appreciate the self-evident risk of damage to the person. You do not have to make a mistake to suffer an injury with serious repercussions, including, if yours is the case in a couple of hundred thousand, the ultimate.

Generally, fatality statistics, even without the population conundrum, are hard to come by, but those glimpses we can garner sometimes throw up surprising results. As a rule of thumb, if you want to pursue a sport with a low mortality rate, do not get into or onto anything with an engine and steer well clear of water. An Australian study of catastrophic injury in sport and recreation in the state of Victoria from 2001 to 2003 returned a mortality rate of 18.5 for water-skiing and power-boating and 9.2 for fishing, on a par with that for motorsport (9.0) over the same period.

Motorsport statistics are as elusive as any, such is the proliferation of events and classes, but the Formula One World Championship is relatively easy to calculate, so tiny is the population and so high-profile the victims. It is manifestly the deadliest mainstream sport on earth. (The more indie pursuit of BASE jumping might claim at least parity.) From its inception in 1950 to 2018, there have been 32 deaths on championship weekends. We might take the population of participants as 24 drivers per year. The early iterations saw more drivers slot in and out of each grand prix, whereas later years have seen a more stable population race each time. This puts Formula One at a disadvantage with other sports, for which the entire population is lumped in together, regardless of how often they compete, but, when one considers that those figures generate an annual mortality rate of nearly 2,000, Formula One might confidently be considered in a class of deadliness all its own, whichever way we calculate it. Since that fateful season of 1994 when Ayrton Senna and Roland Ratzenberger died on the same weekend, the population of drivers each year has settled in the mid-twenties, and safety has improved dramatically. But Jules Bianchi's death in 2015 generates a mortality rate for the sport since 1996 of around 180. Were the sport subject to conventional applications of health and safety, it would not pass.

So small is its population, figures for Formula One are highly volatile. A statistician would advise caution. We are on safer ground with sports of mass participation. In America, the National Center for Catastrophic Sport Injury Research (NCCSIR) provides as comprehensive a guide to fatality rates as anywhere, although restricted to high-school and college sports. They distinguish between direct and indirect fatalities, between those caused by the mechanics of a sport and those (normally cardiac events) that happen to occur during them. Over the past 35 years, gymnastics for boys (0.9 direct fatalities per 100,000 per year) has been the most lethal sport in high school, the mortality rates of which are lower than in college, where skiing is most dangerous (5.7 for males, 4.7 for females), followed by female equestrianism (4.1) and male lacrosse (1.5). American football, surprisingly, is a relatively modest 0.4 at high school and 0.6 at college (note the similarity to rugby's figures).

So much for the realities of a sport's threat to your life. When we try to appraise danger we tend not to pay too much attention to the actual statistics or we would never leave the house. (Mind you, according to the Royal Society for the Prevention of Accidents, the UK's mortality rate for accidents in the home is 9.1.) We go by the look and feel of an activity. Rugby, like American football, feels dangerous. Indeed, there are stats to back this up. Death may not stalk its every ruck and maul but, if it is a high chance of injury that turns you on, rugby delivers.

A person may be around 15 times more likely to die from an accident in their home than on the rugby field, but that does not make rugby, the activity itself, less dangerous. If we played rugby nine-to-five, the mortality rate, as with any sport, would rocket. For all the headlines when they occur, deaths in sport are very rare. A measure used more often for the risk of a sport is the rate of catastrophic injury. Definitions are not always consistent. The NCCSIR's definition includes severe injuries with no permanent disability, as well as fatalities and those with permanent disability. Now we start to see American football take a more prominent role, although it is worth noting that at high school – and school statistics are particularly poignant for obvious reasons – the cheerleaders are more at risk than the players. Cheerleading at high school over the past 35 years has borne a risk of 3.5 catastrophic injuries per 100,000 per year, about the same as gymnastics, which is what the sport amounts to. The high-school rate for football is 2.7. At college level, gymnastics (for men, not women) remains the leader at

16.4. Skiing (for women, not men) is next at 11.4, followed by American football at 10. Ice hockey (for men) has a risk of 8.8.

Rugby's risk of catastrophic injury seems a little lower, although some studies exclude injury without permanent disability. All comparisons – between studies as well as sports – must be treated with caution. Fuller compared results implied by other studies across the world since 1970, some of which concerned themselves only with spinal injuries, some with spinal and fatal injuries. That figure of 0.8 catastrophic injuries per 100,000 in the UK between 1992 and 2002 is low. In 1997, Fiji had a spinal/fatal injury rate of 13, which is an outlier; from 1977 to 1997, Argentina's was 1.9. In Ireland from 1995 to 2004, that figure was 0.9. In Australia and New Zealand, the spinal injury rates of various studies across 1976 to 2005 averaged out at a little over 4. In South Africa, according to the BokSmart database, the catastrophic injury rate, including those who made a full recovery but excluding cardiovascular events, between 2008 and 2018 was 2.3. On the whole, the more recent the figure the lower it is. Catastrophic injuries in rugby are, it seems, on the way down, as the sport's emphasis shifts from the relatively dangerous scrum towards the tackle.

If only that were an end to the problems. On the contrary, rugby's player-welfare status is as critical as it has ever been.

Professionalism might be held to blame once more – the professionalisation of rugby players, yes, but also of scrutiny, of health and safety, of the ability to express opinion loudly and in high dudgeon. The game may be faster and more skilful than ever, but the injuries keep coming. Rugby is becoming a PR disaster for itself, its brutality replayed in Ultra HD from a variety of angles in front of an audience equipped with the technology to make their views known. There was a time when the gladiatorial aspect was relished by fan and television producer alike, but as welfare concerns mount that contradiction jars more and more. There have been no deaths so far in first-class rugby in the professional era. This could be because the players are fit for purpose, it could be because there are so few of them. But if a fatal injury should ever happen live on air expect everything to change.

Without doubt, rugby is a more 'dangerous' activity these days. The incidence of catastrophic injury may have improved this century, but that is far from the end of the story. Do those fatalities in France in 2018 signal the start of a new crisis? Two of them were on the fringes of the first-class game, one a player from ProD2, the French second division (although his was a case of commotio cordis, a very rare cardiovascular event precipitated by a blow to the wrong part of the heart at the wrong millisecond of the cardiac cycle), another a member of the Stade Français academy. In the same year, four Australian schoolboys in Queensland in the space of a month suffered serious spinal injuries. In South Africa, those seven adult deaths from 2016 to 2018 represent a spike, and there was a youth fatality, too, in 2016. Authorities around the world, including the French government, are on high alert as rugby continues to turn this way and that. One does not particularly have to be a gentle flower to be troubled by the feeling that collision sports generally are hurtling towards an apocalypse. Rugby is in the vanguard. Everyone has seen *Rollerball*. The conceit becomes less amusing each year.

Many studies have been undertaken by academics concerning catastrophic injury in rugby, but there are surprisingly few consistent databases recording the everyday toll of a life in the sport. The RFU, together with Premier Rugby and the English Rugby Players' Association (RPA), have been well ahead of the game here, initiating the Professional Rugby Injury Surveillance Project in 2002, which has documented injury rates and types among the 12 Premiership clubs in annual reports ever since. Seven years later, the RFU initiated a similar project for community rugby.

The tackle is now by some distance the most dangerous facet of rugby, leaving the scrum trailing in its wake, at whichever level a player plays. To study the nature of South Africa's catastrophic injuries even just this century is to see how the dynamic has changed, manifested in a shift from spinal injury to traumatic brain injury (TBI). Six of those eight fatalities from 2016 to 2018 were from TBIs. Catastrophic injuries in South Africa may have declined, but the proportion of TBIs to spinal injuries has shifted, as the tackle takes over. From 2001 to 2007, only 16 per cent of catastrophic injuries were TBIs; from 2008 to 2015, 21 per cent were; from 2016 to 2018, that figure was 50 per cent. This has been achieved partly by a reduction in the rate of spinal injury, partly by an increase in that of TBI.

It is too early for statisticians to be alarmed here, so low are the numbers, but in conjunction with some of the findings of English rugby's injury surveillance projects in recent years, not to mention developments in France and Australia, rugby holds its breath to see how this will pan out. The scrum is under control now, but the tackle feels as if it is not. Why this should be a problem since 2016 specifically is a mystery, since the shift in rugby's emphasis from set piece to tackle has taken place over decades. If the tackle count continues to climb, it has done so steadily for years, with no obvious spike of late. Perhaps rugby has reached a tipping point, after which the consequences will prove severe, or perhaps these recent figures are simply anomalies.

Either way, there has been a dramatic shift in the dynamics of the modern game. In 2005, Corris Thomas, the former referee, performed an analysis for World Rugby comparing 16 Test matches from the early 1980s with 16 comparable Test matches 20 years later. His findings are displayed in the accompanying table, together with data gathered from a handful of Test matches in the early 1970s and that gathered by Opta since.

	1970s	1980s	1995 RWC	2000s	2011 RWC	2015 RWC	2019 6N
Tackles	104	104	112	174	197	236	322
Rucks/mauls	38	46	94	148	162	177	213
Scrums	43	31	23	19	17	13	11
Lineouts	60	52	38	37	24	26	25

In the early 1970s a typical Test match contained 43 scrums and 60 lineouts. There were fewer rucks and mauls (34) than either set piece and about as many tackles (104) as both combined. As many tackles as set pieces . . . it is worth pausing to consider that. Anyone who complains today about the modern game as a spectacle would do well to remember it was hardly a laugh a minute back then – but in those days no one particularly cared. That's amateurism for you. The notion of multi-phase rugby simply did not exist. Rugby was overwhelmingly dominated by the set piece.

By the 1995 World Cup, the eve of professionalism, the balance had shifted. There was an average of 23 scrums and 38 lineouts a game, compared with 112 tackles and 94 rucks and mauls. Twenty years later, at the 2015 World Cup, the average number of set pieces a game had almost halved again, down to 13 scrums and 26 lineouts, a reduction in the set piece of more than 60 per cent since the 1970s, and the tackles had rocketed to 236 (more than doubled), with 177 rucks and mauls (nearly quintupled). In the Six Nations of 2019, the average tackle count was higher again at 322, the rucks and mauls 213. For the first time in history, there were more tackles per game than passes.[*] Rugby has become almost a new sport, with new threats to the player – and there is no sign of a let-up in the rise in collisions.

Clearly, under the 'old' dynamic, the scrum was more dangerous than the tackle – and not just because there were relatively so many more of them. Players were slower, smaller and less powerful at all levels, so collisions were less intense. Law changes, principally the 'use it or lose it' culture that was first enshrined in 1994, have forced teams to make more of each ruck and maul. Meanwhile, the simple improvement of basic skills and the introduction in the early 1990s of

---

[*] It is important to note that the methodology of the tackle count changed in the 2010s, whereby double-tackles started to count as two – one tackle registered for each of the two tacklers. This exaggerates the increase in tackles in the 2010s. The ruck/maul count might be a more accurate gauge for the development of the game's attrition rate in the professional era. This has more than doubled since 1995. The contrast with the game in the amateur era remains stark.

synthetic balls have reduced the error count, which halved in the 20 years of Thomas's study. All of which has led to the fall in scrums – dramatic at the highest levels. Tweaks to the sequence of engagement have, moreover, improved the safety of those that do take place, culminating in the introduction of the 'crouch, bind, set' routine, settled upon in 2013, which has improved stability.

Meanwhile, the number of tackles has ballooned, as teams, in short, have got their acts together, filling the airtime gained from the set piece with the blandishment of their improved skillsets, both in attack and defence. The organisation and simple urgency of defences is one of the biggest changes in the professional era. Attacks have had to respond accordingly. Fewer dropped passes, more continuity, more points of contact. That's professionalism for you.

Finally, to complete the transformation, the players are fitter and, with the introduction of tactical substitutions in 1996, they pack so much more of a punch for longer, rendering tackles not only more numerous but more ferocious. Much has been made of the transformation in the dimensions of the modern player. With professionalism, it is true, heavier players have been sourced and selected, and improved standards of conditioning have made the most of the attributes of everybody. The size of players was on the rise anyway. A study by Tim Olds of the University of South Australia in 2001 found that the height of elite rugby players from around the world since 1905 had increased broadly in line with that of the wider population of young men in developed countries (a centimetre a decade), but that the body mass had risen significantly. The weight of young men in the wider population has grown by approximately a kilogram a decade in that time; among Old's sample of rugby players the growth was 2.6 kg a decade, with the rate of increase since 1975 three to four times what it had been from 1905 to 1975. Other studies have demonstrated a further step change since 1995.

Less, though, has been made of the end of that trend. Fuller has shown that the dimensions of the Premiership player reached a plateau in 2006, where it has more or less remained ever since, an optimal balance between heft and aerobic capacity having apparently been reached. Only the fly-half has continued to grow significantly since, in height and weight, and props have become taller. Anecdotal evidence among conditioning staff suggests player size may even be coming down again as the game becomes faster, the ball in play for longer.

But the power of those athletes, the speed and the strength, has never stopped improving. A popular index for measuring explosive power in an athlete is the countermovement jump (CMJ), whereby the displacement achieved from a standing jump is taken as indicative. Phil Morrow, the Saracens performance director, has worked in rugby throughout the professional era, first with Ulster, then Ireland, before joining Saracens in 2011. He estimates the CMJ of a typical professional rugby player to have risen by more than 10 per cent since 2009. In that year, a front-five forward might have registered somewhere between 35 cm and 50 cm, higher for locks than props; in 2019 those brackets had shifted to between 40 cm and 55 cm. The main gain has been an improvement of the players in the lower ranges, a closing of the gap between the best and the stragglers. In 2009, back-row forwards Stephen Ferris and David Wallace registered CMJs of more than 55 cm and were considered freaks; likewise, wingers Tommy Bowe and Andrew Trimble at 60 cm. Now those figures are considered quite normal. In 2019, most back-row forwards came in between 50 cm and 55 cm. It is common for all backs in a squad to record jumps of more than 55 cm.

An increase in the wear and tear of the players under these circumstances cannot be avoided, whatever the level. As the annual injury audits roll in, English rugby manifestly tortures itself as it tries to wrestle with the urges, both valid, on the one hand to keep concerns in perspective, to follow the data, and on the other to protect the players, to ensure matters are not careering out of control. Each year for over a decade we were told that the incidence and severity of injuries in the English Premiership were within the limits of expectation, the statistician's way of allaying fears. But in the 2016–17 season, and then again in 2017–18, we were finally presented with data that exceeded the upper limit of expectation.

Not relating to incidence, though. The number of injuries in the Premiership per 1,000 player hours has fluctuated quite steadily around the long-term mean, actually dipping below the lower limit of expectation in 2015–16, which may, interestingly, be because there was a lengthier preseason, the World Cup in England having required a late start to the Premiership – or it may just be because clubs were laxer with their reporting. The average severity of injuries, though, broke through the upper limit in 2016–17. And even if previous seasons had seen the mean remain within the limits of expectation, that mean has risen steadily since the injury audit's inception in 2002. The average length of absence per injury in the 2002–3 season was 16 days; in 2017–18, it was 37, a 130 per cent increase. Injuries, it seems, are much more severe now.

Or are they? Even here, there are grounds for mitigation. Standards of care are much improved, the counterargument runs, the players better looked after. Squads are bigger too. Fuller has noted an increase in the average squad size of a Premiership club from 37 in 2002 to 46 in 2011. Playing squads, like most aspects of rugby, are difficult to define, some clubs listing academy players separately, but all making regular use of them in the first team. An audit of squads published in the media guide and on club websites suggests 46 remains the average size of a squad today. Clubs are able to give players longer to recover and do. That does not make the injury suffered more severe, but it does increase the length of the player's absence in recovery, which remains the only realistic measure of injury severity. Still, 130 per cent is 130 per cent. Such an increase is not wholly, or indeed much more than partially, down to more forgiving recovery programmes.

Every so often a player breaks rank to open up about the burden of a career in rugby in the early decades of the professional era, the constant battle with aches and pains, the pressure from a stern-jawed director of rugby to play when not fully fit. These tales enrage many among a modern audience brought up on notions of liberalism and compassion. Ranged against such sensibilities is the movement known widely as that of the 'old school'. This holds much traction still in rugby. Indeed, the sport might be said to owe its very soul to old-school virtues. Until professionalism came along there was scarcely a need to entertain any other modus operandi than a robust culture of sucking up grievances and getting on with it. There are plenty of current players who feel that professionalism, as well as raising the duty of care among employers to look after their staff, makes it incumbent upon that staff, now they are being paid for their services, to push their bodies ever harder for the cause.

In 2016, the *Guardian* conducted an investigation into player welfare. Among the several players and coaches interviewed, opinion was split more or less evenly between those who thought the game was hurtling towards a crisis of player welfare, where, to adopt the popular adage, 'something has to give or the players' bodies will', and those who felt the players had never been better looked after, that if they did not like being bashed about they were in the wrong job. The dichotomy was best summed up by the attitudes of two international props of the highest renown, one the bristling firebrand, Alex Corbisiero, the other the earthy stoic, Dan Cole – loosehead and tighthead, fire and earth.

'I want rugby to change,' said Corbisiero of the omertà around pushing players to play before they are ready. 'I want us to look after players by talking about it, listening to each other and having a united front.'

'My grandfather worked down a coal mine,' said Cole, 'and broke his back when the pit collapsed. Would I prefer to do what I do and risk long-term health problems? Yeah. I know what I've signed up for.'

Both attitudes are admirable, both valid, poignant even. But they are at opposite ends of the spectrum. Rugby spins in confusion, torn by the warring consciences they have inherited. Corbisiero and Cole know of what they speak. They were starting props when England beat the All Blacks in 2012. Corbisiero played in the match before he was ready, after major knee surgery, and did not play again for five months. It would prove the last time he started a Test for England. In the same season, which culminated for him in a Lions tour to Australia, Cole played an astonishing 41 matches. A tighthead. The following season, he was out for nine months with a bulging disc in his neck, which had to be replaced. He accepts it was not a coincidence. He insists he would do it all again.

Cole racked up that extraordinary tally because of the Lions tour. Rarely does the sport reveal itself as more hopelessly conflicted over player welfare than when the question of the Lions comes up. There is not a conditioning coach in Britain who sees the Lions as anything other than a menace to their players' welfare. There can be no legislating for it. One cannot manage a player's game time throughout a season on the off-chance that he might be selected for the Lions. So players play out a full season, as Cole did in 2012–13, only to embark at the end of it on the most gruelling tour in rugby. If rugby were serious about improving player welfare (and there is a reasonable, if far from unanswerable, line of argument that it need not be, that matters are under control), the first sacrifice to be made would be that of the Lions. But the financial implications for the three countries lucky enough to receive the increasingly corporate travelling circus would be disastrous.

And so the point of engagement in the welfare debate shifts to finance. This feels like safe ground. If there is one injustice we can all agree on, it is exploitation in the pursuit of Mammon. The players play too much. And why do they play so much? So that their paymasters can, as the saying goes, make a quick buck. Why do some countries play a fourth match in the autumn, outside the international window?

To make a quick buck. Why do almost all leagues have a series of play-offs to determine the winner? Quick buck. Our poor champions are being flogged to death for the sake of a few dollars more.

Which would be a legitimate complaint if any of the accused were laughing as the slave-players poured wheelbarrows of cash into their golden baths. The truth is these extra matches are less about making quick bucks, more about not haemorrhaging more of them. And what is by far the biggest cost on rugby's balance sheet? Player wages.

The players are playing so much in order to pay for themselves. Anyone who calls for a reduction in player workload must first address that not insignificant problem. The players' wages are too high.

Except they are not really. If we consider what the players have to go through, how short (increasingly so) the careers, how much of a toll they might suffer in later life. Very, very few can take retirement after a career playing rugby – and those who could are those who will be in demand for the rest of their lives anyway, taking jobs in front of the camera or behind the lectern or in the coaches' box from those who need the work. One look across at The Sibling and what its slaves are paid – as much for some in a week as the very best in rugby are paid in a year – will further heighten the sense of injustice. Rugby players are paid a pittance by that standard.

Nevertheless, it is more than revenues can accommodate, and therefore it is too much. Not that that stops the constant calls for a reduction in the fixture list. Simple economics will not allow that in the current environment. In an ideal world, the players would take a pay cut, but that, in practice, would be next to impossible to engineer.

Every now and then, a high-profile player muses in public that he would happily take a reduction in salary to facilitate fewer matches. Directors of rugby (who do not come cheaply themselves) will tend to roll their eyes when they hear that line and quip that the message does not seem to be getting through to the players' agents. The salary cap is supposed to address this problem, but we have already seen how the salary cap is constantly under pressure from those clubs wanting to push ahead of the rest, even before they are ready. The salary cap is also under constant pressure from those whose income is determined by the salaries they can secure for their clients. All that happens when the salary cap goes up is that the players' agents are able to counter more easily the old excuses about tight budgets. All that happens is the players' wages go up. Rarely does a raising of the cap translate into a bigger squad. Indeed, we have seen that Premiership squad sizes have remained steady for around 10 years, but the average age of a player has fallen, particularly in the front row, where the regulations of 2009 regarding cover on the bench have placed added pressure on squads. In other words, increases in the salary cap have facilitated bigger salaries for established players, with squad numbers maintained by the recruitment of academy products on low wages.

This policy is made possible by the calibre of those youngsters emerging from the academies. Players' careers are becoming shorter, but that is not just because of the greater toll on the players' bodies. Eighteen-year-olds now step out from their schools unrecognisable from their equivalents of 10 to 15 years ago. When strength-and-conditioning coaches whip young players into shape, they are working from starting points far more developed than in the past – and nowadays have the science to accelerate physical development anyway. The pressures on a player as he passes 30 no longer amount solely to the wear and tear of a life in the sport; he has much more of a challenge now just keeping his place in the team. That 20-year-old junior world champion might simply look a better player. The same is true even for the sensational 20-year-old. If he were picked for his country at that age, time was when he could have expected a consistent 10 years or so of international rugby; now he might feel the pressure within a couple of years from the next brilliant talent. And this new dynamic in turn increases the wear and tear on everyone's bodies, as those callow youths of yesteryear who needed a few more seasons of conditioning are replaced by formidable physical specimens already fit for purpose.

Careers must become shorter under those circumstances, must become more intense. The pattern is familiar in this supercharged century, let alone in rugby – everything tighter, more furious, more now, the fear some breaking point is imminent all the more suffocating.

And at what long-term cost? No one knows what repercussions a career in professional rugby will have in later life. The first generation to have known only the professional era were those born in the 1980s, barely even at middle age now. We know what toll a career in amateur rugby can exact, because there are plenty of gentlemen in their 50s, 60s and 70s who have required replacement body parts before their time, whose limbs ache, all because they played too much rugby in their youths.

Such fellows made an impression on one of professional rugby's most durable players, George Chuter – 18 years and more than 400 matches in the front row for Saracens, Leicester and England – as he mingled with them post-match in the Welford Road bar. If that was what rugby in the amateur era did to the players of the past, what awaits those from his own generation who played in a far more punishing era? What awaits those now?

'I'm under no illusions,' he said to the *Guardian* in 2016. 'You have a great career, you have a great time – and it is a great career – but the human body can't take that sort of punishment and escape scot-free. If you want to get to the top you've got to make sacrifices. And it's not just your time or a bag of chips; it's your long-term health. You want to have that time in the sun. Unfortunately, it's a deal with the devil.'

And the devil calls for his first payment the day he takes that career away.

It is one of life's crueller ironies that those with the most to lose (the young) are those who tend to feel the most invincible. Intellectually, we all know we are going to die, just as surely as our youth shall, God willing, segue eventually into a middle age of diminished physical powers. But, until the first groans of the rest of their life creep up, no right-minded youth engages with the thought.

The better at sport, the more susceptible one might be to this sense of immortality. To be feted throughout school, used to winning, to greet each year as the next long step into a great adventure, focuses the mind on the here and now. The future happens to other people.

Disillusion can set in quite quickly for those who launch themselves into a career in professional rugby. Along the journey, lots of their contemporaries will have fallen away, and more will before the careers of the most successful are out. In many ways, it pays for that reckoning to occur sooner rather than later, because the longer a player hangs on or, perhaps worse still, thrives in the professional environment the greater the readjustment when it ends. To see out a career in professional sport requires a peculiar strength of character, as well as the obvious genetic gifts, just to negotiate that transition from local hero to foot soldier, let alone to maintain one's position. Rugby, with its maddening rituals of violence and pain, represents a particularly vigorous challenge to its wannabes. That focus on the here and now intensifies, the next match, the next training session, the next minutely timetabled day. It is easy to be lulled into thinking the cycle of tomorrows will go on for ever. The cruellest cut is when that next match, session or day springs a sudden end to it all. And the rest of a young player's life gapes before them. Even when a player retires on their own terms the future looms ominously.

Rugby was not so good at dealing with the question of a player's place in the wider world. When launched into its belated, dizzying leap to professionalism, the sport had more immediate concerns. The small matter of what happened to players after they left the payroll was some way down the list of priorities, as was the question of developing them as humans rather than solely as players. In the amateur culture, many of the elite honed their skills at a university. Beyond that, everyone led alternative lives in the day job. Rugby's insistence its players leave all of that behind in the early years of professionalism became almost a badge of honour. The first 10 to 15 years after 1995, elite rugby was all about rugby. Thus the sport might prove itself really, really professional.

Eventually, the realisation dawned that better people make better players, happier even. Now all clubs and unions incorporate the provision, or at least encouragement, of extra-curricular life skills into the services they provide their playing staff. In the late 1990s, groups of players formed unions across the world, in Australia, France, South Africa, New Zealand, which have since grown into ever-more-coherent voices. The RPA in England began life as a one-man band in 1998, set up by Damian Hopley when injury forced him into early retirement and he realised there was no support network for people in his position. Now the RPA is an operation of dozens of employees trying to raise awareness among its membership that there is a life beyond the tackle shields – and that it will summon them all eventually.

Some embrace the message more readily than others. Rugby players have hours of downtime throughout the week, but they are invariably exhausted. The Xbox controls perched coquettishly on the arm of the sofa amount to a more appealing proposition than laptops, emails or work experience. The players are young, fit and powerful, in the shape of their lives. And the purpose of those lives, it might be all too tempting to imagine, has been to convey each player to this, a career in rugby, their raison d'être.

That raison d'être will expire for each within a decade or so. This transition, the last, has always been the hardest for any sportsperson. Elite rugby players have at least had the mitigation in the past of a full life beyond the sport. In this respect, rugby has no more than joined other professional sports in confining its participants to an institutionalised existence of which it is harder to take one's leave. It might be stretching an argument to claim that rugby players face a harder transition than other athletes in professional sport, but there are elements that make the drop out of a career in rugby particularly vertiginous.

Most can be attributed to the physical intensity of the sport. Careers are relatively short, and that gladiatorial quality of the experience when set in a team environment renders each player more dependent on the camaraderie of team-mates than often they realise. The first observation of players just retired is how alone they feel, banished from the company of team-mates that might have been their milieu for 20 or 30 years. Another is the dissolution of a regimen by which to live their lives. Even the most grounded, the best prepared can strike out into a new job after rugby, come home at the end of the day and realise they have not eaten. Why? Because nobody has told them to.

Rugby players find themselves in a dangerous no-man's-land with regard to money. The salaries of elite players, particularly in Europe, may not set them up for life, but they are now high enough to create unrealistic expectations when it comes to the wider world. A lot of players think everyone is on a hundred grand. No one likes taking a pay cut, but unless they can land one of those much-sought-after jobs in the media or on the coaching staff most professional rugby players will do just that when they fall off the end of the conveyor belt. Some take jobs they are ill-suited to, usually desk-bound, purely to mitigate the drop in income. The contrast is jarring. Lots of them do not last. In a 2018 survey by the RPA, nearly half of more than 200 retired players (46 per cent internationals, 77 per cent with more than a hundred first-class appearances behind them) fell into financial problems in the first five years of their lives after rugby. Troubling questions regarding self-worth and a person's place in the world inevitably follow, and in the worst cases coalesce into serious conditions. Professional athletes are driven by a ferocious competitive desire, which sits side by side with unforgiving perfectionism. That is how they get to where they are. When it is all over, that energy can turn on them viciously, the very perfectionism that made them the players they were suddenly a scourge of their souls. In the RPA survey, 62 per cent of players had suffered some sort of mental-health issue, with only 48 per cent feeling in control of their lives within two years of retirement.

Control of one's life is, of course, an elusive condition for many in the wider world, young and old. The irony is rugby players, at just the most vulnerable age, do have control over their lives – or rugby has control over them. Then, suddenly, they are turned out into the chaos – and for most it is an expulsion without argument. Only 29 per cent of the RPA survey respondents were able to retire on their own terms.

The question of transition beyond playing career is a live issue for rugby, but not unique to it. There are other sports and professions whose participants face similar issues, so rugby does not want for models of best practice. The resources available to players negotiating life after rugby are more extensive now than they have ever been, but players need to be open to seeking help, which is not a mindset that comes naturally to a lot of them. That is changing, too, in line with the wider world, as the 'OK not to be OK' movement gains traction. More and more former rugby players are helping others just by going public about their struggles with depression and anxiety. They are helping current players as well, for whom the 'dream job' so often proves to be something other than that. Again, the adjustment is disconcerting when a youngster who has grown up as a local hero accustomed to winning becomes an occasional player in a team, say, battling against relegation. When a player has a history of winning, is paid to win and spends night and day in slavish pursuit of the win, then starts to lose on a regular basis, the dream job can close in like a prison.

Which is professional sport for you, those of the Dan Cole school would assert. Rugby players are well used to pain and adversity. Different personalities will respond to the trials differently, and the attitudes of each, whether stoical or demonstrative, should be equally respected and accommodated.

But for all the conflicting opinions about their workload and wellness, for all the worries over their fitness for a life after the games, there is a greater fear that has gathered over the past few years. It is terrifying because it is so unknowable, its threat so diffuse and open-ended. A player can negotiate a career in rugby and the transition to a life beyond, but this menace may yet descend years after the others have passed.

There is no way to avoid concussion in rugby as currently played. And no one ever knows if the effects of concussion are done with them.

XIII

Concussion

Rugby and American football share a relationship. Of all the team sports, they, along with league, are the most obviously brutal, the most obviously dangerous. Rugby may have begotten American football, but where American football now leads rugby fears to follow. Both sports have suffered their fair share of crises over the years. None has been as sinister or threatening as that hanging over them in the first decades of the 21st century. Direct fatalities can be seen and counted, as can traumatic injuries. With them we can gauge risk. The spectre of concussion, however, has never been so easy to apprehend.

For decades, it was viewed as a source of pride. To labour on after a blow to the head was evidence of commitment to the cause, of uncommon bravery, the more blood the better to prove your worth, a brief stagger nothing other than notice of the gravity of the blow ridden. Any damage to the circuitry of the brain was purely notional, a bruise to be suffered like any other. Out of sight, out of mind. (If only.) On, on with the fray! 'Jeez, you're a tough bastard!' – commendation comes no higher in a contact sport; 'Get back out there! It's just a knock!' – castigation no more bracing. It had been like that for more than a hundred years.

In 2013, a class-action lawsuit brought against the NFL by thousands of former players suffering from long-term effects associated with concussion was successful. The NFL agreed a $765 million package, part towards further research, mainly as compensation to its former employees. But there is no upper limit to the compensation package. Already, as more and more players come forward, it is projected to soar past a billion dollars. Suddenly, concussion has been transformed from a vague, unknowable background word scooping up all episodes of head injury without blemish into a menace that might not only ruin a player's life but bring down a sport.

The link between American football and chronic traumatic encephalopathy (CTE), a neurodegenerative disease caused by repeated head injuries, although yet to be proven, is becoming ever more established. That debate will continue, but the NFL's decision demonstrates that it failed the players in its duty of care. Thus two questions face the sport. Just how much damage does it inflict on the brain? And how best can its authorities look after those players who suffer from concussion? These same questions apply to rugby.

The second is easier to answer. If the second question were the only one, rugby may already be able to carry on with a clear conscience. Implementing the answer has proved far from straightforward, but the answer has been clear for some time and has been arrived at, actually, with quite impressive speed, despite the long history of a very masculine culture. In the space of a few years, rugby has completely transformed that culture with regard to concussion.

There is no doubt the lawsuit in American football proved a significant wake-up. Again, rugby's unique set of circumstances has left it vulnerable to the explosion of claim and counterclaim that has burst over contact sports in the early decades of the 21st century.

A hundred years of amateurism kept rugby's profile low. Not only were the players relatively underpowered physically, the sport was absolved of scrutiny, or just of the call for scrutiny. In short, no one really bothered themselves with what little old rugby got up to. American football's history with concussion, on the other hand, has been more vivid.

For decades the sport has wrestled with the science. In 1994, the NFL set up the Mild Traumatic Brain Injury Committee, a first public acknowledgement of a problem that had long been building. Then that committee set about proclaiming there was nothing to see here and smothering any attempts to prove otherwise. As the old century gave way to the new, increasing pressure was applied from science. The American Academy of Neurology issued policy directives and guidelines on concussion in 1997. And yet it was not until 2001 that science would settle on a unifying definition of concussion, despite all its well-known features. As the most unknowable organ of the body, the brain remained pliable and grey, to be argued over for as long as vested interests could find give.

In 2005, a paper was published announcing the first confirmed finding of CTE in a footballer's brain, that of Mike Webster, whose latter years before his death from a heart attack in 2002 had been plagued by dementia. Soon more cases were presenting themselves; still the authorities of the NFL held out against the mounting evidence. The lawsuits began to pile up, until the NFL was forced into their settlement and a more transparent approach to the relationship between their sport and brain damage.

By the time matters came to a head for the NFL in 2013, rugby was sitting up straight and paying attention. Rugby has quickly appreciated the need to respond to similar questions gathering over its own sport. That realisation did not dawn quickly enough in American football's case to avoid its devastating lawsuit. Rugby hopes it has ridden the first warnings without similar.

The importance of changing the culture of these sports is not to be underestimated, but neither is the size of the task. This is not to condemn certain factions within them for intransigence; it is merely to acknowledge the way the world goes. No culture of any consequence has been changed as if by the flick of a switch. Some of the most obvious injustices in a civilised world have required hundreds of years of campaign and revolution to overturn. The culture of a sport that is itself only a century and a half old ought to prove more receptive to change – and so it has proved. On the issue of concussion, rugby has not changed as quickly as many would like, but in much less than a decade attitudes have been transformed, and the slower wheels of process follow on.

To claim that rugby had no dialogue in the amateur era regarding concussion would be disingenuous, but the urgency of the matter never registered among the playing population. In the 1990s, the International Rugby Board issued a policy that made mandatory a three-week stand-down period for any concussed player. Rarely was it respected as much more than a technicality to be circumvented. As an amateur sport, it was up to the player to decide if any risk of playing, let alone soldiering on after a blow to the head, was worth it. Some people jump out of planes for fun, some people ride motorbikes, some play rugby. That was more or less the sum total of the philosophy on the subject until the mid-1990s.

The dynamic starts to change in a professional environment. Not only do profile and scrutiny increase, but the field of play becomes a workplace, the clubs and unions employers. American football came to terms with its duty of care too slowly for a court of law to condone. Rugby is in position to benefit from the lesson handed down.

Against the backdrop of events in America, the death in 2011 of a schoolboy in Northern Ireland, Ben Robinson, might be said to have brought home the gravity of rugby's own problem. The tale of the 14-year-old's last game, watched by his mum, who remained troubled throughout, long before the harrowing last few moments, was relayed in detail by the *Guardian* in 2013. To feel the emotions of the incident, even via second-hand words on a page, is to feel uneasy about any sport that creates the possibility of such a scenario unfolding. It is a reminder that for all the decimalised rates per 100,000 that we compare and contrast, each statistic has a heart-rending story behind it. If we could somehow feel unmediated the full force of each one, would sport have any chance at all?

As often as not, the news from those in the darkest of places, whether bereaved or suffering the repercussions of a catastrophic injury, is that the sport, in our case rugby, still feels a worthwhile pursuit, for all the agonies it has visited on them. Ben's parents have campaigned relentlessly to improve knowledge surrounding brain injuries in rugby. In 2013, the coroner's verdict was that Ben had died of second-impact syndrome, a rare condition whereby a victim suffers a second blow to the head while already concussed by a previous one. This is thought to trigger a catastrophic dysfunction in the body's regulation of blood supply to the brain. Again, science is not ready yet to pronounce boldly on so rare and poorly understood a syndrome, but it is reckoned to be fatal in around 50 per cent of cases, and the vast majority of those who survive suffer permanent disability.

In May 2013, four months before the coroner's verdict in the Ben Robinson case, Rowan Stringer, a 17-year-old schoolgirl in Canada, died from a blow to the head in a third match in six days, having suffered the symptoms of concussion from other blows taken in the previous two. The state of Ontario has passed 'Rowan's Law' in response, a protocol governing the management of concussion across all youth sports. Every state in America has similar. The rugby unions of New Zealand, Australia and South Africa had introduced injury management and education programmes the decade before, which have since increased their emphasis on concussion. In 2013, the RFU launched its 'Don't Be a Headcase' campaign in community rugby, which together with the work of the Robinsons helped to deepen in the public consciousness what had been only a gradual change in culture.

Other influences helped. High-profile examples of players returning to the field of play started to turn the stomach, when they might have been celebrated only years earlier. George Smith for Australia in the third Lions Test of 2013 was an early example; a bloodied and punch-drunk Florian Fritz seemingly ordered back on by the Toulouse coach a year later was another. Former Scotland international Rory Lamont, who claimed to have been knocked out at least 10 times himself in his playing career, came out in protest against a culture that saw players deliberately try to cheat what protocols had been put in place. In 2012, Dr Barry O'Driscoll had resigned from the IRB over its early attempts to institute what he felt was an inadequate five-minute pitch-side test for concussions, the very one Smith would pass in 2013. O'Driscoll has warned rugby of a civil action, à la the NFL, waiting to happen. Meanwhile, a sustained campaign in the media, led by the sports journalist Sam Peters in the northern hemisphere, Peter FitzSimons in the south, kept up the pressure urgently.

As evidenced by the strife at almost every turn, rugby cannot be said to have changed its ways overnight, to have held up its hands and accepted the scale of the problem at once, but for a culture so established and bullish to shift so completely on this point in less than a decade is an impressive result and a tribute to all those who made it happen. Players with head injuries now are far swifter to leave the field, far less likely to return and not allowed to return at all if knocked out for even a second. Cases of the latter have been missed – to much criticism – but one must assume in good faith. There may be those who instinctively adhere to the tenets of the old school, many of the benefits of which remain valid today, but most are sold on the sanctity of the new ways regarding concussion. And those who might not be are in a vanishing, and necessarily silent, minority.

Similarly, the education of players, at all levels, on the dangers of 'toughing out' a head injury is pervasive. It would be almost impossible now for a player, from international to part-time social, not to be aware of the shift in attitude. The reluctance of even the most hardened international, meanwhile, to return to play before feeling absolutely right after a concussion, however many weeks or even months that may be, is not only an example regularly set but one almost unheard of before 2015. At the end of the 20th century it simply did not happen.

Rugby's recognition and treatment of concussion is unrecognisable. The standard of care, after a few missteps, is irreproachable in terms of attitude, which is not to say there are never any procedural mistakes. That standard is set to rise, too, as science unfolds to a point where certainties might be arrived at, further improving the prospects for a career in the sport to be navigated with relative safety. The imminent availability of a test for biomarkers, in saliva, blood or urine, which would establish without argument the diagnosis of a concussion, is a significant breakthrough. With that, there could be no further mistakes or abuses of the system, at any level, by coaches or players pumped up on the adrenaline of competition. Further down the line, the facility for a community player to drop off a saliva or blood sample at the chemist the day after a match would have saved the life of Rowan Stringer. Further again, to be able to test a sample at pitch-side would have saved Ben Robinson. And others like them.

If a sport's responsibility ends with the proper recognition and treatment of concussion, rugby could be said to be in a healthy place. One might even argue that those years of amateurism have helped here, placing rugby in a position to watch the mistakes made by a similar collision sport with a longer history of professionalism and to avoid making the same. But from here the questions become more complicated.

Establishing appropriate standards of care, no matter the affront they might represent to the old ways, is relatively easy. When it comes, though, to just how dangerous a sport is to its participants' long-term health, the answers become more elusive, subject to argument and counterargument for as long as there is doubt, for as long as there is a sport, an industry, a way of life to preserve.

And if it can be determined there is a threat on the field, what next? Can it be mitigated? Should it be? How much is enough? These are questions that might threaten a sport's very existence.

There is a school of thought in America, more mainstream than one might think, that football has had its day. Influential voices are calling quite coherently for an end to it, the worth of American football as entertainment industry and cultural pillar no longer justification for the suicides, murders and dementia it seems likely are elicited in some by a life in the sport. The anger over the way the authorities tried for so long to deny the scale of the brain-injury crisis has created much ill-feeling, but far more fundamental a problem is the uneasiness, indeed the revulsion, many feel at each and every spectacular collision, now that even just a theory about the repercussions of such violence is beginning to materialise.

Malcolm Gladwell, the bestselling author, is in no doubt that American football is more trouble than it is worth. Even Michael Lewis, fellow bestseller, has his concerns. Lewis is steeped in sport. One of his books is a treatise on American football. Others, of course, have centred on the rise and fall of money markets. He professes to dislike making predictions, but when pushed in an interview in 2017 on what his tip was for the next 'big short' he ended up citing American football. Meanwhile, the steady trickle of horrifying ends met by former players, desperate and afraid, serves only to reinforce the association between the sport and a future life of problems, no matter what the science whispers in its tentative and technical language about the need for further research.

The world wants clear answers to the many questions now, but science does not work like that. Evidence is gathered meticulously over many years and studies, which are themselves studied and cross-referenced as yet more evidence is dissected – and on and on, inching towards consensuses, arriving at the truth by agonising degrees, each rigorously tested and peer-reviewed, while an impatient world screams its fears and arrives at its own various conclusions.

Even science turns up findings that bring 'good news' and 'bad' from paper to paper. One study in 2016, for example, found that among a sample of retired American footballers with more than five years in the professional game, from the 1950s to 1980s, there were fewer than half the suicides that would be expected among a comparable demographic in the US at large and a significantly reduced mortality rate in general. A year later, to much publicity, results were published of a study of the brains of 202 deceased subjects, all of whom had played the sport, their brains donated to science by their families. They found CTE in 87 per cent of them, and in 110 out of the 111 brains of those who had played professionally. There were more suicides among this small sample than in the 3,439 cases reviewed in the 2016 study. The scientists protested long and hard about the selection bias of the sample – a family was likelier to submit a player's brain if they thought he might have been suffering from CTE before he died – but the dialogue between media, science, sport and the public, not to mention the players, is impossible to control.

The drama that has played out has shaken American football, not just financially but existentially. The multiple clashes of skulls and interests have captured the imagination of even Hollywood. The movie *Concussion* (2015) retells the story of the pathologist Dr Bennet Omalu, a Nigerian immigrant, who originally discovered CTE in Mike Webster's brain and stood against the might of the NFL. The ever-more-dramatic tales of fallen heroes committing suicide in such a way as to preserve their brains for further study have a feeling of high tragedy about them, each a final, noble gesture to the sport that raised them up and brought them down, each a gesture that may yet bring down the sport itself.

Meanwhile, that multibillion-dollar industry will necessarily lean as hard against the prevailing scientific direction for as long as it is threatened by the findings, for as long as it thinks it can find room for doubt. Hard scientific fact cannot be denied once established, but there are precious few such certainties over the brain. The ethical questions are complicated. At the ever-raging interface between finance and welfare, the lines are more clearly drawn on brain injury than anywhere. To betray one's employees by suppressing, in the name of commerce, information about an unarguable threat would be to step into criminality. But the question of whether a sport can or should continue in the face of mounting evidence is more complicated, as is that of the degree to which it should fight to clear its reputation. If science were ever to establish – and it 'feels', albeit in our age of media and emotion, as if that time is nigh – that even a small fraction of people who play American football are guaranteed to develop a neurodegenerative disease that will kill them because they played, what then? Could a civilised society countenance the ongoing indulgence of such a pastime? American football is not just an industry, although its status as employer of hundreds of thousands gives it some moral weight there. More than that, it looms large in the American story, brings joy and direction to millions, the benefits of participation in any team sport well known and loudly proclaimed. At what point would the price for all of that, borne by a cohort of doomed heroes, become too great?

And then there is the question of the children. Adults may be big and ugly enough to choose to take on such a risk – and society may decide they should remain free to do so – but children, the vast majority of American football players, and at least a majority of rugby players, are not old enough to make an informed decision. In a debate such as this the smoking/drinking argument is usually trotted out. To have those pleasures taken away from us would amount to an infringement of rights, however dangerous they could be to our long-term health. Freedom of choice tends to trump all arguments – but not when it comes to the children. Findings from studies in 2015 and 2018 suggest a correlation between the age of first exposure to tackle football and the age at which first symptoms of cognitive decline set in, the developing human brain all the more vulnerable before the age of 14. Playing numbers, despite the tentative nature of the research, are falling among America's children, as parents turn away from the sport. The pressure to take steps in junior American football, at least, is building. But if tackling were banned for children, a sudden disconnect would be created in the bloodline servicing the senior game. Players would almost have to relearn the sport when they became adults, which may bring its own dangers.

Rugby looks on in horror. The same sort of issues apply, if on a less dramatic scale. At the moment, the sport feels as if it is insulated against the worst of the CTE crisis faced by the NFL. The absence of helmets, paradoxically, may yet prove a saving grace. The helmets and the padding in American football, it is hypothesised, have lent their wearers over the years a false sense of security, transforming the nature of the sport. Rugby has had to adapt its techniques and laws to allow for the fact that its players, bar the odd stretch of tape here or fabric there, enter the fray without protection. Hayden Smith, who played professional rugby and American football, reckons a player in rugby might suffer as many head-on-head, front-on collisions in a season as a lineman would in a single match of American football. The very dynamic of the latter – short and explosive with barely any aerobic component – ratchets up the forces. In gridiron's scrimmage, of which there might be 60 or 70 for a player to negotiate a game, helmets collide with great power. These helmets are designed to prevent skull fractures, but they do not protect against concussion, or the bang-bang-bang of sub-concussive blows, which may not register as concussions but take their toll all the same. The brain is shaken and stressed by any collision of the head, whether encased in a helmet or not. The active use of the helmet as weapon that had evolved in American football has lessened the importance of tackle technique, on which rugby is so particular, even if there are signs of a renaissance now. This is where rugby has placed much hope – that, when it comes to damage to the brain in team sports, American football has been in a class of its own.

But nobody knows. Progress is being made towards diagnosing CTE pathology in the brains of the living. All the research so far, though, has been possible only on brains post-mortem. And nobody knows for sure whether the CTE discovered was directly responsible for any dementia suffered while the subject was alive, or whether it is merely the residue of brain injury, existing in parallel. These unknowns – the state of the brains of living subjects and the causality of any clinical illnesses – hang over collision sport at this point in history. The worst-case scenario would be unification of the various strands, an unarguable chain of cause and effect that links these sports to an early grave for some of their participants. The next question would be just how many are likely to be affected. Again, nobody knows why some people develop CTE and others seem not to.

Early signs are not encouraging. Following the 2017 study that found CTE in 110 of 111 brains of deceased former NFL players, others in 2018 tried to estimate the extent of the problem. One extrapolated a minimum 1 per cent chance that an NFL player will develop CTE, based on the highly unlikely assumption that the 110 brains represented all the cases of CTE among the 10,000 players from the era in question (1963–2008). In reality, the chance will be higher. Another study in the same year put the starting rate at 10 per cent, based on the number of deaths (1,142) of former players from the same timeframe of the 111 of the sample (2008–16). Again, the real figure is likely to be higher. The NFL itself acknowledged during its lawsuit that 28 per cent of former players would develop conditions eligible for compensation, a figure it was hoped would represent an overestimate, based on the medical conditions reported by the 5,000 plaintiffs. Their estimates, in fact, look shy, at least in terms of the sum total. Two years after the settlement date of January 2017, the NFL's bill for compensating former players had shot through $600 million, 779 claims successful following 8,295 medical assessments of nearly 21,000 former players or representatives registered with the programme. The initial estimate of $1 billion for the NFL's total compensation pay-out over the 65 years of the agreement has been upgraded to $1.4 billion.

These developments are of grave concern for any comparable collision sport. Rugby's fear is that it is no more than a little behind American football on the same narrative arc. Far from putting its players' brains through lesser stresses, is rugby merely following the path of a sport that has been professional for far longer? Indeed, there are indications that rugby is at least as bad, if a simple comparison of concussion incidence is the measure.

As ever, there are complications to such an approach. The standard adopted by the injury audits in English rugby is to rate injury incidence per 1,000 player hours, where a player hour is an hour spent on the field by a single player. A thousand player hours amounts to 25 games (80/60 × 15 × 2 × 25 = 1,000). In America, the preference is to rate injury per 1,000 athlete exposures, i.e. the number of times an athlete plays in a match. Player hours feel less appropriate for American football because, although each gridiron match is 60 minutes, the whole event lasts more than three hours and contains an average of 11 minutes of action. And players come and go throughout. The athlete-exposure approach, though, is a little flattering, as each team contains 46 of those coming-and-going players, which means 1,000 athlete exposures amounts to just shy of 11 games and, in some cases, not an awful lot of exposure.

A more appropriate comparison might be the number of concussions per match. The accompanying table shows the incidence of reported concussions in the NFL regular season from 2012 to 2018 and the equivalent figures in the Premiership, as released by the respective organisations, alongside the rate of incidence per match.

		NFL			Premiership		
		Concussions	rate per match		Concussions	rate per match	
2012		173	0.68		28	0.21	*
2013		148	0.58		35	0.26	
2014		115	0.45		62	0.46	
2015		183	0.71		70	0.52	
2016		166	0.65		92	0.68	
2017		178	0.70		120	0.89	
2018		127	0.50		98	0.73	
Average			0.61			0.53	

* figure not available but estimated from rate across all competitions (Premiership, Europe and Cup)

It can be seen that the NFL has reported a higher rate for longer, but that the Premiership's has climbed dramatically in recent years from 0.21 in 2011–12 to a peak of 0.89 in the 2016–17 season, higher than American football has ever attained. The steepness of this rise in incidence is almost certainly a result primarily of improved awareness and treatment, that radical change in rugby's culture, but it is equally likely that the fundamental dynamics of the sport have rendered the field at the highest level a riskier arena for brain injury. Professional rugby today by this measure cannot claim to have less of a problem than American football.

This measure too, though, is unsatisfactory. The standards in reporting of concussion are not stable, as seen by rugby's recent experience, and there is no way of comparing them across sports. Then there is the different nature of the sports themselves. American football has 22 players on the field at any one time; rugby has 30. American football condenses its action into, typically, 11 minutes; rugby into between 35 and 45. An American football team shares its burden across a squad of 46; a rugby team across 23. Clearly, one sport is more intense, the other more attritional. American football is a much more dangerous sport on a minute-by-minute-of-action basis, but a rugby player suffers a much longer exposure to their sport's lesser risk. How does that affect the overall risk to an individual? Do the differing dynamics somehow change the nature of the brain injuries?

There is every danger we are quibbling over details. Unless it can be proven that American football subjected its professionals to freak stresses of the brain in the second half of the 20th century and first decade of the 21st, that the problem has now been addressed by law and equipment changes, that it will now go quietly away, the chances are that rugby bears similar health risks.

The concussion incidences of the two sports in the second decade of the 21st century seem comparable, but science has raised just as many questions over the long-term effects of sub-concussive blows, the ones that do not register as concussion events. There is no escaping these – and lots of them – in any collision sport. Even the most perfectly executed tackle involves the sudden deceleration of the player, and thus the brain, from up to 20 mph to zero. As the picture changes with each announcement of a new study, rugby's latest preoccupation is with unregistered blows to the head. There is even a theory, elucidated by a 2018 study in America, which subjected mice to head-impact injuries and blast exposure, that it is the blow itself, and not any concussion caused by it, that causes CTE. A player might not need to be concussed at all to be at risk of problems in later life. The passing of this hypothesis into science and/or public consciousness would be quite the disaster for collision sports. For players to be quietly damaging their brains without a diagnosis . . .

Dr O'Driscoll's warning of a class-action lawsuit remains live. Science is investigating the health in middle age of rugby's last generation of amateur players. There is a perfectly coherent case to be made for compensation for any of those found to be struggling. They may have played for the love of it, but much revenue was reaped on the back of their efforts. The great cathedrals of British rugby, for example, now such gleaming assets, were built and upgraded through the battery of unpaid men. But it is when the first generation of paid employees reaches a certain age that we will start to know. Not only have their brains been subjected to more stress and trauma through the higher intensity of training and matches, they will have become, as paid workers, eligible for the type of compensation the NFL is paying out, which is essentially that for industrial injury, akin to asbestos poisoning or black lung or Grandpa Cole's broken back.

It could also be argued, though, that these players are well paid and taking the employment because it is desirable and they want it. Their lot is hardly comparable to that of the miner on low wages, working in the pit because he has to, for the benefit of an industry that makes (or has made) huge profits from his labour. Professional rugby players are meticulously looked after, each one an asset of some value to their clubs, even if they are in exchange placed in positions of extreme duress that might finish the rest of us. They hardly seem emasculated by the experience. To look into the face, however battered from the day's match, of a rugby player in the prime of life, is to struggle to imagine them bent and afraid at old age. They do have a look of the invincible about them. How ridiculous, it might feel, to think about their possible incapacitation at some unknowable time in the future. No wonder they give it not a second thought. Next match, next session. They may be made to sit through concussion seminars explaining the possible dangers, but it is a moot point how many really engage with the information. Is it reasonable even to expect them to? Young people just don't. Whose fault is that: the players for not thinking as if they were 20 years older, or the clubs for not convincing them to? And then, when they come out the other side, retired and with full perspective, practically every single one of them swears they would do it all again, whatever ills they may have suffered, whatever may still await. What does all of this do for any debate about their right to compensation?

As long as they know. As long as they are properly looked after. Personal choice.

It is with the children, though, that this argument breaks down. Rugby is unlikely ever to face some sort of winding-up order over the inherent threat to its participants. As established, in the grand scheme of dangers to a person's life, it still ranks lowly, even when compared to some other sports, however reliable and pervasive the dissemination of each tragic tale by the era's media facilities. But that does not render the sport immune to a gradual withering from the bottom up, a process of which there is already evidence. The PR directive never lets up and, because of those evolving media facilities, it becomes more intense the further we journey into the future. One perception guaranteed to fail the test is endangerment of the children. Rugby has always been serviced by the attitude that painful physical exercise in the company of team-mates forges character, is good for the soul, and so on. Children are still sent out onto windswept fields in the spirit of such a culture. Some hate it and will give up as soon as they can. Others discover their love for the sport through those formative experiences and find their lives enriched by it. May that culture be forever perpetuated. But it is, again, a culture of the 'old school', firmly in the no-nonsense, get-on-with-it movement of human endeavour – and thus very much at odds with some of the energies increasingly shaping the 21st century, one of the derivatives of which is a fastidious culture of health and safety, another the propensity to sue.

The idea of an end to tackling in youth rugby has been broached. In 2016, an open letter to ministers in Britain and Ireland, signed by 70 doctors and academics, called for a ban on tackling in schools. The reaction was uproar in the rugby community and beyond. For now, the old arguments regarding the cultivation of character and the newer movement against obesity are carrying the day, as is the very pertinent point that formative years are the crucial ones for inculcating sound techniques that might avert problems in adult rugby, when the danger quotient rises. If rugby holds back its players from contact until, say, the age of 18, then suddenly unleashes them on each other, the consequence would surely be an even more dangerous game for adults than we have now.

Tackling in junior rugby is here to stay for the time being but, as ever, we can look to American football for an inkling of what the future may hold. Here, it is not just the boffins who are calling for reform. Heavyweight names from gridiron's storied past – players of great legend, some of them with minds failing, others with old friends thus afflicted – are calling for an end to tackling before the age of 14 or publicly opting their children out of it. In a national poll, 53 per cent of Americans felt tackle football was not safe for kids before high school. The problem here, for both sports, is not the disruption to schoolwork of the odd broken arm or dislocated shoulder; it is that shadowy threat to a later life of lucidity. The harrowing tales of fallen players provide a compelling backdrop. Some of those stars of yore are now starting to say, we *wouldn't* do it all again. That is a reckoning of some gravitas for a sport, when its very heroes start to turn against it.

Science wades in with further details. The head of the child is anchored less surely than that of the adult by underdeveloped muscles in the shoulder and neck. The volume of the brain does not peak until the mid-to-late teens, while the neurocranium, the cavity in which it sits, is fully grown by the age of eight. The net result is greater scope for the shaking and stressing of a child's brain in contact. Should we really expose our children to such dangers for the sake of a few extra years of character building?

This is a debate with some mileage yet – and it will all hinge on the science. The implications of collision sport for people of all ages are continually being investigated. The studies will return their conclusions in time, and a message materialise. Already it feels unlikely the verdict will read, 'As you were, chaps. Everything's absolutely fine.'

Which is a serious problem in the struggle for people's engagement. Confronted with it, rugby now focuses its frantically turning mind on how to alleviate the stresses on the body that are inherent to playing the game, or even how just to be seen to. Due care and attention post-injury are achievable. That is a box rugby might be said to have ticked already. The issue of the sport's inherent danger is harder but will be answered eventually by science.

In the meantime, the authorities wrestle with the problem of preventing injury in the first place. And that could prove the most intractable of them all.

Before anyone ventures down this road, it is worth pausing to consider what its logical end point is. Rugby's roots – the depth of love for the sport, be it of rheumy-eyed sentimentalists or those feral 10-year-olds desperate to smash into each other – are surely strong enough to prevent arrival at that ultimate terminus, but be under no illusion. The only way to make rugby safe is to stop playing it. Or – and many would contend it amounts to the same thing – to remove its collision element altogether.

The latter is not such an absurd idea. Touch rugby is already a thriving participation sport, brilliant to play, particularly if you number yourself among rugby's quick and skilful types. Not so brilliant to watch, though. Lacking a certain edge. It is difficult to imagine Ellis Park bursting at the turnstiles for a game of touch.

Rugby is currently of a mind to try to change some of the dynamics of what happens on the pitch. Perhaps we should not be uneasy about this at all. There is ample precedent. Indeed, has there ever been a sport so given to meddling with its own laws? Most changes are a response to some perceived deficiency, or an undesirable development, the maintenance of an ever-mutating organism. Some are motivated by a desire to simplify, some to close loopholes, some for as subjective a consideration as aesthetics, to make the game more 'attractive'.

But some, too, have been for safety reasons, from the ban on hacking right back at the start to the more recent prohibition on kicking the ball in a ruck. The latter modification was easy to decide on, the removal of a peripheral aspect of the game that had no obvious upside and plenty of downside in the risk of a boot connecting not with the ball at all but someone's head. The former was met with more resistance, some believing that hacking was somehow integral to the sport's vigorous nature. Both amounted to the neat, clean removal of an aspect perceived to be undesirable.

In the campaign to address the gathering concern about rugby's threat to a player's brain, there is only one area to target. In a 2017 study by World Rugby, it was found that 76 per cent of 611 incidents that led to head-injury assessments over a three-year period occurred at tackles. If rugby wants to lower the incidence of concussion, the tackle is the overwhelming priority.

The trouble is, this is not some superfluous quirk in the system that needs ironing out. This is the very bedrock of the sport as we know it, or at the very least its second most common event. There can be no indicator more illustrative of the shifting dynamic of rugby and of its relationship with head injury than that exploding tackle count. Although the studies of the brain health of players from the amateur era are to be welcomed, we can almost discard the results as irrelevant to current concerns, so radical the transformation of the sport in the professional era. From around 100 tackles per match as late as the early 1990s to more than 300 today, the only event more common now is the pass – and even that is a close-run thing. Indeed, in the 2019 Six Nations tackles outnumbered passes for the first time. For every pass a player receives, they can be confident a tackle will follow hard on its heels. That simply was not the case in the amateur era. Add in the transformation in power of those involved in the tackle, on both sides, and it is easy to see why there is a problem.

This one cannot be addressed by a simple lift-and-remove

procedure. To do away with a sport's second most common event is to change the sport into something else. So rugby, in its desperation to do something, is forced into tinkering, an attempt to change by degrees, to try to lessen the impact on the brain of the imperative to tackle. Which means rugby is on that path whose logical end is the end of rugby. These are first steps not to be taken lightly, but they are necessary if the aim is to reduce, somehow, the incidence and/or severity of blows to the head.

To step out onto this path does not, of course, make reaching its logical end inevitable. The scrum, which the tackle has replaced as rugby's most dangerous event, has shown that evolution is possible without extinction. A lessening of the forces exerted there has been arrived at in recent years by judicious alterations to the sequence of engagement without any fundamental alteration to the principles that make the scrum the scrum. It has helped, too, that the scrum has become so rare, relative to its ubiquity in the amateur era. The very dynamics that have led to this diminishment of rugby's signature set piece are those that have led to the present head-injury crisis – and they boil down, as ever, to professionalism, the erosion of incompetence. The players, in short, are much better now. They drop the ball less, aided in no small part by improvements in equipment, not least in the balls themselves. They are not allowed to settle for the messy irresolution of the ruck and the maul of the amateur era, to wait in a tangle of writhing limbs for the referee to signal scrum to the team moving forward. Taken together, these factors have precipitated a reduction in the number of scrums and an improvement in the safety of those that do take place. Thus, the scrum has settled into a less threatening pose, almost by accident.

It is harder to foresee a similar settlement for the tackle. There are just too many of them, and they happen so quickly. They are not set pieces, entered into step by step, managed by an official. These are the sporting equivalent of cats to herd.

And what is the aim of any alterations to the tackle? Do we have a target result? The danger of trying vaguely to reduce the incidence of concussion is that, however much is achieved, there will always be something else. Before we know it, we might suddenly find ourselves at or near that logical end point, a game without tackling. That may feel an absurd idea now, which it probably is, but it is valid to wonder whether there will come a point when we say, 'That's it. Our work here is done. Rugby is now Safe Enough.'

There are plenty of laws and regulations out there governing a sport's duty of care to its participants, most of them concerning the treatment of injury and recovery, but there is no recognised standard for how 'safe' a sport needs to be. Self-evidently, some are more dangerous than others, which would make problematic the universal application of such a standard. The very aim of boxing, for example, is to inflict concussion on one's opponent. Nobody steps into a ring squeamish about the idea of repeated blows to the head. So any sense that rugby needs to make itself safer comes from within. It is a voluntary measure.

There is a compelling argument that rugby should leave well alone, that no good can come of meddling with such a complicated facet of the game as the tackle. You can – and should – be sued for a breach of the duty of care, but no sport has ever been sued for being too dangerous. The common-law doctrine of *volenti non fit injuria* (to a willing person, injury is not done), the idea that no one who chooses to expose themselves to a known risk can claim for damages suffered as a result, offers a defence for any sport it would be almost impossible for injured players to undo. As long as they knew. As long as they were properly looked after. All of which requires rugby to focus on education; focus on recognising, removing and rehabilitating – or the 'controllables', to borrow one of sport's favourite terms.

There are other measures, although relevant only to the community game. Simple preparatory techniques have been shown to render players at community level more resistant to injury. According to the RFU's audit of injuries in the community game, the profile of injury incidence since 2009, the year the audit began, has followed a similar pattern to the severity of injuries in the Premiership, which is to say there is a sudden spike from the 2016–17 season. Interestingly, the severity of injuries (the number of games missed per injury) in the community game does not seem to be increasing, even if the number of them is, which lends weight to the idea that improved player management is placing upward pressure on the apparent severity of injuries in the elite game.

The good news is that the community game is much safer for its participants than the elite. It is often postulated that, although the increased power of elite players must take its toll, their very fitness for purpose might counteract this effect. In other words, they may be better equipped to dish it out, but so are they able to take it. The figures from the community game would suggest this is not so, that there is no substitute for depowered players as a mitigation against injury. The injury incidence in the community game for the 2016–17 season was a third of that in the Premiership (22.3 per 1,000 player hours, or an injury per team every 2.2 matches), while the incidence of concussion was a seventh (3.0 per 1,000 player hours, or a concussion per team every 16.7 matches).

More encouraging still is what a simple warm-up can achieve. The RFU has put together a programme of exercises, which it has called Activate. These are designed to improve core strength, balance, flexibility and neck muscles. In a controlled experiment, clubs and schools who followed the programme throughout a season were shown to reduce their incidence of concussion by 59 per cent. The schools reduced their incidence of injury in general by 72 per cent, while the clubs reduced their incidence of lower-limb injury by 40 per cent. Although not applicable to the professional game, where conditioning is already maximised, these are encouraging results for the community game, which show what can be achieved in the way of player welfare without so much as a tinkering with the laws.

Other possible measures include new regulations on equipment. There is a coherent lobby in the medical profession who consider rugby's headgear a problem. This is the same argument that attributes so much of American football's problems to the helmet. Headgear in rugby is good for guarding against lacerations and, in rarer cases, skull fracture. It does not help with concussion. There are those, indeed, who believe the opposite. Although difficult to prove, the theory goes that wearing headgear changes behaviour by instilling the wearer with a false sense of security. Players feel emboldened to charge into tackles with less concern for what happens to their heads – or those of their opponents – and they do so mistakenly, with dangerous results. Science may yet supply a solution in the shape of a new generation of headgear that does protect against concussion, but to date this technology does not exist.

In the current environment, fraught with fear and emotion, to try to do something about what happens on the pitch is an almost-irresistible compulsion for any sport that cares about what it can do for its players, which rugby, for all its faults, generally does, and – let's not beat around the bush – about what it can do for its image. Neither should we criticise any adjustments for the sake of the game's image as cynical posturing. World Rugby may not be liable for any danger inherent to its sport, but rugby can certainly lose friends, and therefore participants, if its show product does not find favour with the new culture for health and safety. In the current environment, a high tackle to a player's head is simply a very bad look.

The trouble is, a chest-high smash with the shoulder is still the most valuable defensive ploy in the game. Certainly until recently, they were openly celebrated. Coaches would coach them, players would practise, crowds cheer, television directors replay over and over again from a variety of angles in high-definition super-slow-mo. Come and see what our sport has to offer! Huge collisions such as these! This is the culture of the 'Big Hit!', and rugby, for the majority of the professional era, has loved it.

Now there is the sense of a shift against. More and more people can be heard to grumble, when did the tackle become the hit? The answer is the same as ever – when the game became professional. To watch a match from the amateur era – some of them can be found on the internet – is to be astonished at the way the game once was.

The most obvious difference is the chaos among the forwards, an ongoing melee of jostling pugilists, crucially never more than a few yards from each other. Set pieces are constantly forming and dissolving like the patterns of a kaleidoscope; rucks and mauls are interchangeable; passages rarely extend beyond one or two phases. The next most obvious difference, intimately linked to the chaos among the forwards, is the space and time available to the backs. There is a glaring lack of discernible defensive systems, certainly ones of any urgency. This all changed when the game turned professional. The arrival of the league coach (and player) was transformative.

There need not be any rancour or sense of conspiracy over that. It should come as no surprise that league became the template. League is the sport most closely related to rugby, and it had been professional for a hundred years. One might argue it is no more or less than the sport rugby would have become if it had turned professional in 1895. There are those who argue it is the sport rugby will become now that it has. If a sport is professional, even if not entirely full-time, it develops systems and, yes, skills that the amateurs do not. That is not a reflection of the qualities of either sport, just of what happens when one has a financial imperative and the other does not.

Many lament the game rugby has morphed into since the influence of league. What they are really lamenting is the passing of the amateur way. Those who resent how teams fan out across the pitch in resolute lines, how players no longer commit to the ruck, are asking teams, in effect, to give each other a little more space to do their thing. They are asking for the sport to become less competitive, which is an understandable yearning, but hopelessly unrealistic. It is the same when we bemoan the power of the modern player. What we really want them to do is to become a little less fit, spend less time on the weights, less time on the track; drink more beer, less protein shake. Would they, in short, mind terribly if they just took it all a little less seriously, gave everyone the space to breathe, not least their opponents?

Needless to say, for as long as they are paid, all players and teams will strive to make life as hard as possible for the opposition. Indeed, they do not even need to be paid to follow the same spirit (see the community game). Short of banning midweek training and making them all have a curry and a load of beers the night before a Test match (as used to happen right up until the 1990s) it is hard to see how this yearned-for dialling down of intensity can be achieved.

Absolutely integral to this mindset is the big hit. Just the sound of the phrase is edgier and more 21st-century than that of the quaint old tackle. Big hit. It is televisual, sensational and goes well with an exclamation mark. But it is also tactically unanswerable. The big hit wraps up the ball-carrier, preventing the offload, so dangerous to a regimented defence; it creates the possibility of driving the ball-carrier backwards; it makes opponents think twice in future.

And it looks great. The incentive for a player is irresistible. They will be feted for it, that adrenaline rush of a roaring stadium because of something they did, the validation of team-mates' slaps on the back, the lingering slow-mos of their prowess replayed in living rooms across the country or world, the coach's approbation in the video review next week. No wonder big hits have become the currency of the age, the higher the better.

But not too high. There is a line across a player's shoulders, right at the base of the throat, above which a tackle is illegal. In the amateur era, this threshold was breached quite regularly and the admonishment of a penalty occasionally (far from always) meted out, but generally tackles were aimed at the waist or legs, and there were only ever around a hundred of them in a sport far less powerful and, crucially, slower. In the arms race for that vital edge, the professional era has seen the height of the typical tackle march remorselessly up the body as the culture of the big hit has bitten, so that the upper body of the ball-carrier was being regularly peppered – and less so with the flailing arm of a player beaten, more with the crushing blow of the shoulder. Nor should it be underestimated just how much such a development has been encouraged by a sport pumped up for a couple of decades on its new-found professionalism, its mandate to wow with the ever-more-spectacular.

Then came the concussion crisis. Suddenly, rugby was confronted not only with the mounting evidence of the science of brain injury in collision sport, but a litany of examples in its typical match of blows to or near the head more ferocious and frequent than had ever been witnessed.

The analysts at World Rugby delved deeper into the mechanics of those 611 head-injury incidents, or more specifically of the 464 that were tackles. It was found that 72 per cent of those were suffered by the tackler, which was one surprising finding. Another surprise was that, no matter what the tackler did, the safest posture for everybody was for the ball-carrier to be bent at the waist. Less surprisingly, one of the two exceptions more dangerous for the ball-carrier was when a tackle was illegally high (the other was the relatively rare 'tip' tackle). So when a ball-carrier has their head taken off by a reckless tackler, it is indeed as dangerous as logic insists it must be. Illegally high tackles are 122 times likelier to cause a head injury than legal, which at the very least justifies that most basic of safety laws against head-high tackles. But of the 611 head injuries, only 18 (3 per cent) were the result of a tackle deemed illegally high, so rugby's problem with head injury extends rather further than that.

Plenty of other logical findings were arrived at. From a head-injury perspective (but not necessarily from that of other injuries) 'active shoulder' tackles were more dangerous than 'passive shoulder' tackles, head-on tackles more so than those from the side or behind, as were those when the tackler was running at speed and those when the tackler was accelerating. More surprisingly, the propensity for head injury decreased when the ball-carrier was accelerating, although this much more common event resulted in more head injuries in absolute terms.

The anatomising of the myriad tackle types and their various threats was comprehensive, offering all manner of strategies, some more realistic than others, for future policy directions, if a reduction in the incidence of head injury is the desired end. And, it is worth remembering, if initial measures are not deemed sufficient, all of these will present themselves as further avenues of exploration, each one edging us closer to that theoretical end point of a game without tackling.

It was decided the most realistic policy was to try to address the height of the tackler. When the tackler is upright, the chances of a head injury are 44 per cent greater than when the tackler is bent at the waist, with a clash of heads the collision likeliest to cause one. Get the heads away from each other, runs the theory, and rugby might become somewhat safer. One way of achieving that is to move the threshold for a legal tackle from the line of the shoulders to somewhere lower on the body of the ball-carrier, for example the line of the armpits or the bottom of the chest – or, as World Rugby memorably put it in 2018, to much unhelpful hilarity, the line of the nipples.

The trouble with moving that threshold is that the big hit would be compromised. There are plenty in rugby who do not want the sport to lose that aspect. Another problem with lowering the legal tackle height, which was the primary concern of the working party of coaches, players and referees that gathered to determine an appropriate response to the data, is the avalanche of penalties that would likely ensue, as players come at each other from all angles. Sometimes it is impossible not to make contact with the upper body. Sometimes, indeed, it is safer to do so.

So, at the end of 2016, World Rugby announced that, rather than institute any law changes, it would issue directives that recommended more draconian policing of the current law regarding the high tackle. Lower the height of the tackler by making the consequences of a high tackle so severe no tackler would dare go anywhere near the upper body. In the strident language of the original directives, even 'accidental' high tackles, which could be demonstrated to be no fault of the tackler, were to be punished with the minimum of a penalty. For tackles deemed 'reckless', whereby the tackler 'knew or should have known' that contact with the head was a possibility, red cards would be perfectly acceptable – to be encouraged even.

That phrase 'should have known' resonated, rugby at its most headmasterly and yet so open to interpretation as to capture all manner of ills. Step on to the field, and a player *should* know that contact with the head is a possibility, some might say an inevitability. The pressure on the referees, who would have to decide on the hoof and in front of thousands of spectators whether a tackler 'should have known', was to be intense.

Even before the directives came into force, on 1 January 2017, referees were secretly told, for one weekend of European rugby in December 2016, to apply them as if they were. Across the 20 matches in question, there were six red cards, 26 yellows and much uproar throughout the game about how impossible the job of a rugby player had become. They play far harder and far faster than the players of the amateur era, they play far cleaner, and yet here they were being sent off more often in one weekend than their predecessors could expect to be in a decade.

Worse still, it was the poor, hapless fools doing the tackling who had to suffer the worst of both worlds. Not only are they the ones who incur

72 per cent of tackle-related head injuries, they are shown 100 per cent of tackle-related red cards. Who'd be a tackler? But if only they would bend at the waist when they made their tackles, the counterargument ran, their chances of avoiding both head injury and red card would improve. 'We are doing this for your own good' was the refrain, as another player caught out by impossible physics trudged to the sidelines.

The chaos of that weekend in December 2016 (and the one before had seen 3 red cards and 22 yellow in the same two European competitions) was never repeated. Almost immediately it was clear the directives would not be followed to the letter, because to do so would be to show a card of either colour several times a match. To qualify as 'reckless' tacklers just had to make contact with a player's head when they 'should have known' it might happen. That happens many times in a match. Referees are manifestly reluctant to send players off for events they can see are unavoidable. In the chaos of a match, player decisions have to be made in split-seconds and bodies, ungainly as they are, have to follow just as quickly but cannot. The tackler's target is always, infuriatingly, *moving*. A perfectly aimed tackle at the midriff, let alone the chest, can become, in the blink of an eye or the step of a foot, grounds for dismissal. Referees understand this because they are there, in the middle of it, right up close. They understand it far better than the subsequent playing and replaying of each incident in slow-motion detail can ever lead a braying mob to appreciate. Their restraint, despite those incendiary directives, has been admirable.

And yet within months the complaint was regularly aired that referees were being too lenient, that more cards were needed, more cards desired. Two years later, when the RFU issued the results of its 2018 Professional Rugby Injury Surveillance Project, it came with the exhortation, handed down from World Rugby no less, that referees needed to punish high tackles more often, with as many cards as they did, for example, the deliberate knock-on, for which a player was three times likelier to be thus sanctioned. The operative word there, though, is 'deliberate'. Referees have never had any problem punishing anything deliberate, nor should they. It is when a 'crime' is manifestly accidental that they balk. But by now, in its panic, rugby had been reduced to wishing red cards on its players.

Too easily the association is being set between cards and a perceived reduction in head injury, via the persecution of those ugly hits to the head. The waving of a red card is thus fetishised by some as the waving of a wand to beat concussion. It is worth reiterating that only 3 per cent of those 611 head injuries were from illegally high tackles. Even if we could eliminate all of them, the impact on head-injury incidence would be negligible.

But it is also important to remember that to eliminate the high tackle is not in itself the aim of World Rugby's directives, just a by-product of the underlying object, which is to reduce the height of the tackler. The aim is to change behaviour, essentially to scare players away from targeting the upper body, while retaining the option of the upper body as a legitimate target because big hits to the upper body are still great to watch, great to coach. Rugby prefers to see examples made of a few than to institute anything as radical as an actual change to the law. If the desired aim is a reduction in the height of tackles, a logical solution might be to lower the threshold for a legal one but, years after the upright tackle was identified as a threat to player safety, the upright tackle is still legal.

This conversation is ongoing. There are those in World Rugby who would like to see the legal tackle height lowered to the waist, but a lowering to the base of the sternum, or even just the armpit, was resisted as unworkable. So we ended up with that ugly fudge whereby upright tackles and chest shots remained legal, but the unlucky few were to be scapegoated if anything went wrong.

Any concerns about applying a new law regarding tackle height are entirely valid – to expect tacklers to avoid altogether contact above the sternum would be unreasonable, impossible even, and in some cases dangerous. Alas, the same logic applies to contact above the shoulders. That area may be further away from the target, and thus contact there rarer, but in a fast-moving sport such errors are unavoidable. Which means, if the zero-tolerance culture is applied strictly by referees, red cards are unavoidable. Lower the legal tackle height, however, and we would be presented with a glut of unavoidable penalties, but at least the culture of dismissing players would become unnecessary. One paradigm would see fewer penalties but more red cards; the other would see more penalties but no need for red cards at all, except for obviously deliberate offences.

The impulse to lower the tackle height is reasonable, however cautious we should be about tinkering with the fundamental dynamics of the sport. But how effective could we expect it to be? According to World Rugby's data, a head injury is 44 per cent likelier when the tackler is upright than when bent at the waist. If, theoretically, it were possible to turn every upright tackler into one bent at the waist, the 164 head injuries from the study that occurred when the tackler was upright might be reduced to 114 (164 divided by 1.44), which would reduce the total of 611 head injuries by 50, or just over 8 per cent. That is *if* upright tackling were eliminated altogether and there were no unintended consequences. In reality, the best we could hope for is a reduction in upright tackling, so any reduction in head injuries might be rather less than 8 per cent. Whether that is a result worth all the controversy, or the chaos a lowering of the legal tackle height would undoubtedly precipitate, is impossible to answer.

Then again, perhaps we are going after the wrong player. What about the ball-carrier? When the ball-carrier is upright, relative to bent at the waist, the likelihood of head injury is reported to increase by 113 per cent – and, in absolute terms, an upright ball-carrier is the factor that leads to the most head injuries. Turn all of those into bent-at-the-waist ball-carriers and, theoretically, we might reduce the 304 head injuries thus incurred in the study to 143 (304 divided by 2.13), a reduction of 161, or 26 per cent of the overall count. A far more effective result. But what kind of law could be passed to ensure every ball-carrier runs around bent at the waist? Not only is the idea ridiculous, it feels as if there might very well be unintended consequences from that.

This is where care needs to be taken. Ball-carriers bent at the waist are not safer per se. Indeed, most of the controversial red cards we have seen since the 2016 directives involve a ball-carrier in a posture lower than the one the tackler expected. The head-injury rate is favourable when ball-carriers are bent at the waist because usually that posture means they are driving at close range, which means the speeds are lower and both players are braced for contact. If ball-carriers suddenly started bending in the high speed of open play the head-injury rate would rocket as they met their tacklers head on.

Which brings us to the real problem. Rugby is not static. An alteration in the posture of one player has implications for the other. When 30 players are altering their postures constantly, at speed, on a relatively small patch of grass, the unintended consequences are virtually unlimited.

In 2018, they introduced a new law to American football. To lead with the head was no longer allowed. That is easier to observe – and thus enforce – because what a tackler does with the head is almost entirely within the tackler's control. The point at which a tackler makes contact with the body of a ball-carrier, however, is not. Rugby's law regarding the height of a tackle is framed not with reference to the tackler, but to the person being tackled. When the ball-carrier moves, so does the line of legality. If a ball-carrier bends at the waist, there are fairly profound implications for the tackler, who is always one step behind, always the one having to react. If they were low enough beforehand, they must get lower again, and quick.

Sometimes, inevitably, it is too quick to be humanly possible. At other times it might be too quick for one type of player, if not for the other. The requirement to tackle low is self-evidently harder for some than others, as is the requirement to move quickly. In the excitable spirit of the age, some of the more intolerant proponents of the red-card regime found themselves arguing, in the wake of a red card for the Leicester lock Will Spencer in 2018, that to be six-foot-seven should make no difference to a player's ability to tackle low. 'If so-and-so [usually one of the greatest players of the age] can do it, why can't they all?' runs that particular line of argument, ignoring that even so-and-so sometimes gets a tackle wrong despite being, well, one of the greatest players of the age. If only we could all tackle like so-and-so . . .

A truth too often overlooked in the persecution of players caught out is that the tackle is a skill as technical as any other. Some are simply better at it than others, just as some can run faster. Other studies have demonstrated the truth that tackling becomes more dangerous after a defensive system has been breached – in other words, when tacklers are panicking, off balance, unsighted, no longer ready. Those dastardly ball-carriers do so like to make life as difficult as possible for the tacklers. 'If only they could become more predictable,' we are practically on the point of saying, 'there would be far fewer head injuries.'

That horrible reality presents itself once again – the more rugby players improve, the more dangerous they become to each other. In the absence of malice, a card for a high tackle is essentially the dismissal of a player for a failure of technique, for not being quite good enough at a skill, or for simply being caught in an impossible situation. That is a sorry position for a sport to arrive at.

Enough people in rugby's legislative know this, hence the ongoing attempts to arrive at more equitable, not to mention effective, solutions. The aggressive, borderline irresponsible, language of the 2017 directives has been toned down, with allowances made for the role of the ball-carrier in any incident. Education is being prioritised over clumsy enforcement.

Already there are signs of a change in culture, the big hit seemingly less in evidence and more frowned upon when it does happen, even when technically legal. There is a moral onus now on coaches and players to work on tackling techniques, with or without the application by referees of a zero-tolerance culture. The strategic benefits are obvious, too, in working on the technical ability of tacklers to keep themselves safe. This is the way forward – behaviour change by education not red card – but it is subtler and less demonstrative. Defence coaches, even at international level, have admitted they spend most of their time working on systems rather than tackle technique. More investment in the coaching of safe technique may yet benefit everyone, tackler and ball-carrier.

Everybody knows about concussion. Nobody wants to inflict or receive one. Convincing the wider world of this, in an unforgiving age, is rugby's best hope.

These are desperate times for a sport thrust into a treacherous arena on the horns of players quicker and more powerful than ever. Rugby will continue to try anything it can to mitigate the threat of concussion, just as it tries to win the battle for hearts, wallets and eyeballs in a market of ferocious competitiveness. Each step taken to satisfy one imperative has repercussions for others, often even for the original.

To be in the middle of the chaos is to wonder sometimes how the dear old game can survive. Those ancient dynamics it has always played to, by turns brutal and poetic, the arcane rituals, the laws, the mysterious gesturing of officials trying to enforce them, now unfold onto a wider stage, where the scrutiny is eviscerating and ruthless.

What are these strange goings-on, the passing customer asks, is there any reason for me to linger? After a century of wallowing in its own peculiarities, content with the loyalty of a devoted cult, rugby has now woken up to the demands of the entertainment industry. That spotlight is merciless. The endearing quirks, so ingrained and beloved of the traditional clientele, must now find favour more widely or be smoothed over in pursuit of a newer, more fickle audience. The tension is familiar, between the old and the new. To negotiate the demands of both without losing the interest of either is a feat requiring sophistication and a lightness of touch. Desperate times, indeed.

Part 6

A Beautiful Beast Bewildered

XIV

Caught in the Floodlights:
Of Scrums and Australians

If anyone ever tells you they understand rugby, you can dismiss their opinion as worthless. If they think they have understood it, they have not.

You can know your rugby. And know it and know it until you don't think you can know any more. And then it makes a fool of you anew.

No other sport could so confound its very best practitioners that they can often be heard asking the referee what they can and cannot do during a match. This delicious scenario was best played out in the 2017 Six Nations match between England and Italy, when the wily Italy assistant coach, Brendan Venter, devised a strategy that exploited a loophole in the laws regarding offside (what else?) at the ruck. They called it 'The Fox', and for an entire half of rugby the second best team in the world at the time did not know what to do, or even just what they were allowed to. Senior players were reduced to asking the referee for help.

Much hilarity ensued, but the subsequent reaction in the press, on social media and down the pub revealed yet another trait that may not be peculiar to rugby but is undoubtedly accentuated by the depths of its mystery – the phenomenon of the Know-It-All. Out they came in the days that followed, stroking their chins in wisdom after the event, showing off their knowledge, closing rank against any Johnny-Come-Latelies who might not be so well-versed in rugby's ways, who might not, like some of the very best players in England that day, have known what the hell was going on.

Any sport has an element of this, a barrier between the initiated and the not, but rugby's is particularly formidable, and so too the importance to some of proving themselves on the right side of it. This, fundamentally, is also a barrier against rugby's growth – and that is a problem in this consumer age.

'Have you ever played the game?' may sound like an innocent question, but it is actually the rugby snob's most caustic put-down. The implication is clear – if you haven't played, you can't possibly understand. And so a sort of hierarchy of opinion is created, where one's playing history determines the degree to which one's views should be taken seriously.

Of course, such a notion is absurd. By that rationale, we would listen to no one other than Gareth Edwards or Richie McCaw or whoever else is esteemed the Greatest Of All Time. And they, in turn, would all agree with each other about absolutely everything because they would know The Truth.

Nobody agrees on anything in rugby, because nobody understands it, much like this life it mimics so poignantly. That need not be a problem in itself. Many of the sport's faithful are attracted to it precisely because of its complexities. But there are many, many more who just cannot be bothered with the investment of attention required to pick out any patterns from the chaos of a typical match.

Good, some of the faithful might say, in an echo of that spirit of exclusivity that used to define so much of the sport's mood, in which for so long it was content to wallow. Nor should such an attitude be entirely condemned, for it recognises the way the sport is now against the way it might have to go if more of those floating votes are to be won. Rugby has changed into a sport almost unrecognisable from the one of the amateur era, but it still is rugby, just about. Those set pieces are hanging on in there, central, if in subtly different ways; the primacy of the contest is still observed (again, just about), the tackle, the requirement to pass backwards, those goalposts. Any or all of them might come under threat should the game capitulate completely to the whims of consumer sovereignty. But so too do they mitigate against the sort of mass appeal enjoyed by The Sibling.

Part of the problem is those laws. There have always been so many. And they keep changing. Just keeping up with the latest requires quite some immersion in the sport. Casual observers do not stand a chance.

World Rugby is unconditionally signed up to the notion of a sport of mass appeal, sometimes to an almost undignified degree. The constant tinkering with the laws is one obvious manifestation of this, but it spent two years, too, actually tinkering with the wording of those laws. So sensitive is World Rugby these days to any charge of exclusivity, it worried about what impression rugby's plodding 160-page law book might make on anyone of a mind to venture into it, which is precisely nobody bar the most fully paid-up rugby geeks. If a person ever reaches a point in life when a sortie into rugby's law book feels necessary, it is safe to say they are already converted. Nevertheless, at the very start of 2018, World Rugby published with much-trumpeted pride a new law book, 42 per cent slimmer than the unwieldy legacy of the amateur era. Its score on the Gunning fog index, the measure of a text's penetrability, had been reduced from 10.6 to 7.26, which means the new law book is appropriate for a 12-year-old to read, rather than the 16-year-old one had to be to have a chance with the old one.

No laws were changed in this process of simplification, but of course they have been since. That law book looks different again, the torturous growth by mutation that delivered the previous monstrosity already under way with yet more definitions, clauses and sub-clauses, as rugby continues its eternal search for the perfect blend.

All of which invests disproportionate significance in the role of the referee. Could the universe have conceived of a sport more intricately and continuously shaped by the judgements of the human being appointed to supervise it? In rugby, the referee is elevated from a position of passive arbiter to that of third party. Rugby is not a simple contest between two teams.

The template for the relationship between referee and contest is well established in the sporting world. None can be said to have the perfect set-up, but the more the referee or umpire can be kept out of proceedings the better. Ideally, they can be left seated in a chair, required only to adjudicate occasionally on a binary decision. A sport like tennis would seem to have this arrangement most aptly realised.

Thence we move along a spectrum through sports like cricket with its occasionally debatable decisions, through those like football with its referee obliged to try to keep up with play but still only now and then required to make a contentious decision of significance. League, of course, requires plenty of the marginal calls inherent to rugby to be made by a referee on the hoof, but it absolves its officials of the need to arbitrate over a set piece of any influence or over the constant and shifting contest for possession.

In rugby, at virtually every point of contention – and quite a few without – there is a whole range of decisions and interpretations open to the referee, whose reactions to each are constantly shaping the direction of the match. At the lineout alone there are 22 technical infringements a referee could blow for. Within that there are six different ways for a player to be offside. Anyone with a recording of a match and enough patience could pick out more than one infringement, more than one reason for a referee to blow the whistle, at so many different events. Some of them the referee may miss, some choose to ignore, some consider secondary to another – or, to borrow from the refereeing community's lexicon, less 'material'. Each decision changes the course of the narrative, much to the exasperation or approval of those watching, according to their allegiances, which invariably incline a fan to identify other infringements again, imagined or otherwise. No knife to a fan or coach is quite so sharp as the sound of that whistle, and the arm thrust skyward against their team, so confident and authoritarian, as if there were only one conclusion to be arrived at from out of the general chaos. To those whose interest is passing or merely exploratory, a perusal of what this strange game might have to offer, the reaction is simply one of bewilderment. Even those who know the game inside out are continually wondering why.

The disproportionate influence of the referee is one of rugby's most fundamental flaws, a barrier in general against anyone's appreciation of the game, particularly those who are not used to it, but more specifically and on a regular basis a barrier against the elemental justice of the right team winning. Even a judgement as apparently simple as whether a pass has gone forward is replete with complexity – and where there is complexity there is constant disagreement.

World Rugby has tried to clarify the standard by which a forward pass should be judged, but too many people just do not want to hear, ranting about the markings on the pitch, when an indicator as static as a line drawn on the ground bears no relation, or even relevance, to something as dynamic as a pass delivered on the run. Some players can run at 10 m/s. If one throws a pass that leaves the hands in a direction parallel to the tryline (i.e. flat), which is within the laws, that pass, while it flies laterally across the field, must also continue to travel in the same direction and at pretty much the same speed as the person who threw it. So if a long pass thus delivered travels through the air for one second it will travel the best part of 10 metres towards the tryline and still be legal. Many refer to this as 'that new momentum law', but this one, identified and described in the 17th century by Sir Isaac Newton in the first of his three laws of motion, pre-dates even those of the RFU. And the fundamental principle of it goes back to the very dawn of time. It has always applied, in rugby as much as anywhere, and cannot be circumvented. All that has changed, in rugby's case, is the proliferation of televised matches, camera angles and replays, which alert us to the apparent paradox of a ball passed backwards actually travelling forwards. In the old days, with the naked eye, we just never noticed.

Watch a highlights reel of tries on any given weekend and with the power of pause and rewind measure by any fixed mark, on pitch or advertising hoarding, each pass delivered on the run. Most of them are forward by that standard, although they clearly leave the passer's hands in a backwards direction. If you threw a pass from a speeding train, you would not expect it to go backwards relative to a fixed marker, however hard you flung it against the prevailing direction. It is the same principle. The only standard by which to judge a pass is the orientation of the ball relative to the passer the moment it leaves the hands. If the passer is able to carry on running at the same speed in the same direction, an easy measure is if they are in front of the ball when it is caught, but that is not available if they are stopped by a tackle, which is when legal passes can look particularly forward.

Whatever the measure, the truth is that sometimes it is all but impossible to tell, no matter how many angles are viewed. Cue the raging arguments. The sooner a technology such as Hawk-Eye, so adeptly deployed by tennis and cricket, can come to the rescue the better. Indeed, technology could go a long way to solving a lot of controversy. A microchip in the ball, for example, might one day be able to tell us whether it has been grounded on or over the line. For now, though, the arguments are set to rage for the foreseeable future.

And those are just the ones over what should be binary decisions, questions of yes or no, but rarely is anything so simple in rugby. Hardwired into this chaos is the galling imperfection, the virtually suicidal flaw, of a sport so vulnerable to the referee's whims. In reality, the referee's decisions are constantly leading each game in certain directions, but there are few faux pas more ruinous for a sport's credibility than a match decided at the death not by the excellence of a competitor but by something that the ref saw. The more debatable, trivial or even just imagined the infringement the greater the damage to credibility. Well might a spectator, certainly a casual one, wonder why they should bother if they do not understand why one team won and not the other – and no less so if they do understand but just do not agree.

So many of the 'infringements' in a rugby match cannot be avoided. There are times when the injustice of being penalised for such feels acceptable, namely when the team benefiting has forced the opposition into the impossible situation. If a side is unable to press home the advantage of, say, a slashing break because one of the opposition is trapped on top of the ball, preventing release, it feels right that that team should be rewarded somehow, whether or not there was anything the offender could do to avoid the infringement. All too often, though, a penalty is awarded when neither side has done anything to earn it, when the game has simply meandered to some sort of stalemate and the referee, acutely aware of all the watching eyes, wants someone to blame, wants simply to try to inject a new development into the narrative.

Some phases of play are more vulnerable to these arbitrary shifts in momentum than others, but none more than that incomparable signature of our sport, its icon every bit as much as its blight. Rugby may be the most unfathomable sport on earth, but nobody, repeat nobody, understands the distillation of chaos theory that is the seething, twisting multiplicity of muscle and bone for which rugby is most famous. Nobody understands the scrum.

There are those who might tell you they do. They will tend to be as wide as they are high, the bearers of misshapen ears and war-torn faces.

They will tend to be veterans from the frontline of the scrum, having engaged hundreds, maybe thousands, of times in rugby's most brutal ritual, one of the most brutal in sport. If they tell you they understand, under no circumstances disagree.

Ask them, instead, some questions. Why does a scrum collapse? How much control do props have over their actions? What role do the second and back rows play? Listen to their answers and marvel at the variety, the incompatibility. None of them agrees. If the good people of the front-row union are party to some higher truth regarding the scrum it is just as well the rest of us are protected, lest our delicate crania be exploded by the multidimensionality of the knowledge.

Sometimes, a front-row forward will confess. Not often, because to do so is to admit to not Knowing It All, to bring into question one's right to our respect and awe for operating amid the unspeakable horrors and surviving, but hang around long enough and there is a chance they will break. Phil Vickery might not have been the scrummager's scrummager, but he won a World Cup as a tighthead, so if anyone knows he should. In 2004, three months after England's great triumph, he told the *Observer*: 'Ninety-five per cent of scrum penalties are not deliberate. Anyone who says they know why a scrum collapses is a liar.'

That came after lengthy questioning on a February afternoon in Gloucester, but up against a late-night bar is another fertile environment for honesty from a prop, the harrowing tales of the sound of that shrill blast while your face is planted in mud, the weight of hundreds of kilograms of flesh pressing down on it, scarcely daring to extricate yourself for fear of what the verdict is, certainly not daring to guess – and then the devastation at finally raising your face from the ooze only to discover, long after everyone else, that the referee has decided it is you who ruined everything, you who has cost your team.

A familiar trope for a commentator is to chuckle as a prop retires from a penalty, shaking the head in protest. 'What, me, sir?' the commentator will laugh. 'Butter wouldn't melt!' As if props know exactly what they are doing at all times, as if, consistent with the legend, they are all in there trying to con each other, trying to con the ref, to con the rest of us. The reality is, no one has a clue what is going on, not the commentators, not the fans, the scrum-halfs or flankers, not even the props themselves. And certainly not the referees.

Games, sometimes, are decided by these random decrees. That World Cup final in 2003 was very nearly one of them. The scrum is, yes, an expression of pure chaos theory, with cauliflower ears. Just as the notional flap of a butterfly's wing in Hampshire may precipitate a hurricane in the Caribbean, so may an itch in a loosehead's toe bring down a scrum, decide a World Cup.

Scientists have measured the impact felt by a player at engagement in an elite scrum at up to 20 kilonewtons, or two tonnes. As transmitted through the bony, sinewy outcrops and crevices of human heads, necks and shoulders, coming at each other from all angles, with the gravitas of further irregular shapes and sizes following on behind, the cocktail is volatile, the scope for malfunction virtually limitless. We should not wonder at the inherent instability, the chaos, the mystery.

The scrum is rugby. The world marvels at it, just as it recoils, part beauty, part beast, compelling and poetic, infuriating and tedious.

The scrum *was* rugby, literally. The scrum was football. In certain shady corners of the internet you can watch footage of those few folk-football matches that still take place today. They amount to a mass brawl with a ball in a street. On Shrove Tuesday. It is nothing more or less than an excuse for a fight. This is what football was for centuries. Then, when the public schools – or, more specifically, the unsupervised boys of the public schools – started to develop their own interpretations, they all involved some form of mêlée. At Rugby School, the mêlée was pretty much it. You stood around, pushing and shoving. And hacking. Then a degree of separation evolved between the pushers and shovers and those who stood at the back, to guard against any breakout from the melee and then those who stood half-back, or three-quarters, or full. Next, when this adolescent pursuit was adopted by adults, the notion of the pushers and shovers bending at the waist and interlocking in formation was introduced, but still the pushing and shoving was the main event. Until the All Blacks burst on to the scene at the start of the 20th century, alerting the sport to other possibilities.

Even then, though, the scrum and all its repercussions dominated for much of the 20th century. As late as the 1971 Lions Test series in New Zealand there were 50 scrums a match. Back then, it is possible to believe that those in the front row might have been practising their fair share of the 'dark arts' – and doing so deliberately. The players were smaller. Each scrum would form in a few seconds, the two packs marching up to each other and engaging without so much as a word from the referee. The subsequent contests would last far longer. Sometimes, if the referee required it, the scrum-half would put the ball in three times to the same twisting, scuttling scrum without the front rows breaking up or collapsing. In this environment, with scrums lasting sometimes for tens of seconds, the scope for deliberate chicanery might well have been present.

Key to this facility was the lack of a two-tonne force through each spine. The reduction since the 1970s from 40-plus scrums a match to a dozen nowadays is just as well considering the size and power of those partaking in the professional era. In that time, the scrum has changed by degrees. Some posit the power of the Argentina scrum of the 1970s, with its infamous technique of *bajada*, an all-out assault through the hooker, others the French and their policy in the 1980s of picking a third prop at hooker. Others again cite the All Blacks in the 1990s and the timing of their shove, just as the ball came in. No doubt all played their part, but the net result, as ever, was an intensification wrought by the arms race in power at the turn of the century, exacerbated by professionalism. Gone is the art of hooking, gone the straight put-in, gone the jog-up-and-bind engagement. Now these gargantuan athletes assume their positions meticulously before erupting into each other;

now the referee must guide them step by step to try to keep the explosive forces in check. No one can be deemed in complete control of their actions when they are absorbing the transmission of two tonnes of power through their being.

The scrum has almost always been in or near an existential crisis, despite its status as rugby's calling card – more probably because of it. The fate of the scrum in those related sports that introduced the commercial imperative early is instructive. American football and Australian rules did away with it almost as soon as possible. League agonised over it for years. They removed a couple of players barely a decade after they had broken away from union, tilting the balance between backs and forwards in favour of the former. By the end of the 20th century, the scrum in league was nothing more than an exercise in corralling half the players into a confined space to allow the other half room to express themselves – and a chance for everyone to have a breather.

In rugby, the insularity of an amateur sport that need answer to no one allowed the scrum to take root, to focus in on itself, explore techniques and innovations, until it started to succumb to the same pressures of the late 20th century that every other aspect of society has, turned up even more so in rugby's case by the leap to professionalism. The pressure on each scrum was ratcheted up, physically, tactically, emotionally. Fifteen years into the professional era, and the scrum was becoming, just before concussion took over, the bane of rugby's life, the perfect symbol for a sport ancient and soulful thrust suddenly into a spotlit arena, twisting and turning in bewildered confusion, beautiful, charismatic but lost, quite lost amid the glare. Entire minutes out of the precious 80 could be taken up by a single scrum as it tried to find itself, its super-charged collectives coiled opposite each other again and again, not willing or able to cede the newton of collision that might give the thing a chance. 'We're not here to watch you fail to scrummage!' an exasperated sport raged. Who can guess what the world beyond thought.

As ever, when faced with a crisis, rugby responded with a suite of desperate measures, some effective, some wild, borderline insane. Has, for example, a sport anywhere under the sun contrived to banish its contestants from the field of play for being weaker than their opponents? Has a sport ever thought it sensible, let alone effective, to punish a team already struggling by reducing their number? In its panic, rugby has taken to sending props to the sin bin for failing to deal with the opposition drive, that distant legend of incorrigible props constantly up to no good lingering on in the conviction that these poor goons are somehow doing this all on purpose, ruining our enjoyment deliberately.

Down a scrum goes again, one team clearly weaker than the other, and the referee approaches the beaten front row to issue that final warning. Everyone in the conversation, including surely the referee, knows what is coming next, because it is exactly what has just happened again and again. There is a peculiar sort of insanity in thinking that to send anyone off is to help improve the situation. There is a peculiar insanity in sending anyone off for being, essentially, not as good as their opponent. A referee might as well say to a beaten winger, 'Your opposite man is skinning you on the outside every time. I want you to run faster, or you'll leave me with no option.' Referees can dress up their lectures to beaten props all they like with technical jargon such as packing square, shoulders above hips, binding long, and so on – what they are really asking is for the props to become stronger and better than they are, and to do it NOW. It should come as no surprise when it turns out they cannot.

The problem seems to lie in the primeval urge of the scrummager to scrummage. If it is not impolitic to single out one scrum from all the others in history, there was an illustrative example of uncommon stability in a match in January 2016. Harlequins had just lost their powerful lock James Horwill to the sin bin, and Saracens set up a position on their five-metre line. Quins next conceded two penalties for illegally stopping driven lineouts, and then proceeded to be penalised four times in a row at the subsequent series of scrums. Had Horwill not been absent, someone would have gone to the bin by then, but this time the referee did issue that warning. And the next scrum was, at last, perfectly stable. It also retreated neatly over the Quins line, where Saracens scored at their leisure. The key ingredient? One of the two teams, for possibly the first time in scrummaging history, chose not to push.

The whole spectacle was so outlandish to anyone familiar with rugby and its bull-headed ways that it provided a momentary insight into the problem. Scrums, these days at least, do not collapse because of devious props trying to ruin the game; they collapse because of the coming together of ferocious forces that can scarcely be controlled. If one side is weaker, the cocktail is more unstable still.

The extraordinary decision not to push was a tactical masterstroke by Quins. It must have gone against every instinct of the props, who happened to be two of the most experienced in the game, Joe Marler and Adam Jones. Rather than suffer the inevitable penalty try and loss of yet another player to the bin, they concentrated on staying up at the scrum, which meant not pushing. They let Saracens have the try, forced them into taking a conversion on the angle and, as it happened, welcomed back Horwill from the sin bin a minute later, having used up most of the time without him with those series of resets. They also went on, against the odds, to win the game.

This is not a realistic template for future policy, but it does highlight the fallacy of issuing yellow cards to beaten props. Their only crime is to try to resist under hopeless circumstances. Penalise them, by all means, including with penalty tries, but keep them on the field.

Far more effective have been changes to the sequence of engagement. The innovation of 2013, which requires props to reach out and bind on their opponents before they come crashing together, has improved the stability and safety of scrums. The sequence has been demonstrated to reduce the force of the initial hit by around 25 per cent. The language, issues and policies surrounding the scrum crisis, it is worth noting, are just the same as those of the concussion crisis that has followed – 'hits' and anger and players sent to the sidelines for technical deficiencies or their entrapment in impossible situations. These are the signs of a sport panicking, punishing its players, and thus itself, for the way things are.

The scrum has been taken off the critical list for now but, like rugby, it is beset still with angry protestations about its very nature. How people of a certain age long for the days when a powerful scrum was a means to win front-foot ball. Now it is predominantly a penalty machine. This sets up a paradox, elevating the importance of the scrum just as it seems to diminish. For as long as penalties are awarded or conceded at them, scrums remain tactically valuable, but their number has plummeted – and clean ball from them even more so. Many scrums never see the ball emerge, concluded instead with a blast of the referee's whistle. The scrum's purpose as a means to restart the game has all but withered entirely.

This is lamentable on one level. The scrum is not only what people think of when they think of rugby, it is the set piece at which players are assigned their very positions. Without the scrum, notions of loosehead and tighthead, hooker and prop, openside and blindside, to name just a few, are meaningless, which means they are in danger of becoming just that.

The openside and blindside distinction, in particular, lingers on as a concept even more obsolete than the scrum itself. The idea behind the openside (or the 'out-and-out seven', as people still like to call it) is a legacy from those days when scrums outnumbered breakdowns, when it mattered which side of the scrum a flanker packed down on because there were around 50 of them a match. In the 2015 World Cup, the ball emerged from the scrum an average of nine times each game. Meanwhile, there were 178 breakdowns. Under those conditions, any mission to be 'first to the breakdown' from each scrum, the raison d'être of the old openside, is all but irrelevant.

Besides, the skill most people associate with the modern concept of the openside is to steal the ball at the breakdown, or to 'jackal', as it has become known. This was never a significant facet of the amateur game, because there were so few breakdowns to attend. The openside used to be a support player in attack and the lead tackler in defence. Only when the breakdowns started to multiply in the 1990s did the idea of the jackal take hold, and it was a role immediately associated with the openside. As the breakdowns swiftly multiplied into their hundreds, however, the jackal grew in importance but, in another related paradox, the role of the player most associated with it diminished accordingly. It is physically impossible for one player to be at all those breakdowns, so the requirement developed that others become proficient at the skill. Now, a team needs a number of players effective over the ball. The number on their back does not matter.

This amounts to the erosion of specialisms, the erosion of that other famous claim of rugby – that it is a game for all shapes and sizes. Central to that idea was the supremacy of the set piece. One could perform the above analysis on pretty much all of the positions – of the forwards at least, but even some of the backs. The number eight, for example, used to require the skills to control the ball at the base of the scrum and the athleticism and power to pick up and charge; nowadays, the ball is at the number eight's feet a handful of times a match. Similarly, the hookers no longer hook, the props and locks, without all those set pieces, must run and handle more than ever before. Already, the notion of the back-five forward has been established, the forward who can play anywhere behind the front row. Some could even play in the backs. It is fashionable right up to the highest levels to play locks as flankers and flankers as locks. And there is absolutely no reason why not. Maro Itoje, for example, can perform any skill required of a lock, flanker or number eight. All of which versatility is good and is bad, paradox after paradox for a sport caught between the past and the future, confused about what it wants, confounded each time it tries to make a move. The debates rage about what needs to be done, but for every adjustment apparently for the good there is a repercussion for the ill.

For years, the accent has been on an increase in 'ball in play' time. Nothing speaks more loudly of rugby's blissfully oblivious state as an amateur sport than the fact it was content with less than 30 per cent of its 80 minutes actually involving any action. Indeed, before Corris Thomas performed his retrospective on the 1980s (ball in play, 29 per cent), it is unlikely rugby was even aware of it. World Rugby measured a 31 per cent figure at the 1991 World Cup, 33 per cent for 1995 – and then professionalism happened. By 2003, ball in play had rocketed to 44 per cent. In the Six Nations nowadays, some games nudge 60 per cent, nearly 50 minutes out of 80.

Cue the reaction. More minutes mean more collisions, which, under the cloud of concussion, mean more cause for alarm. Aesthetically too, the sight of overgrown athletes thudding into each other again and again has worn thin and has us yearning for the old days.

There is no fix for this that does not run the risk, or even likelihood, of undesirable side-effects. One obvious solution to the relentless attrition might be the revocation of tactical replacements. The tactical replacement was introduced in 1996 and changed everything, almost as much as the professional era with which it coincided. And the grounds for its introduction were typically spurious.

Rugby officials have a long history of taking the easy way out. Professionalism itself was motivated as much as anything else by the realisation that players were being paid anyway, so they might as well make it official, to 'come clean', as it was so often described. Similarly, everyone knew that players were faking injuries so they could be replaced tactically. Rather than try to police it, rugby chose simply to make it legal. Again, with huge repercussions. One might just as logically legalise speeding, on the basis that everyone does it. But rugby has never been very good at policing its laws. Just too many of them.

So rugby is stuck in a quandary regarding the tactical replacement. In 2009, following Bloodgate, when Harlequins were caught abusing the system, a working party set up by the RFU to investigate the state of the game recommended rolling substitutions as a possible response, actually deepening the use of tactical replacements, as in league. The counterargument is the reverse policy – to abolish them altogether. Retain three front-row replacements for safety purposes and, say, another two to cover the rest of the team, allow them to come on only in the event of injury and install an independent doctor to keep any malpractice at bay.

The theory goes that without tactical replacements players would need to de-power, to increase their aerobic capacity, so that they might last the full 80. Exhaustion would surely set in for all, creating more opportunities in the endgame. Front rows would be able to spend that full 80 working each other over, winning that battle within a battle, rather than see a tiring opponent replaced in the 55th minute by someone even bigger. Gasping front-row forwards might mean extra space for wingers who could go back to being normal-sized.

Yet if aerobic capacity became the currency, would that not further erode the importance of specialists and the mandate for all shapes and sizes? With a withering set piece and the accent on (yet more) fitness, what would be the point of those props at all, what point the locks? Flankers, flankers everywhere. Which is why we should hold fire on bewailing the notion of the scrum as penalty machine. There are so few scrums now, the only way to keep them tactically relevant, to keep the panting fatty of yore in the game, is to reward the dominant ones handsomely. Winning front-foot ball a handful of times a match wouldn't cut it, but a well-timed penalty for a big scrum might, or just the ability to avoid conceding the same. Then again, some of those who pass as props these days dismantle all such theorising. Tadhg Furlong, Kyle Sinckler, Joe Moody and the like look like props, but they move and handle like centres – and could no doubt do so quite happily for the full 80.

And on we go, pushing the pieces backwards and forwards in the impossible, eternal puzzle.

One radical attempt to overhaul rugby as we know it was launched in 2008, the infamous Experimental Law Variations, which advocated simplification of rugby's laws to the extent of abolishing all penalties everywhere, bar those for offside and foul play, replacing them with free kicks. The southern hemisphere gave that a go for a season, dreaming of a rugby world not shaped by the referee's whistle, but the north resisted, dubbing it a cheats' charter. Another classic impasse was set between rugby's traditions and the urge to modernise. Other law changes were trialled in both hemispheres, some adopted (the five-metre offside line at scrums, for example), others not (the ability to pull down a maul, handle in a ruck, field unlimited numbers at the lineout).

The old ways won out, rightly in most cases, particularly vis-à-vis the lineout and maul, but much ill-feeling arose, the factions at loggerheads, organised according to their respect for the way things are and their anxiousness to move rugby on. It boiled down in most people's eyes to a face-off between complexity and crassness, gravitas and razzmatazz. A face-off, in short, between everybody else and Australia.

For a team that have won two World Cups, played in two other finals and supplied rugby with some of its greatest players, Australia have suffered their fair share of ridicule among the rugby fraternity. Part of it is, or was, those scrums and their apparent aversion to them for long periods. They have never much cared for a maul, either. Just the name of Andrew Sheridan, the mighty English loosehead of the mid-to-late 2000s, is enough to make certain Australians weep. It was around the time of the Sheridan Indignities that they were perceived, certainly by those in the north, as trying to push rugby towards a future without set piece or substance, a frothy, tasteless sop for mass consumption, much like their beer.

But rugby dismisses the Australians and their concerns at its peril. Their mindset is forged not only by their natural disdain for tradition but by their unique circumstances. Where the rest of us could tolerate endlessly reset scrums, for example, as little more than a tedium to be endured, for Australians such consumer turn-offs represent a structural crisis that threatens the very viability of the sport in their country. Among rugby's leading nations, Australia is the only one that ranks the sport a distant fourth of its codes of football. Australian rugby is constantly fighting for the attention of the consumer. The problems it wrestles with are those heading the way of all rugby, as the competing propositions for an individual's time and money proliferate.

Australia has the 14th largest economy in the world. Australians adore their sport and are singularly good at it. Their pre-eminence as a rugby nation should come as no surprise. Alas, that very affinity for sport cuts both ways. The marketplace in Australian sport is brutal. Let the action relent for even a minute or so while two gargantuan packs assemble themselves for a scrum, and the casual viewer has switched over.

As much as it feels rugby's vanishingly small share of the Australian market is a new crisis, these issues have always pertained. Our impression of Australia as one of the great rugby nations owes itself largely to a period of around 20 years, when the Wallabies could credibly lay claim to being the best rugby team on the planet. From the early 1980s to the early 2000s Australia enjoyed an era of unparalleled success, becoming in 1999 the first country to win the World Cup twice. For five consecutive years, 1998 to 2002, they held the Bledisloe Cup, the trophy they contest annually with New Zealand, a record run for them. At that point, with a third World Cup final reached, on home soil in 2003, Australian rugby was feeling quite bullish, even contemplating a challenge to the supremacy in their country of league and Aussie rules.

Alas, 2003 now looks as if it was the end of an era, an era that has proved the exception not the rule. Such is the talent in Australia, they are never less than capable of mixing it with the best. A Rugby Championship triumph and run to the World Cup final in 2015 represented a notable high amid long stretches of desperate form. But their travails since 2003 fit more snugly into the narrative of the first 100 years than the golden 20 at the turn of the century. Rugby has never been much more than a minority sport there, properly embraced by the private schools of Sydney and Brisbane, but even in their states of New South Wales and Queensland, Australia's rugby heartland, rugby is overwhelmed by the interest in league. Those two states account for a shade over half the 25 million people of Australia – in the other states, rugby barely registers at all. Aussie rules dominates the landscape there. Australia's relationship with rugby is similar to that of a country like Ireland, a minority sport participation-wise, predicated on the private schools.

What Australians do have, which the Irish do not, is a range of alternative professional sports with which rugby must compete for the public attention. Their sensitivity for what constitutes attractive sport to the consumer is thus particularly acute. Too often, the verdict has been that rugby fails to deliver, hence the constant agitation for law changes.

The Australians were agitating even in the dark ages of the mid-twentieth century, when rugby generally moved at a snail's pace and almost always at the behest of the home unions. For the first half of the century, the global game's governing body amounted to the home unions. There was no Australian union at all, just the unions of New South Wales and Queensland, who, along with those of New Zealand and South Africa, were no more than affiliates of the RFU. Only when the three southern hemisphere nations were admitted to the council in 1948 did the Australian union come into being.

The Australians, though, had always lobbied for an alteration to the law regarding kicking for touch. In the dark ages, a team could kick directly to touch from anywhere, and the lineout would take place where the ball went out. Australian rugby knew it could not afford to drown in the resultant deluge of set pieces with so much competition from Aussie rules, which had done away with set pieces altogether, and league, which had done away with the lineout. So, in 1936, New South Wales (and New Zealand, who were also interested in any innovation that might speed up the game) were allowed to play to a different law, whereby kicking directly to touch for a gain in territory was allowed only from the kicker's own 22.

Naturally, the home unions did not approve. The Australian Dispensation, as it became known, would not apply in any Test match involving them, but it was reluctantly accepted that what the Australians got up to on the underside of the world should be their own concern. When the southern three were finally granted seats on the council in 1948, Australia and New Zealand had to revert to playing Tests between themselves according to the old law, but the rest of the world was beginning to catch up with their way of thinking. By the time 1963 came along and the infamous Scotland–Wales match with its 111 lineouts, the Aussies were not the only ones who were dissatisfied with the state of the game. Four Test matches of the era ended in scoreless draws. Even the RFU had to accept the time for change was nigh. In 1968, the Australian Dispensation was trialled across the world, then, with the game vastly improved as a spectacle, accepted into law in 1970.

Looking back from our vantage in the 21st century, the innovation makes perfect sense; indeed, the reverse seems obstinately unreasonable. If every kick directly to touch earned a gain in metres, why would anyone try anything else in a game as territorial as rugby? But each break from the past in any pursuit feels like a violation to those invested deeply enough in the way things are. Rugby has always had a particularly strong affinity for tradition, which has tended to place modernisers like the Australians out on a limb, their schemes not to be trusted. The more out on a limb they find themselves, the more they must agitate, the more fear for the state of their sport.

There is genuine concern, at the end of the 21st century's second decade, about the future of rugby in Australia. Whichever way we measure it, the condition of the sport feels critical. Long gone are any notions of rivalling the two big football codes of Australia. In 2018, the first State of Origin match (league's annual series between Queensland and New South Wales) and AFL's grand final achieved viewing figures of 3.4 million each. The two sports accounted for five of Australia's six biggest TV audiences of the year, the royal wedding coming in seventh (the opening ceremony of the Gold Coast Commonwealth Games was fifth). Both sports have huge television contracts, which dwarf rugby's deals in Europe, let alone Australia, shared between free-to-air and cable. Rugby in Australia has no free-to-air deal at all, partly because the mainstream channels are not interested, mainly because rugby long ago chose/was forced to take the greater money from cable.

The classic vicious circle has set in. Many studies have found that a person who has participated in a sport, or been close to someone who has, is far likelier to follow it. This is particularly so for a sport like rugby. The best way to become acquainted with its mysterious dynamics is to play. But Australian rugby has invested much in the trickle-down strategy of sports administration, whereby investment in the elite game generates success, which generates interest. The fear is that this does not deepen the roots of the sport as much as the bottom-up model, whereby community participation is the investment priority.

In an ideal world, both the top and bottom of a sport would be well funded, but everything is linked to revenue. All too quickly, a sport can find itself spiralling, particularly when resources are limited. Australian rugby has become dependent on the money from cable. Two-thirds of Australians do not have cable, so most cannot watch rugby, even if they wanted to. Which means people are less engaged, whether as players or spectators, which means Australian rugby is more dependent again on the money from cable, and so on. Then, if that cable company encounters financial trouble itself and contemplates drastic cuts to its 'non-marquee' sports, as Foxtel announced it would in 2019, the outlook starts to look ruinously bleak.

In 2018, viewing figures on Fox for Super Rugby matches played in Australia were on a par with soccer's A-League (although the latter's figures were for free-to-air), averaging 71,000. As a spectator sport, rugby still just about trumps soccer in Australia, but soccer, as everywhere, is way, way ahead of all of Australia's football codes when it comes to participation. That controversial report of 2017, contested by Rugby Australia, rated rugby the 26th most popular participation sport in the country, one place behind ballroom dancing, claiming that the number of regular players aged 14 and older had collapsed from 148,000 in 2001 to 55,000 in 2016. The report had soccer at number one with 623,000.

Whomever one believes on the eternally murky question of partici-pation numbers, the decline of Super Rugby crowds is no less alarming, although this is as much a problem in South Africa as Australia, as the best players leave and the format becomes ever more convoluted. Super Rugby has always been less transparent with its attendances – and those that are published these days are regularly queried by the sceptics – but this decline can be seen with the eye. Australians, like Americans, love a winner, attendances inevitably spiking in periods of success. One might posit this as a classic symptom of the trickle-down method, fans who flock during the good times but prove less than loyal in the bad.

The Brumbies, shining light of the small, albeit capital, city of Canberra, ruled the roost at the end of Australia's golden era, when they could expect upwards of 20,000 to their games, 25,000-plus for the latter stages of their triumphant seasons – actually remarkable figures for a city of only 400,000. The Queensland Reds saw their fortunes peak on the field with their Super Rugby-winning campaign of 2011, and they averaged more than 33,000 that year, more than 34,000 the year after. The NSW Waratahs won Super Rugby in 2014, averaging nearly 20,000 in the regular season, which they surpassed the following year, but 10 years earlier, just at the tail end of Australia's golden era, they averaged more than 35,000, although across only five home games. In 2018, the Waratahs' average home gate was 14,000, the Reds' 12,000 and the Brumbies' 8,000. And those are the figures for Australian rugby's traditional heartlands.

Inevitably, something has had to give – and not only in Australia, but in a spluttering Super Rugby. In 2016, the Super 15 expanded to 18, welcoming teams from Argentina and Japan, as well as a sixth from South Africa, but the format proved too unwieldy, not to mention unpopular, so the decision was taken to contract two years later back to 15, retaining the Jaguares of Argentina and the Sunwolves of Japan (although in 2019, it was announced the Sunwolves would be cut too) but losing two teams from South Africa and one from Australia. Who was it going to be?

South Africa could not get their two out of there quickly enough, shipping the Cheetahs and the Southern Kings off with a dowry to the PRO14 in Europe. Which left Australia to decide which of their five teams to axe. The agonising could be heard the other side of the world. The Reds and the Waratahs were safe, the Brumbies reasonably so because of their previous successes, so it became a choice between the Western Force and the Melbourne Rebels, between Perth and Melbourne. One has a reasonable culture for the sport, but is the remotest city on earth; the other has next to no interest, but is two and a half times the size and just an hour's flight from Sydney. Needless to say, the Western Force of Perth were the team chopped.

All of which has created an interesting new dimension to Australia's status as testing ground for future policy and direction. Western Australia raged at its exclusion, betrayed, as they saw it, by Australian rugby's authorities thousands of miles to the east, for whom they had done so much, establishing a foothold for the sport in the west, where Aussie rules is king but, tellingly, league rates lower than union. Rugby Australia's decision was widely decried as short-sighted, a case of following the money.

And yet there is an uncommon amount of money in the hands of the man who had backed rugby in Western Australia, mining magnate Andrew Forrest. Vowing to make his mark in rugby – and rich enough to do it – Forrest set about instituting a new version, by which he might not only make his mark but break out the sport into Asia, making his version bigger than the one over which those traitors on the east coast presided. He initiated Global Rapid Rugby, a radicalisation to confound the radicals. Rugby Australia wanted World Rugby to stop him, or at least not to ratify his venture. To no avail. In November 2018, it was given the seal of approval.

Forrest laid out his vision, 'where elite sport and entertainment collide'. His mission statement went on: 'Like all sports, rugby needs to evolve. In today's world we're spoilt for choice, with easily digestible, fast-paced action in high demand. We believe our unique combination of rugby and entertainment is a perfect avenue to deliver this content.' Matches would be 70 minutes; any try that originates from within the scorers' 22, dubbed the Power Try, would be worth 9 points, no need for a conversion; there would be no gain in ground from a direct kick to touch at all, even from inside the 22; scrums would have no more than 60 seconds to set, lineouts 45. A million bucks to the winners.

Every button pressed was designed to appeal to a new audience, one used to and demanding instant gratification. Teams were lined up in Hong Kong, Malaysia, Singapore and the Pacific Islands, as well as Western Australia. Further plans were announced, as and when the venture felt ready, for expansion into those commercial G-spots of the Middle East, Japan, India and China. In 2018, the Western Force had showcased a series of fixtures against visiting teams played to the new format. Ball in play was said to have increased by 30 per cent; attendances rose from 9,000 the year before to 15,000, more than any of Australia's other provinces managed in Super Rugby that season.

Forrest might have been excused for laughing at rugby's status quo. Then again, could his vision be any more Australian? A cynic might highlight the focus on community development in his mission statement as a point of difference, but otherwise he might just as well be the old Australian union when he trumpets his competition's progressive nature, disruptive and innovative, predicated on the fast and free-flowing, predicated on entertainment.

His plans stalled when he was forced to delay the onset for a year, to much distress in the Pacific Islands, for whom this concept might establish that much-longed-for dream of professional rugby on the islands. But if the credibility of any new venture in rugby – indeed the world at large – resides in the pockets of its backers, Forrest qualifies as firmly in the billionaire category of human. Add in a missionary zeal and the added edge of anger against the establishment, and Global Rapid Rugby has every chance of biting.

If not it, something similar is coming, as surely as rugby's next law change. The continent of Asia is the dream jackpot of all aspirant industries. Rugby would happily break into it any which way, but, if that success is ever realised, it will not be by clinging on to the old. The pertinence of Forrest's call to radicalisation, however hideous to those who love a good set piece and the rumble of a well-conceived maul, cannot be denied. It will take something like Global Rapid Rugby, something easy on the eye and brain, to break new ground in such a way, to convert new followers.

We are talking about further violation of rugby's sacred principles. That concept of the Power Try, for example, is poignant, because for the first time in rugby history it suggests that some types of try are worth more than others, and its corollary that some types of player are worth more too. For all that we talk about the sanctity of set piece and changes of pace, enshrined even deeper than that in rugby's constitution is the notion that it is a game for all shapes and sizes, an egalitarian dream with equal importance afforded the fat, the tall, the short, the quick. From that creed stems everything else. To elevate a certain type of try above the others would seem to shatter this core principle, or at least to begin the process of its undoing. And yet that is, ultimately, the demand of the 21st century, so unconditionally devoted to the spectacular, the easy and entertaining. Nuance and layers are lost in the rush. Under this paradigm, the scrum is indeed an embarrassment, the heaving, steamy maul in the rain an unmitigated turn-off. Astute kicking games are lost on the 21st century.

This fundamental tension between the involved and the simple cannot be reconciled in the same proposition to an audience. One impulse will always pull away from the other. A balance can be struck – and rugby will insist that that is what it is trying to establish – but the demands of the audience a sport does not yet have will constantly be pulling that sport away from what it is.

The drift can be stopped only if the sport comes to accept what it is, learns to love itself. Rugby is as far from that happy release as any on Earth.

XV

Towards Some Easy Answers

Beware the person with all the answers, as someone surely once said. This book has asked a lot of questions, presented flaws and paradoxes, staged a parade of The Things Wrong. But answers are harder to come by.

Firstly, let us pause to appreciate the things right. If we could somehow banish from our minds the several impending crises that hang over rugby and focus on the point of it all, what happens on the pitch, we should realise that we have never had it so good. Don't let anyone tell you rugby was better in the 20th century. How could it have been? The players were a bunch of amateurs.

Nowadays they are paid to spend their days perfecting skills and maximising fitness, each with a tailored programme to fulfil their specific roles with maximum effectiveness. Of course they are better, much, much better – and so is what they produce on the field. Rugby is more dynamic and skilful than ever before, but it is still a contest between two sets of opponents, which means it is prone, as any sport, to lapses of incoherence. Some people like to complain the whole time and are almost constantly obliged by the next episode of the Shit

Match, which is never far away. All sports have them. Always have done, always will. The Sibling's are particularly shit. Rugby's have changed shape over the years – these days they tend to feature endless hit-ups, where once we bemoaned mauls and set pieces – but any mission to eradicate shit matches is doomed.

Rugby need not worry. If only we could count them – and agree on their categorisation – we would find fewer in rugby today and far, far more of the exhilarating contests of high drama and excellence that keep us coming back for more. Any lamentation for the way rugby was played in the old days is purely and simply a function of nostalgia.

In the name of research, a certain amount of time in the writing of this book was spent watching the second and fourth Tests of the 1971 Lions tour of New Zealand, which can be found in their entirety on the internet. This ordeal was suffered so that no one else need go through it. This, the 1971 Lions tour, which still glimmers just over the horizon of scrutiny as one of the greatest episodes in rugby history.

If that was rugby at its best in 1971, God help the rest of it. The endless set pieces and the randomness of their outcomes, the fumbles, the kicking, the almost absurd lack of urgency in defence, the lawlessness. The kicking. In the first two minutes of the fourth Test, there are two scrums and two lineouts, both of the latter ending in examples of tedious violence, the first with a shoulder to the head, the second with an elbow to the same followed by a retaliatory punch to the face. All of them would be red cards today; instead, they are nothing more than material for after-dinner speakers, while the rest of us roar with laughter at those bawdy tales of yore, back when men were men.

No, they weren't. The men we watch today are put through an infinitely more aggravating experience, and if they so much as mistime a tackle, let alone swing a fist, they are sent off. Or at the very least cited – usually by someone who, er, dished it out with impunity in the old days.

Meanwhile, the rest of us, far from laughing at the hilarity of it all, scream in righteous indignation at the barbarity. There is nothing like the replay of a mistimed tackle in high-definition super-slow-mo from multiple angles to enrage an audience, just as a well-delivered anecdote after a few beers can make a casual act of cowardly violence 40 years earlier seem not only OK but a cause for celebration.

Easy Answer Number One: stop the hypocrisy. Rugby is the most beautiful game to those of us who love it, but there has always festered within it a dirty, scurrilous, even scandalous, cesspit of violence and depravity. Any blazer who drivels into a gin and tonic about core values, as if their sport were somehow better than all the others, ought to be reminded that such hypocrisy is the very reason so many loathe rugby types and their misplaced sense of superiority.

The hypocrisy lingers on today in the profound irony that players at the highest levels are cleaner and nobler than they have ever been, despite having to endure levels of physical aggravation beyond the ken of those in the old days, and yet they are sent off more than ever too. The self-restraint of the players today is extraordinary, so other grounds for dismissal are contrived, the observation regularly accompanying the latest red card that there was 'no malice', in other words the dismissed player was caught up in an accident. If there is no malice, there should be no grounds for dismissal, at least in any sport that treats its players with respect. Rugby almost seems to delight now in sending them off and/or hauling them out for trial by social media. That a call should echo around the sport for more of its players to be shown cards, that new low reached during the concussion crisis, is a craven betrayal of good people and a sure sign of a sport in panic, preferring to blame its players for the hideous reality hardwired into its nature.

The threat of concussion looms as the most critical of the crises facing rugby and the hardest to avert. For all the disagreements over how, or even if, to alter the dynamics on the field, rugby, like American football, is at the mercy of science on this one. Should science ever prove rugby to be a health hazard no sane person should countenance, what then? Participation levels are already under pressure from the multiplicity of choices in the 21st century. If rugby's hopeful cry from the periphery came with the added twist of guaranteed brain damage for even just a minority of those who answer, the effect would be catastrophic for the sport as we know it. The smoking counterargument is usually offered here – there will always be smokers, there will always be rugby players, as long as they know the risks – but smoking is in the midst of the mother of all participation crises. On current trends, they reckon it will have died out altogether in the UK within 50 years. If rugby's future is smoking's, there is every reason to panic. And smoking is illegal, anyway, for the children.

Science, though, may also come to the rescue. The advances made in the detection and treatment of concussion are already great enough to foster hope, and there is no reason to think they will stop now. There has been a corresponding shift, too, in rugby's culture, which not only bodes well for a graceful negotiation of the problem but commends the sport as highly as any other development.

If only its player-welfare issues ended there. Such is the intensity of the modern game throughout the levels, but dramatically so at the highest, the question of how much of it a player should be exposed to in a given season is a constant source of contention. In many cases, that question is answered for the coach or medic by an untimely injury, but there is no neat equation by which to achieve the perfect blend between player freshness, longevity and value for money. On the handling of concussion, a consensus has more or less been arrived at. No such agreement exists on appropriate workload, which differs from player to player anyway. Most coaches and medics preach common sense when pressed on the subject, but some institutions, clearly, are better at handling the competing demands than others. Many grand pronouncements are issued by governing bodies and clubs alike about player welfare being their 'number-one priority', to howls of derision for the most part, as the games continue to come thick and fast. That derision, though, is almost exclusively reserved for the handling of the freshness and longevity quotients. Few talk about the money.

Easy Answer Number Two: pay the players less. So many of rugby's problems currently stem from the fact the sport cannot afford the wages it pays its players. There is absolutely no prospect of a reduction in the games they are required to play for as long as this is the case. No club, district or province can afford to cut so much as one home fixture from its calendar. Good luck to anyone trying to persuade even the richest unions to do the same. As soon as new revenue becomes available it is channelled overwhelmingly in one direction – to the players. Nor should that be decried. The players are what we keep coming back for, and they are not particularly well paid when one considers what they go through and for how long they get to do it. Well might they maximise their earnings while they can. But every time the angry cry goes up that their welfare is being neglected, that they play too many games, every time a player makes the same point, this simple question of economics is conveniently ignored.

Rugby is all about the money now. Well, of course it is. This is professionalism. What did people expect? The time for complaining about that idea was in the first half of the 1990s. Not that any of us were given the chance. The direction of travel had been set. All of society is on the same conveyor. Was it ever realistic rugby should remain amateur? No, but back then the question of professionalism seemed to boil down to whether players should be remunerated for their pains. That was a superficial dilemma. In 1995 rugby really faced a profound ideological choice between the quirky and the spectacular, the casual and the intense – between the 19th century and the 21st. What rendered this choice so explosive was rugby's missing 20th century. The opportunity to muddle along merely paying the players, as other sports had for most of that era, was no longer available. Rugby was thrust into the new century as on a rocket, the stresses in its creaking infrastructure palpable, not to mention on the flesh and bones of its players.

Of all the sports, rugby is ill-suited to such a journey, simply because of the violent nature of its game. It is further rendered vulnerable by its close relations with The Sibling. This is a particular problem because football is so big in rugby's overwhelmingly dominant marketplaces, England and France. Here the cultures are firmly rooted in the free-market model. Here the managed growth of a sport is an alien concept. Rugby thinks it can be football. At times, rugby considers being football to be a moral duty. The notion of a seamless game, for example, is defended as fundamental to the very concept of sport, when, in fact, it is only in football, the world's one global sport, that it can be found. And in rugby in England and France. Nowhere else are all teams, professional and amateur, integrated into the same system, the professionalism of those at the top allowed to dribble messily throughout the structures beneath. This infiltration places much strain on those support structures, but so too on the elite themselves, whose fevered attempts to avoid the drop force each other into hideous contortions of discomfort – and everyone else around the world into various states of ruin.

Easy Answer Number Three: stop trying to be like football. Look instead at how almost every other sport organises itself. Strong independent governance, equalisation strategies that bite, a closed league and a system that seeks to help new teams, not disadvantage them.

In reality, undoing the system that has been allowed to develop – or that has been created by rugby's vacuum between two centuries – feels impossible already, for it would require those who have found themselves in control to surrender it. This would be problem enough in just the one administration, but rugby's strong international culture makes a joined-up strategy all the more difficult to achieve. The model on which most professional sports settle revolves around a regular diet of domestic action. Any international component is a supplementary delicacy. Cricket, that other great Empire sport, has suffered, like rugby, from a tension between the domestic and the international games, the entertaining and the nuanced, but cricket's tension is increasingly resolving itself in favour of the former. This has ominous implications for rugby's traditional power base, the 15-a-side international game.

Rugby's civil war between club and country is only now beginning to enter its decisive phase. Even within that, there is, if not a war, competing interests between factions, the legacy of a century in which a minority of nations were free to establish their own rules of governance. No one should be surprised they are reluctant to let that go. The international game, just as much as the domestic game everywhere else, knows it is under threat from the clubs of England and France. The response has been as fractured and uncoordinated as one might expect, the big beasts of the Six Nations with one set of priorities, the deteriorating powers of the southern hemisphere with another, everybody else in the world game with another again. Protectionism is the unavoidable result. The gravitation of resources to the strongest is an inevitability in a free-market model. This is an ugly sight, whichever sphere it plays out in, but rugby's narrative is further enlivened by the role played by the Pacific Islanders, the archetype of a people disenfranchised, defiant and noble, yet powerless against the machine.

Easy Answer Number Four (and this one really is easy): end the system of player capture. The tying of a player to a single nation is as naked a manifestation of the politics of self-interest as any of the travesties concocted by rugby's administration. The Pacific Islander question is more complicated than the easy headlines of outrage would have us believe, but at a fundamental level their gene pool supplies the world with its best rugby players, even if they cannot sustain an economic model to keep them at home. The very least the game owes them is to free up as many as possible. Nationhood is blurred in the global village, but the elemental consideration of where one's fibres originate wields more power in a sporting context than where one has lived for a while. Make qualification harder through residency – perhaps based on passports – but never stop a player when they qualify through blood, whomever else they may have represented. More players available to the international game must benefit the international game, and the Tier 2 nations in particular. If Fiji, Samoa or Tonga could draw from more of their gene pool – and have that pool increased by a reduction of the legion players who have qualified for someone else through residency – we would see far more of them in the knockout stages of a World Cup.

To see fresh faces in the knockout stages of a World Cup is the ardent wish of World Rugby's executive. But more fresh faces mean fewer of the old – and in rugby it is the old faces who are still in control. This status quo has thrown up some ugly postures, some impasses of an unseemly nature. The temptation to rage at these end results is all but irresistible to any right-thinking human, but the assignment of goodies and baddies in the narrative is unhelpful. There are, generally speaking, no bad guys here, only humans and collectives thereof operating under flawed systems of governance. If there is, for example, such a thing as a Tier 1 and you are in it, why would you ever allow yourself to be ousted, or it to be disbanded? If that Fijian qualifies for you under the rules, why wouldn't you pick him? If this country has a multitrillion-dollar economy and that one does not, it would make sense to explore opportunities in the former. If there is strategic merit in smashing that unsighted fly-half, then smash him is what you will.

On the field is where this will play out. Governance structures will continue to evolve, new competitions rise and fall, existing ones expand and contract, but the game is everything. If new audiences are to be won, it is by the game; if health threats are to be averted, it is by the game. Alas, these imperatives are so often incompatible. Not enough happening to entice the viewer? Speed the game up. Too many injuries? Slow it down. The puzzle is interminable, but the path of rugby's evolution is familiar.

A cynic might suggest rugby is trying to reinvent the wheel. That Other Sibling has already done it. League faced the issues confronting a professional version of rugby more than a hundred years ago. As the original revolutionary sport, league's respect for tradition was less entrenched, and it was quick to adapt with an audience in mind. As rugby wrestles with dilemmas thrown up by a different calibre of athlete playing to the rhythms of an amateur sport with the same positions on the same size of pitch, all too many of the suggestions sound familiar. Reduce the number of players? League. Diminish the influence of set piece? League. Increase ball in play? League. Even as rugby despairs at the sight of players in straight lines smashing into each other, league can say it has been there.

Everybody is in the same predicament – to make their sport attractive – but where rugby might still be said to retain a point of difference, beyond the withering set piece, is in the notion of the contest for possession and with it the prospect of the turnover. League has been here too. The thud, thud, thud of unbroken possession was a chronic problem for the game deep into the 20th century. League's response was to give each team six goes at being tackled, before they let the other side have the ball. Rugby finds itself at or approaching a similar impasse, such is the proficiency of teams recycling possession, such is the organisation of defences. The contest for possession has diminished at each and every point of contact. Corris Thomas's analysis found that in the early 1980s a turnover occurred once every six breakdowns; 20 years later, it was once every 23; in the 2019 Six Nations, once every 31. Together with a dramatic increase in the reliability of set-piece possession, particularly at the lineout (ban lifting again?), rugby is suffering from a dearth of changeovers in possession, as league did. But in this instance a different path presents itself – if rugby can resuscitate the breakdown.

The silver bullet would be some sort of innovation that forces players back into the ruck. Defending teams tend to send in a player to 'jackal' at each tackle, requiring at least one or two attackers to clear the area. Thus, attacking teams are so often at a numerical disadvantage when the ball emerges from each ruck. Of all the recent suggestions, the prohibition of hands after the tackle – an outlawing of the jackal – is the most interesting. The jackal, the hallmark of professional rugby, is at the root of so many problems, both aesthetic and medical.

Rugby was introduced to a whole new injury in the first decade of the 21st century, one previously seen only in surfing, when the surfer is hit by a wave. Rugby started to see hamstrings torn away from the bone, such were the forces suffered by players hit by an opponent when crouched over the ball.

More than that, though, the jackal absolves the rest of the team from joining the ruck, which precipitates the escalation of those tackle counts and the rhythm of that thud, thud, thud. Ban the jackal, so the theory goes, and the only way for a defence to win the ball, bar forcing an error or a kick, is to send players into the ruck.

It is a plausible theory but, as ever, there will be repercussions. 'Bring back rucking' has long been the cry of the old school. When they voice it, they tend to mean specifically the use of studs to clear out players on the wrong side of the tackle – 'a good shoeing', as the lexicon once had it. With more people, and thus studs, in a ruck there will be more such contact between boots and the flesh of prone players. There will be blood. Sometimes, because watching your step while wrestling ferociously at a ruck is not a realistic directive, there will be blood from the head. Try getting studs to the face past the PR police. Sit back and count the red cards.

And on with the impossible puzzle.

Easy Answer Number Five: drink.

Beer.

Not protein shake.

This is, by far and away, the least feasible of our Easy Answers, but in it lies the key to everything. The answer has always lain in the glass. For many long decades rugby was beer. Now, suddenly, it is protein shake.

There is no doubt that most of the things very right about rugby now, at the top end at least – the excellence of the players, the awe of the spectacle – owe their emergence to the ideology of the protein shake. But the side-effects are deleterious, and they seep throughout the sport, just as they seep through society. That 21st-century drug of maximisation leaves not a wrinkle of slack anywhere, across our skin, across our souls, across our rush defences. Protein shake maximises performance, but it ratchets up everyone else's too. It is Dr Jekyll's frothing cocktail, demanding as much as it gives back, heightening the collisions and the mania and the sense that some sort of apocalypse is impending, that everything is about to go pop.

Whereas beer de-powers us just a shade. We are still brilliant with beer, but less intense, more of a mind to enjoy ourselves and each other, to plunge into a happy communal bath awash with mud and other people's sweat. Beer is dirty and makes us a bit crap. Beer has soul.

A return to beer, though, is impossible. Because it only takes one. One person not to indulge. One person to reach for the protein shake. Without strong, independent governance, a legally binding commitment to beer is impossible. One person reaches for the protein shake, and the rest must follow to stand just a chance of surviving.

There can be no going back, no answers or remedies, just the compulsion of what happens next. Rugby has been thrust into this transition with unseemly haste, its violent nature rendering the predicaments all the more explosive. But it is in the lingering traces of what it was that we still perceive rugby's soul. The idiosyncratic rituals delight us as much as the stubbornness drives us mad. We watch in wonder a fish out of water, that twisting, seething scrum caught in the floodlights, as confused, ugly and beautiful as us all. What will become of it? Who will love it? Does it even matter?

As rugby's arch practitioners cry in that strange tongue before each match, dressed in black, eyes flaring beneath terrible brows, warlike and of another time, even while the cameras swoop and the world awaits:

'Tis life! 'Tis life!

Acknowledgements

This book was many hours in the writing, but probably even more in the talking, emailing and general suing for information. Many have given up their time for no reward other than the kind found in heaven and the acknowledgements section. What follows is a list of those, but it is almost certainly incomplete. Apologies to any who have slipped our minds – you'll just have to wait for heaven.

Firstly, to those who not only talked but read whole sections of the book relating to their field of expertise, some of them very long. John Daniell's expertise extends from New Zealand to the Pacific Islands via France, so his was the biggest read. Other sections were read by Dr Glen Hagemann of the Sharks in South Africa, Martin Pengelly of the *Guardian US*, Jamie Singer of Onside Law, Oliver Owen of *Sport500*, Richard Beard of literary fame and Christopher Aylwin, arch saver of lives, of St Mary's Hospital, Paddington.

For all things historical and sociological in rugby, no serious researcher would fail to seek out the work and advice of Tony Collins of De Montfort University. Corris Thomas has been similarly generous with his time and research, the first person to anatomise the dramatic changes in international rugby on the field either side of the millennium.

Rusty MacLean, the archivist of Rugby School, supplied key information for Part One and the William Webb Ellis chapter in particular.

For their help with Part Two, our thanks go to Ben Ryan, Stuart Farmer, Edward Griffiths, Andy Friend, Blaine Scully, Dan Lyle and Hayden Smith.

For Part Three, James Harrington, Simon Gilham, Professor Philip Dine, Professor Joris Vincent and Gavin Mortimer did much to unravel the mysteries of French rugby, John Griffiths, Simon Cohen and Alistair Bow those of English rugby, Paul McNaughton and Brendan Fanning Irish, Conor O'Shea Italian and Alasdair Reid Scottish.

Regarding Part Four, our thanks go to Darren Clayton and Jack Royle of Zeus Events and Mark Fletcher of Pitchero for the transmission of our clubs survey and to Bob Reeves, Ben Lowe, Terry Burwell, Chris Burns, Giles Simons and Brandon Walker for their insights into the culture of the community game in England.

Part Five, AKA The Chapter That Wouldn't End, required much input from the medical and legal worlds. Thanks therefore to: Dr Colin Fuller; Dr Ross Tucker and Dom Rumbles of World Rugby; Dr James Brown and Dr Wayne Viljoen of BokSmart; Jonathan Webb, Dr Simon Kemp and Verity Williams of the RFU; Dr Michael Turner; all at Onside Law, particularly Stevie Loughrey; Miles Benjamin; Ben Cisneros of Rugby and the Law; Christian Day and Josh Frape of the RPA; Phil Morrow of Saracens; Karl Binks of Perform Group; and Dick Wetherell, NFL geek.

Part Six, as well as a fascination with the scrum, owes much to the out-sized hands and capacity to endure pain of John Aylwin, stalwart hooker of Richmond FC in the 1960s, who, according to his wife, Angela, had a trial for England once.

For his faith in the whole project, our particular thanks go to Andreas Campomar of the Little, Brown Book Group.

Lastly, thanks to Vanessa, Max and Franky for putting up with the endlessly closed door.

Selected Bibliography

Books

Aylwin, Michael, with Singer, Matt *The Red and the Black: Glory and Uncertainty at Saracens Ltd* (Edinburgh: Mainstream 1999)

Beard, Richard *Muddied Oafs: The Last Days of Rugger* (London: Yellow Jersey 2003)

Collins, Tony *A Social History of English Rugby* (Abingdon: Routledge 2009)

Collins, Tony *The Oval World: A Global History of Rugby* (London: Bloomsbury 2015)

Daniell, John *Confessions of a Rugby Mercenary* (London: Ebury Press 2009)

Dunning, Eric *Barbarians, Gentlemen and Players: A Sociological Study of the Development of Rugby Football* (Oxford: Martin Robertson 1979)

Harvey, Adrian *Football, the First Hundred Years: The Untold Story* (Abingdon: Routledge 2005)

Henderson, Jon *When Footballers Were Skint: A Journey in Search of the Soul of Football* (London: Biteback Publishing 2018)

Hughes, Thomas *Memoir of a Brother* (Boston: JR Osgood and Company 1873)

Hughes, Thomas *Tom Brown's School Days* (Cambridge: MacMillan & Co 1857)

Jones, Stephen *Endless Winter: Inside Story of the Rugby Revolution* (Edinburgh: Mainstream 1993)

Kuper, Simon and Szymanski, Stefan *Soccernomics: Why England Lose, Why Germany, Spain and France win, and Why One Day the Rest of the World Will Finally Catch Up* (London: HarperCollins 2018)

Macrory, Jennifer *Running with the Ball: Birth of Rugby Football* (London: HarperCollinsWillow 1991)
Marshall, Rev Frank, ed *Football: The Rugby Union Game* (London: Cassel 1892)
McRae, Donald *Winter Colours: Changing Seasons in World Rugby* (Edinburgh: Mainstream 1998)
Old Rugbeian Society, Sub-committee *The Origins of Rugby Football* (Rugby: AJ Lawrence 1897)
Samuel, Bill *Rugby: Body and Soul* (Edinburgh: Mainstream 1998)
Selfe, Sydney *Chapters from the History of Rugby School* (Rugby: AJ Lawrence 1910)
Smith, Sean *The Union Game: A Rugby History* (London: BBC Books 1999)

Academic articles

Anderson J 'The legal implications of concussion in contact sports' (2016) *LawInSport.com*
Anderson J, Heshka, J 'Concussion in sport – How employers' duties compare in the U.K., Ireland & North America' (2017) *LawInSport.com*
Anderson J, Partington N 'The scope of the duty of care in sport – A submission in relation to UK Government's review' (2016) *LawInSport.com*
Asplund C, Best T 'Brain Damage in American Football' (2015) *BMJ*
Badenhorst M, Verhagen E, van Mechelen W, et al 'Catastrophic injury incidence rates in South African rugby union: are there regional differences?' (2017) *British Journal of Sports Medicine*
Barnes A, Rumbold J, Olusoga P 'Attitudes towards protective headgear in UK rugby union players' *BMJ Open Sport & Exercise Medicine*
Brown J, Lambert M, Verhagen E, et al 'The incidence of rugby-related catastrophic injuries (including cardiac events) in South Africa from 2008 to 2011: A cohort study' (2013) *BMJ Open*
Christian I, Nye S 'Could incidents of concussion in sport be an issue of negligence?' (2015) *LawInSport.com*
Cohen J, Cottrell S 'An overview of concussion protocols across professional sports leagues' (2014) *LawInSport.com*
Cunningham J, Broglio S, Wilson F 'Influence of playing rugby on long-term brain health following retirement: A systematic review and narrative synthesis' *BMJ Open Sport & Exercise Medicine*
Davies M, Judge A, et al 'Health amongst former rugby union players: A cross-sectional study of morbidity and health-related quality of life' (2017) *Scientific Reports*

Selected Bibliography

Drawer S, Fuller C 'Evaluating the level of injury in English professional football using a risk-based assessment process' (2002) *British Journal of Sports Medicine*

Fuller C 'Catastrophic injury in rugby union: Is the level of risk acceptable?' (2008) *Sports Medicine*

Fuller C 'Implications of health and safety legislation for the professional sportsperson' (1995) *British Journal of Sports Medicine*

Fuller C 'Injury risk (burden), risk matrices and risk contours in team sports: A review of principles, practices and problems' (2018) *Sports Medicine*

Fuller C 'Managing the Risk of Injury in Sport' (2007) *Clinical Journal of Sports Medicine*

Fuller C '"Recognize and remove": A universal principle for the management of sports injuries' (2018) *Clinical Journal of Sport Medicine*

Fuller C, Ashton A, et al 'Injury risks associated with tackling in rugby union' (2008) *British Journal of Sports Medicine*

Fuller C, Brooks J, et al 'Contact events in rugby union and their propensity to cause injury' (2007) *British Journal of Sports Medicine*

Fuller C, Brooks J, Kemp S 'Spinal Injuries in Professional Rugby Union: A Prospective Cohort Study' (2007) *Clinical Journal of Sport Medicine*

Fuller C, Drawer S 'The Application of Risk Management in Sport' (2004) *Sports Medicine*

Fuller C, Fuller G, Kemp S, et al 'Evaluation of World Rugby's concussion management process: results from Rugby World Cup 2015' (2016) *British Journal of Sports Medicine*

Fuller C, Myerscough F 'Stakeholder perceptions of risk in motor sport' (2001) *Journal of Safety Research*

Fuller C, Taylor A, et al 'Changes in the stature, body mass and age of English professional rugby players: A 10-year review' (2012) *Journal of Sports Sciences*

Fuller C, Ward C 'An empirical approach for defining acceptable levels of risk: a case study in team sports' (2008) *Injury Prevention*

Gallo V, McElvenny D, Hobbs C, et al 'BRain health and healthy AgeINg in retired rugby union players, the BRAIN Study: study protocol for an observational study in the UK' (2017) *BMJ Open*

GBD 2016 Alcohol Collaborators 'Alcohol use and burden for 195 countries and territories, 1990–2016: a systematic analysis for the Global Burden of Disease Study 2016' (2018) *Lancet*

Grey-Thompson T 'Duty of care in sport' (2017) Independent Report to Government

Harmon KG, Drezner JA, Gammons M, et al 'American Medical Society for Sports Medicine position statement: concussion in sport' (2012) *British Journal of Sports Medicine*

Heiborn C 'How Australia's top contact sports manage concussion' (2017) *LawInSport.com*

Hislop M, Stokes K, Williams S, et al 'Reducing musculoskeletal injury and concussion risk in schoolboy rugby players with a pre-activity movement control exercise programme: A cluster randomised controlled trial' (2017) *British Journal of Sports Medicine*

Hoh B, Pearce A 'How the latest technological advances in diagnosing concussion could influence sports policy' (2018) *LawInSport.com*

Holle R 'Annual Rates of Lightning Fatalities by Country' (2008)

Lehman E, et al 'Suicide mortality among retired national football league players who played 5 or more seasons' (2016) *The American Journal of Sports Medicine*

Massey P, Massey S, Hogan V 'Competitive balance and match attendance in European rugby union leagues' 2012 *UCD Centre for Economic Research Working Paper Series*

McCrory P, Meeuwisse W, Dvorak J, et al 'Consensus statement on concussion in sport – the 5th international conference on concussion in sport held in Berlin, October 2016' (2017) *British Journal of Sports Medicine*

McMillan T, McSkimming P, Wainman-Lefley J, et al 'Long-term health outcomes after exposure to repeated concussion in elite level: rugby union players' (2017) *Journal of Neurology, Neurosurgery & Psychiatry*

Mez J, Daneshvar D, Kiernan P et al 'Clinicopathological Evaluation of Chronic Traumatic Encephalopathy in Players of American Football' (2017) *The Journal of the American Medical Association*

Olds T 'The evolution of physique in male rugby union players in the twentieth century' (2001) *Journal of Sports Sciences*

Quarrie K, Hopkins W 'Changes in player characteristics and match activities in Bledisloe Cup rugby union from 1972 to 2004' (2006) *Journal of Sports Sciences*

Reboursiere E, Bohu Y, Retière D, et al 'Impact of the national prevention policy and scrum law changes on the incidence of rugby-related catastrophic cervical spine injuries in French Rugby Union' (2016) *British Journal of Sports Medicine*

Roberts S, Trewartha G, England M, et al 'Collapsed scrums and collision tackles: What is the injury risk?' (2015) *British Journal of Sports Medicine*

Safinia C, Bershad E, et al 'Chronic Traumatic Encephalopathy in Athletes Involved with High impact Sports' (2016) *Journal of Vascular and Interventional Neurology*

Selected Bibliography

Seminati E, Cazzola D, Preatoni E, Trewartha G 'Specific tackling situations affect the biomechanical demands experienced by rugby union players' (2017) *Sports Biomechanics*

Smith D, Johnson V et al 'Chronic traumatic encephalopathy – confusion and controversies' (2019) *Nature Reviews Neurology*

Stewart W, McNamara P, et al 'Chronic traumatic encephalopathy: a potential late and under recognized consequence of rugby union?' (2016) *QJM: An International Journal of Medicine*

Tagge C, Fisher A, Minaeva O et al 'Concussion, microvascular injury, and early tauopathy in young athletes after impact head injury and an impact concussion mouse model' (2018) *Brain*

Tierney G, Denvir K, Farrell G, et al 'Does player time-in-game affect tackle technique in elite level rugby union?' (2018) *Journal of Science and Medicine in Sport*

Tierney G, Denvir K, Farrell G, et al 'The Effect of Tackler Technique on Head Injury Assessment Risk in Elite Rugby Union' (2018) *Medicine & Science in Sports & Exercise*

Tierney G, Simms C 'Can tackle height influence tackle gainline success outcomes in elite level rugby union?' (2017) *International Journal of Sports Science & Coaching*

Tucker R, Raftery M, Fuller G, et al 'A video analysis of head injuries satisfying the criteria for a head injury assessment in professional rugby union: A prospective cohort study' (2017) *British Journal of Sports Medicine*

Tucker R, Raftery M, Kemp S, et al 'Risk factors for head injury events in professional rugby union: a video analysis of 464 head injury events to inform proposed injury prevention strategies' (2017) *British Journal of Sports Medicine*

Williamson B 'Premiership Rugby Union: Through the Antitrust Looking Glass' (2015) *The Competition Law Review*

World health statistics '2018: monitoring health for the SDGs, sustainable development goals' (2018) World Health Organization

Resources:

Companies House

Ligue Nationale de Rugby annual reports

National unions annual reports

RFU Adult Competition Review 2014, Professional Rugby Injury Surveillance Project reports 2002–18 and Community Rugby Injury Surveillance Project reports 2009–17

World Rugby annual reports and documents

Index

Index

Index

Index

ranking 54–6
Springboks *see* South African national
   team
Sri Lanka 74, 90
Stade Bordelais 120
Stade Français 108, 115
stadium ownership 112, 114–15
Stead, Billy 53
steroids *see* performance-enhancing
   drugs
Stringer, Rowan 237, 239
Sunwolves 294
Super League 129
Super Rugby 82, 83, 104, 196, 293, 294
Swansea 150

tackles 173, 217–18, 219, 252–4, 256–7,
   258–67
   ball-carriers and 258, 259, 260,
      264–5, 266
   behaviour change 267
   exploding tackle count 218, 219, 220,
      252
   junior rugby 173, 243, 249–50
   legal tackle height 260–1, 263, 264
   reckless or illegal 258–9, 261, 262,
      263
   tackle types 260
   see also concussion
tactical replacements 286, 287
tag rugby 173
team sports, declining popularity of
   177–8
technical infringements 274–5, 277
television audiences 88, 292
television revenues 80, 82, 128–9, 131,
   292–3
Telfer, Jim 148
Test matches 59, 60, 62, 68, 76, 80, 83,
   142, 218–19, 224, 280, 291, 299
Thomas, Corris 218, 286, 306
Tier 1 nations 42, 44, 47, 59, 61, 67–8,
   69, 77, 85, 86, 90, 138, 170
Tier 2 nations 43, 45, 62–3, 74, 86, 139,
   305
Tier 3 nations 43, 74

Tom Brown's School Days (Thomas
   Hughes) 18, 23, 40
Tonga 69, 87, 88–9
Top 14 129, 130
totalitarian regimes 8, 109, 110
touch rugby 10, 177, 251
traumatic brain injury (TBI) 218
Tri Nations Championship 59, 82
trickle-down strategy of sports
   administration 292
Trimble, Andrew 221
Tuigamala, Va'aiga 38, 73
Tunisia 90

Uganda 92
Ulster 139, 140
USA *see* American football; American
   rugby

Vale of Lune 183
Varsity Match 21
Venter, Brendan 271
Vichy regime, France 109–10
Vickery, Phil 278
Victorian Football League 168
violence 35–6, 57, 108–9, 173, 213, 299,
   300
   see also injuries and fatalities
Voivenel, Paul 109
Vunipola, Billy 71

Wallace, David 221
Warburton, Sam 142
Wasps 21fn, 71, 116, 118, 125, 149, 165
Web Ellis Cup 15, 27–8
Webster, Mike 235, 241
weight-graded rugby 53
Weir, Doddie 148
Welsh national team 65–6, 68, 69, 73,
   85, 86, 87, 109, 291
   eligibility for 62, 74
   Five Nations 147
   grand slams 147
Welsh rugby 34, 37, 41, 145–7, 150–1
   attendances 150, 151
   Champions Cup 145